DEVELOPMENT BANKING AND INDUSTRIALISATION

DEVELOPMENT BANKING AND INDUSTRIALISATION

A Case Study

By

BHASKAR PURKAYASTHA

ANMOL PUBLICATIONS PVT. LTD.

NEW DELHI - 110 002 (INDIA)

ANMOL PUBLICATIONS PVT. LTD.
4374/4B, Ansari Road, Daryaganj
New Delhi - 110 002

Development Banking and Industrialisation

First Edition, 2001

ISBN 81-261-0952-1

PRINTED IN INDIA

Published by J.L. Kumar for Anmol Publications Pvt. Ltd., New Delhi - 110 002 and Printed at Mehra Offset Press, Delhi.

Dedicated to my Parents
Shri Gunendra Nath Purkayastha
and
Smt. Gita Purkayastha

Contents

Preface

Since independence India ushered in the era of Planned economic development. The Directive Principles of State Policy laid down that the state must formulate policies designed to prevent concentration of wealth in the hands of a few. The Industrial Policy Resolution was a step to uphold the directives of the State Policy.

The Banks and Financial Institutions play a vital role in this endeavour. The First Five Year Plan emphasised that the monetary and Credit Policy is a powerful instrument in development planning. The financial institutions take on a direct and active role for financing developmental activities and ensuring credit flow in the desired direction. The State level Financial Institutions of various states act as an intermediary between the All India Financial Institutions and the entrepreneurs in channelising loans. The role of the State Industrial Development Corporations (SIDCs) in the industrial development of the north-eastern states of India has been exemplary in this respect. SIDC in hill-bound, land locked areas is the maiden institution to facilitate industrial development.

The road from Monarchy to Democracy was not strewn with roses. The smooth transition required the Government of India to open many avenues. The economy was characterised by a glut of loan assistance and this instilled an awareness of democratic norms and values into the minds of the people of Sikkim. The Sikkim Industrial Development and Investment Corporation Limited (SIDICO) was established in 1977 to hasten the pace of industrialization on a small and medium scale basis. The Corporation has established a liason amongst the Government, Financial Institutions and Entrepreneurs and till date provides financial assistance to more than ninety per cent industries in the State. The story of the industrialization in Sikkim is but the story of the role played by the Corporation in this regard.

The object of this study is to examine how far industrialization been taking place in Sikkim. The study addresses itself in particular to the following questions related to Sikkim: What was the general state of economy? What was the contribution of SIDICO (SIDC for Sikkim) to the process of industrialization? What were the sectors developed in consonance with financial credit policies and sustainable ecological balance?

There have been many studies on Sikkim's socio-political development in recent years. But no research oriented studies have so far been made on the industrial development of the state. This work is aimed to be the pioneering one in this field.

The work is divided into twelve chapters. The first three chapters look into the brief history, the state of economic affairs and the importance of small scale industries in the given ecological perspective of such a beautiful state in the eastern-Himalayas. The fourth chapter takes an overview of importance and methodology of the study. While the fifth chapter is devoted to analysing the pivotal role of the Corporation in the process of industrialization, the following four are on the Organisation, Resource mobilisation, Credit policy and Recovery position of the Corporation. The tenth chapter has revealed the industrial and human resource development. The eleventh is on the Financial Management. The last chapter sums up the findings and draws certain specific and broad conclusions.

Some of the salient findings of the study are worth noting here. Since 1975 the year Sikkim joined the mainstream of India the sectoral growth was phenomenal. The development in agriculture, power and roads was considerable. The industrialization was limited to the small scale and a few medium scale units. The per capita development expenditure was the highest in the country. The Corporation at one point of time had no dearth of finance but poor recovery from borrowing industries led to a serious resource crunch in the mid-nineties. As per Article 371F of the Constitution of India Sikkim enjoys some privileges whereby the king's law is operative in respect of certain matters. This hinders the recovery drive of the Corporation through the All-India enactments. The patronage of the state government towards the entrepreneurs — mostly of the first generation, was not sufficient. The tourism sector, however, witnessed a steady growth with the loan facility of the Corporation. The sectors related to small vehicles, hotels, tiny and cottage industries have generated maximum employment in the State. However, caution should be exercised to protect the values of the traditional society from the tourist culture. The sustainable development can be achieved by a eco-friendly development policy.

In completing the study my debt is indeed very extensive. Apart from the works cited in the text and the bibliography, I benefited immensely from discussing problems with Planners, Officials, Entrepreneurs during the period of study. I express gratitude to Dr. Manas Dasgupta, Professor, Department of Economics, University of North Bengal for his guidance in the successful completion of the study. I am obligated to Shri C. Raju, DGM, SIDICO for information and valuable opinion throughout the study. I must record my thanks to the related departments of the Government of Sikkim, especially, Planning and

Development, Directorate of Industries, Bureau of Economics and Statistics, SIDBI and other Commercial banks for their co-operation and suggestions. Among the libraries that came to my help of particular importance were National Library, Calcutta, North Bengal University Library, The Ramkrishna Mission Institute of Culture, Calcutta. The favourable environment at my previous workplace in Sikkim Government College contributed immensely and I am grateful to those who contributed to it. I am also thankful to all my colleagues of Heramba Chandra College.

Finally, no word can adequately express profound gratitude to my parents for their blessings to overcome all the odds. It is needless to mention indebtedness to my wife Aditi for her sacrifice and co-operation in the completion of the study.

Bhaskar Purkayastha

List of Tables

Abbreviations

AFIs	—	All Financial Institutions.
AIFIs	—	All India Financial Institutions.
APIDFC	—	Arunachal Pradesh Industrial Development & Financial Corporation.
B.E. & S.	—	Bureau of Economics and Statistics.
GIC	—	General Insurance Corporation of India.
GOS	—	Government of Sikkim.
IDBI	—	Industrial Development Bank of India.
IDC	—	Industrial Development Corporation.
IRBI	—	Industrial Reconstruction Bank of India.
MANIDCO	—	Manipur Industrial Development Corporation.
MIDC	—	Meghalaya Industrial Development Corporation.
MSIs	—	Medium Scale Industries.
NIDC	—	Nagaland Industrial Development Corporation.
PIPDIC	—	Pondicherry Industrial Promotion, Development and Investment Corporation Limited.
RCTC	—	Risk Capital & Technology Finance Corporation Ltd.
SCICI	—	Shipping Credit & Investment Corporation of India Ltd.

SFC	—	State Financial Corporation.
SIDBI	—	Small Industries Development Bank of India.
SIDC	—	State Industrial Development Corporation.
SSIs	—	Small Scale Industries.
SVO	—	Small Vehicle Operator.
TDICI	—	Technology Development and Information Company of India Ltd.
TFCI	—	Tourism Finance Corporation of India Ltd.
TIDC	—	Tripura Industrial Development Corporation.
UTI	—	Unit Trust of India.
WBIDC	—	West Bengal Industrial Development Corporation
WEBCON	—	West Bengal Consultancy Organisation Ltd.
ZIDCO	—	Zoram Industrial Development Corporation, Mizoram.

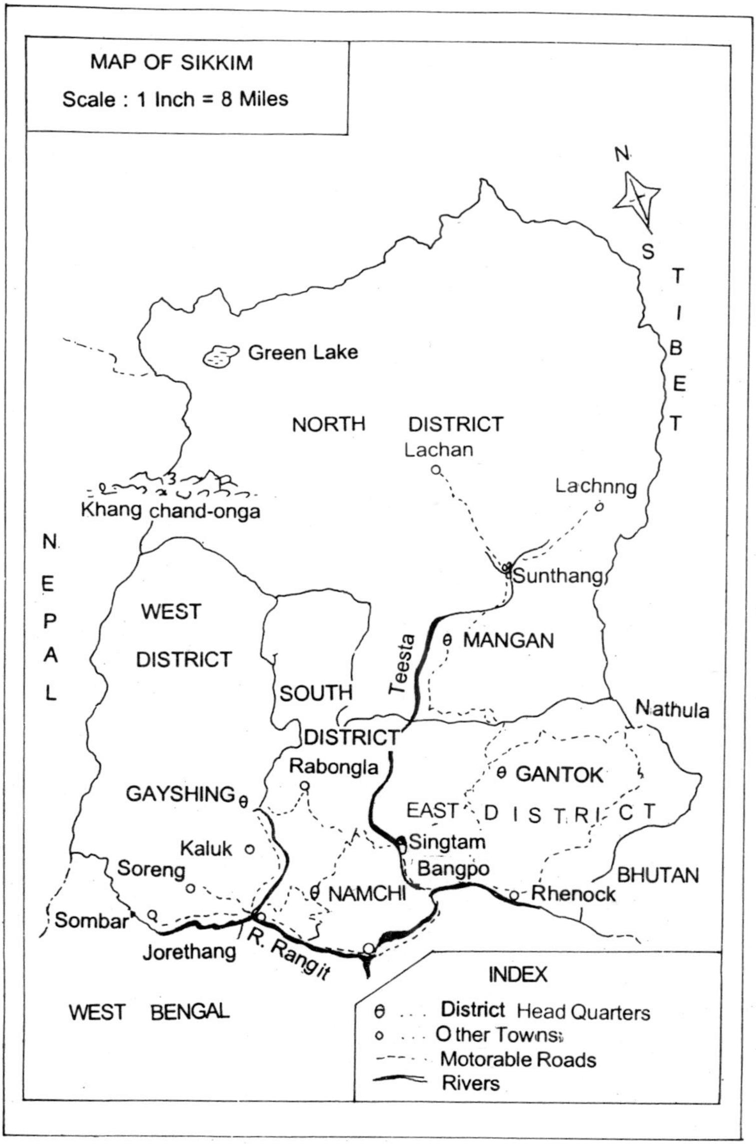

MAP OF SIKKIM

1

Introduction

The sweeping panoramic view of the picturesque mountains with snow-fed silver shining, emerald lakes, fluttering prayer flags, fascinating Buddhist murals and the gentle chant of hymns by Lamas beside the tender butter lamps inside the monasteries are all synonymous with the name of 'Sikkim'.

The state nestles high up in the eastern Himalayas surrounded by vast stretches of Tibetan Plateau in the north, the Chumbi Valley of Tibet and the kingdom of Bhutan in the east, Darjeeling district of West Bengal in the south and the kingdom of Nepal in the west.

Sikkim is located between 28°07'48" and 27°04'46" north latitudes and 88°00'58" and 88°55'25" east longitudes.[1]

The state has an area of 7096 square kilometres. It has been divided on the basis of the dividing lines of two rivers Teesta and Rangit. The state is almost rectangular with a distance of 114 kms. from north to south and 64 kms. from east to west. As the inner part of the Himalayan range of mountains projects southwards, it has no flat piece of ground of good size anywhere. The state is separated from its surroundings by great mountains ranging from 3000 metres to 8500 metres in height. Thus the land is of varied elevation ranging from 300 mt. above mean sea level at the southern foothills to 5500 mts. in the inner part of boundary hills in northern and north western boundaries.[2]

The rainfall varies between 50 cm. and 200 cm. The temperature in the state ranges between 00.0° and 26.5° centrigrade.[3]

The forest cover of the state is around 36.0 per cent of the total geographical area. About one-sixth of the forest area is under perpetual snow. The snow-bound areas are largely in the north district and some parts in the west and east districts.

Historical Perspective

The history of Sikkim dates back to 1641 when a horde of Tibetans overran this area inhabited by a small tribe of Lepchas. The latter are reported to have migrated to this area from one of the tribal regions of north-east India. Beyond their being animists, indolent and fun-loving, the British records do not reveal very much about their origin and culture.

The first phase of Sikkim's history is linked to the 'Blood treaty' in 1641 between the two tribes recognising the leader of the invaders as the spiritual and secular head. This treaty between the Bhutias and Lepchas promoted the growth of a multiple ethnic society with the invaders providing the ruling dynasty. The Lepchas were converted to the Lamaist Buddhism of the Tibetans. The new religion and ruler made a deep impression on the social and economic life of the community. The dominance of the Bhutias was so overwhelming that the Lepchas remained the poorest and the most neglected of the people, barring a few who intermarried with the Bhutia elite to attain the level of equality. Mostly confined to the northern belt of Sikkim in an area called Dzongu, they lived their life of indolence and negligence contributing little against the aggressive exploitation by the Bhutias rich in land and forest. In the late eighteenth century, during British presence, their missionaries converted a few of them to Christianity.

The advent of the eighteenth century saw an aggressive Nepal encroaching on the territory of Sikkim. This was the beginning of the second phase in Sikkim's history. While a small trickle of Nepalese into Sikkim had started at the beginning of the eighteenth century, Nepal's invasion in 1774-75 and subsequent occupation of Sikkim's western region, led to a substantial settlement of the Nepalese on her territory. By 1790, Nepal extended its hold over the entire lower Teesta basin in the East. Helpless against the powerful invaders, the Sikkim ruler sought the assistance of the British East India Company who had by then established their stronghold in eastern India with the weakening of the Mughal rule. Nepal's occupation of Sikkim came to an end in 1812, when the British troops of the East India Company intervened and defeated the Nepalese forces. But, the Nepalese settlers stayed back.

The British interest in Sikkim was linked to their trade and political interest in Tibet. Both Bhutan and Sikkim were the possible gateways to Tibet. Sikkim, besides being the weaker of the two, had an easy access. On Feb. 10, 1817, Sikkim signed a treaty with the East India Company surrendering all her rights to deal with any foreign power and conceded unhindered right of free access to the British upto Tibet border and Sikkim became a de-facto protectorate in 1861 when this treaty was further revised. The Anglo-Chinese Convention of 1890 put a seal on this status.

The ethnic scene of Sikkim began to change rapidly with the advent of the British. Not only had the early Nepalese settlers multiplied in numbers, the British needed more Nepalese labour to develop the communication network for access to Tibet. By 1891, the Nepalese constituted fifty-one (51%) per cent of Sikkim's population, reducing the Lepchas to nineteen per cent (19%) and Bhutias to Sixteen per cent (16%). This excluded Darjeeling which had been gifted by the Sikkim ruler to the British as a health and recreation resort forming part of the State of Bengal under British occupation.[4]

In 1830, an official of the East India Company, J.B. Herbert wrote a valuable travel-account of Sikkim namely *'Particulars of Visit to the Sikkim Hills'*.

The *Sikkim Gazetteer* compiled by H.H. Raisley in 1889 is the main source of knowledge about Sikkim of a hundred years before.[5] The book is in the form of travel account and official reports. The book also discusses various ethnic groups in Sikkim.

The ethnic composition changed in Sikkim by 1947 when the British left India and India became independent. The Nepalese constituted 75.0 per cent of Sikkim's population reducing the Bhutia community to 11.0 per cent and the Lepchas to 14.0 per cent. In terms of inter-ethnic group interaction, it acquired the attributes of a plural society with the focal point of its management being the ruler whose shrewd manipulations succeeded in co-opting at the top, the ethnic notables in the economic, administrative and political fields.[6]

Economic Perspective

Being a very humid region, Sikkim has a variety of flora and fauna as resource-base. The state possesses 4000 species of flora of wild relatives of crop plants, native bamboos, medicinal plants like Ginseng, Chirota, Jatamansi etc., beautiful orchids and many species of Rhododendrons. Sikkim occupies the first position in the country with 600 species of orchids in the state. As reported, in respect of faunal resources, the state has 144 species of mammals, 429 species of birds, 39 species of reptiles, 9 species of amphibia, 16 species of fish and 423 species of lepidopterons insects.[7]

The total area under cultivation as per 1980-81 Agricultural census was 1,09,068 hectares divided into 56,198 holdings. More than 80.0 per cent of the holdings are below 3.0 hectares. The agricultural lands are situated at an altitude of 300 mt. to as high as 3600 mt., but the majority of the cultivated area lies below 1800 mt. At lower altitudes it is possible to carry out multiple cropping but at high altitudes only monocropping is possible.[8]

The mineral deposits in Sikkim are notably copper, zinc, lead, dolomite, graphite etc. The copper reserves found at Rangpo have been estimated at 6 lakh tonnes and those at Dikchu at 2,87,000 tonnes. High grade dolomite reserves of 11,00,000 have been located near Rishi.[9]

Sikkim also is rich in hydro-potential. Besides the two main rivers, there are many rivulets like Tholung chu, Lachan chu, Lachung chu, Bokachu chu, Kayam chu and Rangbhang khola. All these rivers drain out through deep mountain gorges and the rapid currents could be used for hydro-electric generation.

The utilisation of all these resources has been, however, very much below expectation. In the following section we take a look at the growth of the economy over the years.

Growth of Economy (Pre-Merger Situation)

Planned economic development in Sikkim started in 1954 by the then Prime Minister of India Pandit Jawaharlal Nehru and Chogyal of Sikkim. The Table 1.1 shows the pattern of actual plan expenditure during the first four plans (1954-76).

TABLE 1.1

PATTERN OF SECTORAL OUTLAY DURING THE FIRST FOUR PLANS (1954-76)

(Rs. in lakh)

Sector	*Total Plan Outlay (1954-76)*
Agriculture & Allied	610.0
PRIMARY SECTOR (A)	610.0 (16.0)
Power	263.0
Industry, Mining & Commerce	291.0
SECONDARY SECTOR (B)	554.0 (14.5)
Road & Transport	1699.00
Education	343.0
Health	234.0
Co-operation	34.0
Miscellaneous	338.0
TERTIARY SECTOR (C)	2648.0 (69.5)
GRAND TOTAL = (A) + (B) + (C)	3812.0 (100.0)

Note: Figures in parentheses are per centages.

Source: Compiled from the Sixth Five Year Plan. Draft Proposal (1980-85), Department of Planning & Development, Government of Sikkim.

The total expenditure incurred over the twenty-two year period was Rs. 3812.0 lakh. In this total, the Agriculture and Allied Sector accounted for 16.0 per cent, and the Secondary Sector for 14.5 per cent. The Secondary Sector, however, also included power and it accounted for 6.9 per cent of the total plan expenditure; thus the industry's share was only 7.6 per cent. The highest allocation was for the Tertiary Sector, accounting for 69.5 per cent to the total plan expenditure. In the aggregate for the tertiary sector, Road and Transport accounted for as much as 64.2 per cent.

As regard achievements, according to a survey conducted by the Reserve Bank of India, 80.6 per cent of the net domestic product in 1965-66 accrued from agriculture, 7.3 per cent from Industry, Mining and Construction, 5.6 per cent from Trade, Commerce and Transport and 6.5 per cent from services. The per capita annual income was less than Rs. 500 in 1975.[10]

The growth in agricultural output was very meagre. Production of foodgrains in 1975-76 stood at only 29,650 tonnes with Maize accounting for 16 thousand tonnes and Rice 8,200 tonnes. Output of Soyabean in that year was 1,200 tonnes and of Rapeseed and Mustard 150 tonnes. Production of potato stood at 4,500 tonnes, of ginger 2,750 tonnes and large cardamom 3,300 tonnes. Among fruits, orange was the most important and its output stood at 5,600 tonnes in 1975-76. The output of fruits as a whole stood at 6,100 tonnes.[11]

The pace of industrial development in the pre-merger period was very slow. Total number of small and medium scale units in 1975 was only 31. The important among them were Sikkim Distillery Limited, Government Fruit Preservation Factory, Sikkim Mining Corporation, Sikkim Tannery Private Limited and Sikkim Jewels Limited. The achievements were more significant in the area of infrastructure. In 1950, Sikkim had only 2 kms. of pucca road in the capital town and 39 kms. of bullock cart road connecting Gangtok with Rangpo. By the end of 1975, the total mileage rose to about 828 kms. Many of the roads were, however, only fair weather ones. In power generation, the installed capacity stood at only 2.87 MW in 1975. The per capita power availability was 0.0022 KW.[12]

A full-fledged department of co-operation to look after the co-operatives was established in 1975 to boost the co-operative movement in the state.

On the Educational front, a total of 264 schools existed in the state during 1975-76. Out of this 228 were primary schools. 29 middle and only 7 higher secondary schools. Total enrolment during that period was 20,959 in which 66 per cent was boys. The plan and non-plan expenditure during 1975-76 accounted for Rs. 7.5 crore and Rs. 4.6 crore respectively. During the period, tax revenue collected was Rs. 1.3 crore and grants-in-aid was Rs. 7.1 crore.[13]

The post-merger period witnessed an unprecedented growth in the economy of the state. In the next chapter, an elaboration and analysis has been made on the post-merger development.

REFERENCES

1. Government of Sikkim (GOS), *Agriculture Census*, 1980-81, p. 10.
2. *Ibid.*, p. 10.
3. GOS, *Sikkim at a Glance*, 1993, p, 2.
4. Das, B.S. *The Sikkim Saga*, Vikas Publishing House Pvt. Ltd., New Delhi, 1990, p. 6.
5. Raisley, H.H, *Gazetteer of Sikkim*, Bengal Secretariat Press, Calcutta, 1894.
6. Das, B.S., *The Sikkim Saga, op. cit.*
7. GOS, *Agriculture Census, op. cit.*, pp. 21-24.
8. *Ibid.*, p. 40 and Annexure 1.
9. State Bank of India, *Lead Bank Survey*, Gangtok, 1985, p. 4.
10. GOS, *Compendium of Achievement*, 1987, p. ii.
11. *Ibid*, p. 4.
12. *Ibid*, p. ii.
13. *Ibid.*, pp. 39-40 and *Statistical Profile (1979-80 and 1991-92)*, GOS, p. 156.

2

State of Economy

The princely State of Sikkim was merged into India in 1975 and this was expected to give a significant boost to the development efforts in Sikkim. In Table 2.1, we present the increase in total expenditure since the merger.

TABLE 2.1

FIVE YEAR PLAN OUTLAY IN SIKKIM

(Rs. in Crore)

Plans	*Primary Sector*	*Secondary Sector*	*Tertiary Sector*	*Total*
1st Plan	0.5	0.5	2.2	3.2[1]
2nd Plan	1.0	0.7	4.7	6.4
3rd Plan	1.4	1.5	6.8	9.7
4th Plan	3.2	2.9	12.7	18.8
5th Plan	11.2	18.8	53.1	83.1
6th Plan	21.4	34.0	66.5	121.9
7th Plan	61.7	73.9	158.2	293 8
8th Plan	—	—	—	550.0[2]

1. First plan was of 7 years duration (1954-61)
2. Approved Outlay.

Source: Economic Survey, 1991-92, Bureau of Economics & Statistics (B.E.&S.), Govt. of Sikkim (GOS), p. 58.

The post-merger period experienced an unprecedented growth in plan expenditure. The total of expenditure during the Seventh Plan rose to Rs. 293.8 Crore from Rs. 83.1 Crore during the four years of the Fifth Plan. The average annual expenditure in the latter period, at Rs. 58.8 Crore was thus around three times the level of expenditure in the former period, which was at Rs. 20.8 Crore.

In the total outlay, during the fifth plan, the tertiary sector accounted for 64.0 per cent amounting to Rs. 53.1 Crore to the total outlay of Rs. 83.1 Crore. The Secondary Sector spent Rs. 18.8 Crore i.e., 21.0 per cent to the total during the plan period. The huge allocation for the tertiary sector was mainly due to the expenditure on roads and bridges. This was extremely necessary to develop basic infrastructure in the State. In the Secondary Sector, Power occupied major expenditure again in order to develop infrastructural base in the State.

In the Sixth five year plan, percentage wise allocation to the tertiary sector came down by 10.0 per cent which was diverted to the Secondary Sector, ensuring for the sector about 30.0 per cent of the total plan allocation. This was to give impetus to the power sector especially to spread electric connection to the whole state.

The Seventh Plan experienced an increase in the primary sector by 6.0 per cent. In this plan, Primary Sector consisting of agriculture and allied activities, amounted to Rs. 61.7 Crore to the total expenditure of Rs. 293.8 Crore registering 21.0 per cent. In the two preceding five year plans i.e., 5th and 6th, Primary Sector accounted for 15.0 per cent of the total plan outlay. The Secondary Sector had 25.0 per cent of the total expenditure.

Table 2.2 exhibited revenue income by the State. The revenue collection from 1975-76 to 1984-85 rose to Rs. 77.2 Crore from Rs. 10.4 Crore. The growth was about 8 times. However, grants-in-aid is the main component in this hike. During 1984-85, grants-in-aid by the Central Government was Rs. 60.5 Cr. i.e., more than 80.0 per cent. The trend, remained unchanged during 1994-95, when grants-in-aid amounted to Rs. 215.2 Cr. to the total of Rs. 263.7 Crore accounting for 81.0 per cent to the total. During the period, Rs. 19.0 Crore was collected from tax revenue i.e. about 7.2 per cent of the total.

TABLE 2.2

DETAILS OF REVENUE RECEIPTS OF SIKKIM

(Rs. in Crore)

Year	*Tax Revenue*	*Non-Tax Revenue*	*Grants-in-Aid*	*Total*
1975-76	1.3	2.0	7.1	10.4
1979-80	2.8	3.7	26.3	32.8
1980-81	2.9	5.5	32.4	40.8
1981-82	3.5	4.8	30.8	39.1
1982-83	3.9	7.6	33.7	45.2
1983-84	4.8	7.9	43.4	56.1
1984-85	6.0	10.7	60.5	77.2
1985-86	7.6	10.8	73.2	91.6
1986-87	9.8	14.6	89.1	113.5
1987-88	11.2	18.0	97.2	126.4
1988-89	15.1	22.9	111.5	149.5
1989-90	15.9	20.5	97.8	134.2
1990-91	15.3	26.7	117.5	159.5
1991-92	15.4	28.6	138.4	182.4
1992-93	16.3	30.9	162.1	209.3
1993-94	20.9	27.6	176.5	225.0
1994-95	19.0	29.5	215.2	263.7
TOTAL	171.7	272.4	1512.7	1956.8

Source: Report on the Financial Position of Sikkim as at 31.3.94, GOS, p. 2 and Economic Survey, 1992, GOS, p. 59.

An account of both plan and non-plan expenditure has been drawn in Table 2.3 since the merger. It is apparent that non-plan expenditure constituted substantial portion in the total expenditure. In the total expenditure, plan expenditure was 51.5 per cent and the rest was non-plan expenditure.

TABLE 2.3

POST-MERGER PLAN EXPENDITURE IN SIKKIM

(Rs. in Crore)

Year	*Plan Exp.*	*Non-Plan Exp.*	*Total*
1975-76	7.5	4.6	12.1
1976-77	11.2	8.8	20.0
1977-78	12.8	11.2	24.0
1978-79	16.1	14.2	30.3
1979-80	21.0	17.8	38.8
1980-81	21.5	21.5	43.0
1981-82	24.5	20.3	44.8
1982-83	23.9	22.8	46.7
1983-84	28.7	38.4	67.1
1984-85	44.8	31.5	76.3
1985-86	60.0	43.9	103.9
1986-87	66.2	48.9	115.1
1987-88	73.5	65.1	138.6
1988-89	82.1	81.7	163.8
1989-90	86.5	80.3	166.8
1990-91	94.6	88.6	183.2
1991-92	121.1	102.3	223.4
1992-93	120.3	123.1	243.4
1993-94	129.6	138.3	267.9
1994-95	138.0	150.0	288.0
TOTAL	1183.9	1113.3	2297.2

Source: *Statistical Profile of Sikkim (1979-80 and 1991-92), and Report on the Financial Position on 31.3.94,* GOS, pp. 12-13.

There is a spectacular growth in total plan expenditure during 1975-90. In the first five years i.e. 1975-80, total plan expenditure was Rs. 125.2 Crore; in the later years i.e. 1985-90, total plan expenditure has risen to Rs. 688.2 Crore, registering an increase of 5.5 times over the years. However, the growth between 1980-85 and 1990-95 has been reduced to 4.3 per cent.

The growth in plan and non-plan expenditure is also akin to the rate of total expenditure.

For 1993-94, as against the total per capita developmental receipt of Rs. 5723.0 the disbursement was Rs. 6233.0.[1]

The Net State Domestic Product at current prices as per quick and provisional estimate was Rs. 25015.0 lakh and per capita income was Rs. 5707.0 for the year 1993-94. The per capita income thereby grew more than 10 times from Rs. 500.0 in 1975.[2]

Table 2.4 shows the growth in net State Domestic Product since 1985. In recent years the growth has come down to a meagre 2.0 per cent.

Table 2.5 depicts the growth in per capita income in Sikkim compared to the All-India level. The per capita income in Sikkim was ahead of the All-India per capita level.

The Consumer Price Index in Sikkim, however, indicates higher prices compared to All-India indices. Table 2.6 noted the differences in Price-Index for five years, the base being 1982. In 1993-94, the general index in Sikkim mounted to 303.8 points.

The growth in the rate of inflation registered comparatively low inflation during 1992-93, as evident in Table 2.7.

TABLE 2.4

NET STATE DOMESTIC PRODUCT (NSDP) IN SIKKIM

(Rs. in Lakh)
Base = 1980-81

	At Current Price		*At Constant Price*	
Year	*NSDP*	*% Change*	*NSDP*	*% Change*
1985-86	11330.0	—	7559.0	—
1986-87	13476.0	18.9	8916.0	17.9
1987-88	15607.0	15.8	10775.0	20.6
1988-89	16665.0	6.8	11490.0	6.8
1989-90	18467.0	10.8	12289.0	6.9
1990-91	21294.0	15.3	13574.0	10.5
1991-92	22817.0	7.2	13851.0	2.0
1993-94	25015.0	—	—	—

Source: Economic Survey, 1994, B.E.& S., GOS, p. 78.

TABLE 2.5

PER CAPITA INCOME: SIKKIM VIS-A-VIS ALL INDIA

Year	*Current Prices(Rs.)*		*Constant Prices (Rs.) (Base = 1980—81)*	
	Sikkim	*All India*	*Sikkim*	*All India*
1985-86	3023.0	2734.0	2017.0	1844.0
1986-87	3886.0	3289.0	2678.0	1902.0
1988-89	4241.0	3844.0	2924.0	2069.0
1989-90	4686.0	4313.0	3118.0	2134.0
1990-91	5259.0	4934.0	3352.0	2199.0
1991-92	5522.0	5529.0	3352.0	2175.0
1993-94	5707.0	6928.8	—	2292.0

Source: *Economic Survey, 1994,* B.E.& S., GOS, p. 78.

In brief, since merger the plan outlay in the State increased in an unfettered way. The larger part of the plan expenditure had to be diverted for infrastructural development. Now the state has attained a level in roads, transport and bridges and in the Power Sector. The State has achieved cent per cent electrification in the late nineties.

TABLE 2.6

CONSUMER PRICE INDEX

Base 1982=100

	Sikkim		*All India*	
Year	*General Index*	*Food Index*	*General*	*Food*
1989-90	207.4	207.5	173.0	177.0
1990-91	238.3	239.9	193.0	199.0
1991-92	266.7	270.4	225.0	230.0
1992-93	277.7	287.5	240.0	254.0
1993-94	303.8	318.1	249.0	258.0

Source: Economic Survey,1994, B.E.& S., GOS, p. 79.

TABLE 2.7

ANNUAL RATE OF INFLATION

(Base 1982=100)

	Sikkim		*All India*	
Year	*General Index*	*Food Index*	*General*	*Food*
1989-90	4.9	5.6	7.0	5.1
1990-91	14.8	15.5	11.2	12.5
1991-92	11.9	12.8	13.5	15.6
1992-93	4.3	6.4	6.8	6.1
1993-94	9.2	10.6	9.1	9.9

Source: *Economic Survey, 1992*, B.E.& S., GOS, p. 60. and *Economic Survey*, 1994, B.E. & S.. GOS. p. 79.

In this chapter an analysis has been made on the Sectoral performance over the years. In some cases a comparative study has been made in between 1979-80 and

1991-92. Special emphasis is given to the Industrial Sector to find out the scope for study on the State level financing institute confined to financing industrial activities in the State.

The economy of Sikkim is reliant on the performance of Agricultural and Non-Agricultural enterprises. Due to geographical barriers, the State has derived majority of the enterprises and employment from non-agricultural sector.

The total number of enterprises and employment thereof is exhibited in Table 2.8. The majority of the enterprises and employment are confined to rural areas. In the total 10,686 enterprises, rural Sikkim accounts for 7366 enterprises, which is 69.0 per cent of the total. Out of the total 47,296 persons employed, 28,363 persons are in rural areas accounting for 60.0 per cent of the total.

TABLE 2.8

ENTERPRISES AND EMPLOYMENT IN SIKKIM (1990)

Location	*No. of Enterprises*		*No. of Employment*	
Rural	7366	(68.9)	28363	(60.0)
Urban	3320	(31.1)	18933	(40.0)
TOTAL	10686	(100.0)	47296	(100.0)

Note: Figures in parentheses represents percentages.
Source: Report on Economic Census, 1990, B.E.& S., GOS, p. 9.

The non-agricultural activities outnumbered agricultural activities in terms of number and employment of enterprises. As evident in Table 2.9, non-agricultural enterprises accounted for 9,997 enterprises out of the total 10,686 enterprises i.e., 93.5 per cent. Likewise, in employment also these enterprises numbered 45,369 persons against a total of 47,296 persons, i.e. 96.0 per cent.

TABLE 2.9

AGRICULTURAL AND NON-AGRICULTURAL ENTS. AND EMPLOYMENT (1990)

Sector	*No. of Enterprises*		*No. of Employment*	
Agriculture	689	(6.5)	1927	(4.1)
Non-Agriculture	9997	(93.5)	45369	(95.9)
TOTAL	10686	(100.0)	47296	(100.0)

Note: Figs. in parentheses denotes percentages.
Source: *Report on Economic Census*, 1990, B.E.& S., GOS, pp. 20-28.

TABLE 2.10

MAJOR ACTIVITY GROUP IN NON-AGRICULTURAL ENTERPRISES (1990)

Activity Group	*No. of Enter-prises*	*% to total*	*Employment* No.	*Employment* % to total
1. Mining & Quarrying	1	0.0	38	0.1
2. Manufacturing	884	8.8	5153	11.4
3. Electricity, Gas and Water	34	0.3	437	1.0
4. Construction	147	1.5	2206	4.9
5. Wholesale Trade	33	0.3	98	0.2
6. Retial Trade	4219	42.2	8622	19.0
7. Restaurant & Hotels	659	6.6	2402	5.3
8. Transport	192	1.9	443	1.0
9. Storage & Warehousing	95	0.9	309	0.7
10. Communication	157	1.6	664	1.5
11. Financial, Insurance, Banking, Business Services	100	1.0	1102	24.3
12. Community, Social and Personal Services	3476	34.9	23895	52.6
TOTAL	9997	100.0	45369	100.0

Source: *Report on Economic Census*, 1990, B.E.& S., GOS., p. 52.

Thus, in terms of business purpose, non-agricultural activities ushered in a major activity group both in the number of enterprises and employment. Table 2.10 enlisted as many as 12 of such activities attributed to the non-agricultural enterprises and employment.

Among non-agricultural activities, retail trade accounting for the largest share in total number of enterprises and community, social and personal activity provides maximum employment.

Retail trade, Community Services and Manufacturing altogether occupy 86.0 per cent of total enterprises and 83.0 per cent of total employment.

In two major activities, an inverse relation has been observed in the number of enterprises and employment thereon. While retail trade accounted for 42.0 per cent of the total enterprises, it only provides 19.0 per cent of the total employment. Similarly, Financial and Business groups constituting only 1.0 per cent of the enterprises offered 24.0 per cent of the total employment.

Intra-District Comparison

The spread of enterprise is highly skewed in favour of the east district. As evident from Table 2.11, this district occupies 55.0 per cent of the total enterprises and 63.0 per cent of the total employment.

TABLE 2.11

DISTRICT-WISE COMPARISON OF ENTERPRISES AND EMPLOYMENT

	Enterprises			*Employment*		
Districts	*Agri.*	*Non-Agri*	*Total*	*Agri.*	*Non-Agri*	*Total*
North	25	850	875	29	3262	3291
East	471	5418	5889	1369	28721	30090
South	128	2105	2233	220	8121	8341
West	65	1624	1689	309	5265	5574
STATE TOTAL	689	9997	10686	1927	45369	47296

Source: *Report on Economic Census*, 1990, B.E.& S., GOS, p.16.

Despite the small areas compared to other districts, the east occupies a dominant position in the concentration of industrial activities in the State.

There are 8 towns in Sikkim and Gangtok as the State Capital, is the nerve centre of all activities. Among the 8 towns, Gangtok shares 58.0 per cent of the total urban enterprises in the State. East district alone accounts for 77.5 per cent of the total urban enterprises.[3]

Rural and Urban

Among Agricultural Enterprises, 680 enterprises accounting for more than 98.0 per cent are in rural areas. In the total employment also more than 98.0 per cent are in rural areas. The female workers constitute 33.0 per cent of the total agricultural enterprises employment.[4]

Among non-agricultural enterprises, 6,686 enterprises out of a total of 9,997 i.e. 67.0 per cent are in rural areas. Employment-wise rural areas constitute 26,459 persons in the total number of 45,369 persons in this sector, which is 58.0 per cent to the total.[5]

Distribution Per 1000 Sq. Km. and 100 Sq. Km.

Overall distribution of enterprises per 1000 of population in the State is estimated at 26 and for agricultural and non-agricultural at 0.2 and 25 respectively. The concentration of enterprises in east district is 33 per thousand, followed by north's 28 per thousand. The lower distribution of enterprises per 100 sq. kms. in the north is due to the fact that 35.5 per cent of the total area in the district is perpetually snow-bound and 31.4 per cent are covered with shrubs, pastures and rocky barren areas of Alpine Zone. Only 12.5 per cent of the total area is available for habitation and cultivation.[6]

Size

The average enterprise size is estimated at 4.4 persons whereas in establishment, on an average 7.1 per sons were found working per enterprise.[7]

Ownership

Among enterprises, 73.8 per cent is under Private Ownership and 1.8 per cent is in the Co-operative Sector. About 83.9 per cent of the enterprises are operating without power. Again in non-power-driven enterprises, 93.0 per cent are engaged in non-agricultural activities.[8]

Ratios

The ratio of distribution of employment between rural-urban areas is 3:2. The ratio of employment between Male-Female is 3:1.

A comparative study of growth of structure, size and pattern of non-agricultural establishment reveals that:

1. The total non-agricultural establishments have gone up from 1976 units in 1979 to 9,997 units in 1990, registering an increase of more than 4 times.
2. The total employment has grown up by 127.0 per cent during 1979 to 1990; and
3. The use of power in establishment is increasing as per the census. In three consecutive economic census of the State the number of power-driven establishments, was 12.8 per cent, 16.5 per cent and 18.2 per cent respectively.[9]

Distribution of Work-force

The Table 2.12 reveals the distribution of population in different categories of workers. In the total population of 4,06,457 in 1991, the main work force constitutes 1,64,392

TABLE 2.12

ECONOMIC CLASSIFICATION OF POPULATION FOR 1981 AND 1991

	Item	*1981*	*1991*
1.	Population	316385	406457
2.	Main Workers	147436 (46.6)	164392 (40.4)
	A. Cultivators	88610	95078
	B. Agricultural Labourers	4887	12851
	C. Household Industry	1586	1267
	D. Other Workers	52353	55196
3.	Marginal Workers	5378 (1.7)	4329 (1.1)
4.	Non-workers	163571 (51.7)	237736 (58.5)
		316385 (100.0)	406457 (100.0)

Note: *Figures in parentheses denote percentage.*

Source: Census of India 1981 and 1991 quoted in Sikkim — Statistical Profile (1979-80 to 1991-92), B.E.& S., GOS, P. 6.

i.e., 40.4 per cent of the total populace. The growth in main work force over 1981 census is 11.5 per cent. In the main work force of 1991, cultivators accounted for 58.0 per cent and agricultural labourers were 7.8 per cent; household industry occupied a meagre 0.8 per cent. However, in total population cultivators and agricultural labourers comprised 26.6 per cent. The household industry occupies 0.03 per cent of the total population. The marginal workers were only 1.1 per cent of the total population during 1991. The large chunk i.e., 58.5 per cent of the total population is in 'non-worker' group. They are children and aged people. According to 1981 census, about 50.0 per cent of the total population were below 19 years of age. The old people i.e., those above 65 years were 2.5 per cent of the total population.

As one-fourth i.e., about 26.0 per cent of the total population is engaged in agriculture, it is thus the single largest employer in the State. The post-merger agricultural development shows spectacular growth in crop production, seed production etc. In power, roads, forests, dairy products, banking etc., the State has achieved notable improvement. The performance of important sectors is discussed in this chapter.

Pattern of Land Holding

In the hill-locked State of Sikkim, only 11.0 per cent of the total area is cultivated. It is evident from the Table 2.13 that the total operated area is 15.4 per cent. The vast area of 36.1 per cent is under forest and 25.4 per cent is barren land.

TABLE 2.13

USE OF LAND

	Type of Land	*Hectare*	*Percent*
1.	a) Net Area sown	78,321	11.0
	b) Fallow & Culturable Waste & Others	31,647	4.4
	Total Operated Area	1,09,968	15.4
2.	Forest	2,56,533	36.1
3.	Misc. trees and groves	5,450	0.8
4.	Pastures	72,937	10.3
5.	Land for non—agricultural use	85,362	12.0
6.	Barren	1,80,250	25.4
TOTAL		7,09,600	100.0

Source: *Agricultural Census, Sikkim,* 1981, GOS, p. 51.

The number of operational holding in the State is 56,200 (Table 2.14). Total area operated is 109 thousand hectares. Thus average size of holding is 1.9 hectare per holding.

TABLE 2.14

DISTRICT-WISE LAND HOLDING

	North	East	South	West	Total
Operational holding (No.)	4800	18200	16300	16900	56200
Operated Area (Hect.)	15300	31700	29500	32600	109100
Average size of holdings (Hect.)	3.2	1.7	1.8	1.9	1.9

Source: Sikkim at Glance 1993, B.E.&S., GOS, p. 2.

The maximum number of holdings is in the east district and it numbers 18,200 holding followed by West's 16,900, South's 16,300 and North's 4,800 holdings But in case of operated area, West district accounts for the largest area of 32.6 thousand hectares followed by East's, 31.7 thousand hectares and South's 29.5 thousand hectares. Again, in case of average size of holdings the north district has the largest holding with 3.2 hectares.

In the size and pattern of operational holding, as disclosed in Table 2.15, small area holding is at the maximum. The maximum number of holding i.e., 25.0 per cent holding is of below 0.5 hectare group. However, the maximum area held is in the size of 1.0 to 2.0 hectares.

TABLE 2.15

SIZE, PATTERN OF OPERATIONAL HOLDING

Size Class (Hectares)	*Number of Holdings*	*Percentage of Holdings*	*Cumulative Percentage of Holdings*	*Area held (hect)*	*Percentage of Area held*	*Cumulative percentage of Area held*
1	2	3	4	5	6	7
Below 0.5	14097	25.1	25.1	3804	3.5	3.5
0.5-1.0	11438	20.4	45.5	8156	7.5	11.0

1	2	3	4	5	6	7
1.0-2.0	13076	23.3	68.8	18797	17.2	28.2
2.0-3.0	7132	12.7	81.5	17378	15.9	44.1
3.0-4.0	3794	6.8	88.3	13124	12.0	56.1
4.0-5.0	2254	4.0	92.3	10015	9.2	65.3
5.0-7.5	2599	4.6	96.9	15630	14.3	79.6
7.5-10.0	935	1.6	98.5	7917	7.2	86.8
10.0-20.0	739	1.3	99.8	9414	8.6	95.4
20.0-30.0	92	0.1	99.9	2080	1.9	97.3
30.0-40.0	24	0.06	99.96	829	0.7	98.0
40.0-50.0	4	0.02	99.98	170	0.1	98.1
50.0 & above	14	0.02	100.00	1754	1.6	100.0
ALL SIZE	56198	100.0	—	109068	100.0	—

Source: Economic Survey.. 1991-92, B.E.&S., GOS, p. 54.

Agricultural Operation

Table 2.16 exhibits a comparison of area under principal agricultural crops between 1979-80 and 1992-93. During 1979-80, maize cultivation was done in the largest area of 30.2 thousand hectares. Rice was cultivated in 14.8 thousand hectares followed by large cardamom, wheat etc. After a decade, till 1992-93 one major change occurred in large cardamon cultivation as almost 10.0 thousand hectares of land brought under cardamon cultivation. Now, cardamom occupies the second largest area under cultivation. In respect of other crops, the area has also increased over the years.

Districtwise, the west accounted for the largest i.e., 32.4 hectares, followed by the East's 28.9 hectares and so on.

Production

In the account of production between 1979-93, maize possesses the highest production of 53.9 thousand tonnes

TABLE 2.16

AREA UNDER PRINCIPAL CROPS

('000 Hect.)

		Districts				*Total*
	1979-80	*North*	*East*	*South*	*West*	*1992-93*
Maize	30.2	3.0	9.6	13.5	14.3	40.4
Large Cardamom	13.8	7.4	7.0	4.7	4.4	23.5
Rice	14.8	1.4	6.7	2.5	5.5	16.1
Wheat	7.0	1.0	2.7	1.9	2.4	8.0
Pulses	3.4	0.1	1.5	2.1	2.5	6.2
Potato	1.8	0.3	1.2	0.6	3.0	5.1
Barley	0.6	0.1	0.2	0.1	0.3	0.7
TOTAL	71.6	13.3	28.9	25.4	32.4	100.0

Source: *Statistical Profile* (1979-80 to 1991-92) and *Sikkim at a Glance,* 1993, B.E.&S., GOS, p. 16 and p. 2.

in 1992-93 as compared to 27.8 thousand tonnes during 1979-80. The production of Potato has shot up more than 5 times, from 6.1 thousand tonnes in 1979-80 to 33.5 thousand tonnes in 1992-93. Rice production has come down to the third position from 10.3 thousand tonnes to 20.7 thousand tonnes over the years. Table 2.17 exhibits the position of production of different crops.

The production of Cardamom is stagnant over the years. This again show negative productivity because the land under cardamom cultivation increased by about 77.0 per cent during the period. In the total of these crops, the growth in production registered 120.0 per cent during 1979-93.

Horticultural Product

Horticulture is gaining momentum in Sikkim. As the

State has potential to develop in this field, so the government is maintaining a sęparate horticulture department to boost up production.

TABLE 2.17

PRODUCTION OF PRINCIPAL CROPS

('000 tonne')

		Districts				*Total*
	1979-80	*North*	*East*	*South*	*West*	*1992-93*
Maize	27.8	4.2	13.8	15.4	20.5	53.9
Potato	6.1	2.5	8.3	4.1	18.6	33.5
Rice	10.3	1.7	8.9	3.0	7.1	20.7
Wheat	10.4	1.7	5.0	3.2	4.2	14.1
Pulses	2.0	0.1	1.4	1.8	2.2	5.5
Cardamom	3.5	1.2	1.1	0.7	0.7	3.7
Barley	0.5	0.1	0.3	1.2	0.5	2.1
TOTAL	60.6	11.5	38.8	29.4	53.8	133.5

Source: *Statistical Profile* (1979-80 to 1991-92) and *Sikkim at a Glance* 1993, B.E.& S., GOS, *op. cit.*

Besides large cardamom, ginger is also produced in abundance in the State. Till 1992, 3.5 thousand hectares of land produced 17.0 thousand tonnes of ginger. A Spices Board (earlier Cardamom Board) under the Ministry of Commerce, Government of India is operating in the State to help and trade the spices especially cardamom, Ginger etc. Another important horticultural product is Citrus with a production of 16.5 thousand tonnes. In vegetables and fruits, leafy mustard, radish, cabbage, beans, tomato and banana are important and production with area cultivated is depicted in Table 2.18.

Forest

Besides the Agricultural Sector, the State exchequer is also enriched by many other Sectors.

TABLE 2.18

IMPORTANT HORTICULTURAL CROPS

Crops	*Area ('000 Hect.) 1991-92*	*Production ('000 tonnes) 1991-92*
Ginger	3.5	17.0
Citrus	6.3	16.5
Leafy Mustard (Rayo)	0.6	4.8
Radish	0.6	4.6
Chayote	0.4	4.3
Cabbage	0.4	3.8
French bean	0.9	3.6
Garden Pea	0.9	3.6
Tomato	0.5	2.6
Banana	0.8	1.3

Source: *Statistical Profile* (1979-80 to 1991-92), B.E.S., GOS, p. 17.

Forest is contributing to the State Exchequer in the form of sale of forest produce and during the year 1991-92, Rs. 91.2 lakh have been contributed which is 17.3 per cent lower than in the last year. Among the forest produce, Sandstone appears to be the largest factor contribution with Rs. 51.4 lakh i.e., 56.0 per cent of the total. Table 2.19 gives the comparative picture of the forest produce for the last two years.

Milk, Egg and Wool Production (Genetic Industry)

The animal husbandry Sector has been providing supplementary income to a large number of families especially in rural areas. The State has already established a good infrastructure not only to look after the animal health but also to bring about qualitative and quantitative changes in animal population.

TABLE 2.19

FOREST PRODUCE

(Rs. in lakh)

		1990-91	*1991-92*
1.	Sand stone	36.9	51.4
2.	Misc. forest products	53.6	21.2
3.	Timber	8.9	8.6
4.	Charcoal	4.3	4.5
5.	Fuelwood	2.6	3.7
6.	Others	3.9	2.4
	TOTAL	110.2	˙91.8

Source: *Economic Survey*, 1992, B.E.&S, GOS, p. 12.

The overall achievement in milk, egg and wool production during the last three five year plans is evident from Table 2.20. The growth in milk production was about 100.0 per cent in the 6th plan as compared to the previous plan period. The growth rate has come down compared to 6th plan to 42.0 per cent with 27,000 million in 7th plan. The growth in egg production was 180.0 per cent in the 6th plan over the 5th plan. In the 7th plan the growth registered 243.0 per cent. The growth rate in wool was negligible over the plan periods.

TABLE 2.20

PRODUCTION OF MILK, EGG AND WOOL

	5th Plan	*6th Plan*	*7th Plan*
Milk ('000 million)	10.9	19.0	27.0
Egg (million)	1.3	3.5	12.0
Wool ('000 Kg.)	24.0	24.0	28.0

Source: *Economic Survey*, B.E.&S., 1991-92, GOS, p. 2.

Per-Capita

The per capita milk consumption per diem is estimated

around 170 mili litre whereas egg consumption is estimated at 30 eggs per person per year in the State.[10]

During 1991-92, milk production increased to 28.6 thousand mega litre (ML). Egg production has gone up to 12.7 million which is 70,000 more than 1990-91. Wool production has gone up to 31.0 thousand kg. during the same period.[11]

Distribution of Input

The distribution of inputs for helping the poor and to bring about qualitative improvement in live-stock population is another important activity under this sector. Table 2.21 shows the distribution of inputs during two years.

TABLE 2.21

LIVE-STOCK POSITION

Items	*1990-91*	*1991-92*
Milch Cattle (no.)	115	80
Breeding Bull (no.)	52	15
Birds (no.)	2084	3000
Piglets (no.)	796	540
Fodder Plants (Rs. in lakh)	6.5	9.7
Fodder Seed (mt. tons)	—	150
Mini kit (kg.)	—	3000
Feed (kg.)	—	200

Source: *Economic Survey*, 1992, B.E.& S., GOS, p. 11.

As evident from the table, distribution in milch cattle and breeding bull has been reduced by 30.0 per cent and 70.0 per cent respectively. However, distribution of birds increased by 50.0 per cent between 1990-91 and 1991-92.

The department has increased expenditure on Fodder plants by Rs. 3.2 lakh over the years. New avenues have been opened for Fodder seed, Mini kit and Feed. The distribution during 1991-92 in Fodder Seed, Mini Kit and Feed were 150.0 Mt. tons, 3000.0 Kg. and 200.0 Kg. respectively. This, obviously, ushers in a new era in seed and feed for genetic industries in the State.

Fisheries and Fish Production

Despite the adequate resource endowment of fresh water rivers, lakes and streams, the pisciculature is yet to make a dent in enabling the rural people to derive substantial income.

The feasible area of pond fishery development is estimated around 110.0 hectares. Table 2.22 shows the production of fish, seed and area in operation etc.

TABLE 2.22

FISH PRODUCTION

	1981-82	*1991-92*	*1992-93*
Fish Production (tonnes)	24	95	97
Fish seed production (million)	0.5	1.0	1.0
Fish seed firms (no.)	1	5	5
Nursery Area (Hect.)	0.6	2.0	2.2

Source: *Sikkim — At a Glance*, 1993, B.E.& S., GOS, p. 2.

In a decade from 1981-82 to 1991-92, fish production has risen from 24.0 tonnes to 95.0 tonnes, i.e. an increase of about 4 times. The fish seed production has doubled from 0.5 million to 1.0 million during the same period. Fish nursery area was 0.6 hectares in 1981-82 and occupied 2.0 hectare in 1991-92. During the year, 2,80,000 fingerlings were distributed.

Communication

The State since its first economic planning in 1954 had only 19.0 Kms. of rough road from Rangpo to Gangtok and only 2.0 Kms. pucca road in Gangtok town. During 1992-93, total road network in the State has gone up to 1556.0 Kms (Table 2.23). As the State has only roads as lifeline, vehicular traffic and passengers have to use the only way of communication by road. At present, no rail or air service is available in the State.

TABLE 2.23

LENGTH OF ROAD

(in Kms.)

	1991-92	*1992-93*
National Highway	40	40
State Highway	225	225
Major District Road	446	446
Other District Road	820	845
	1531	1556

Source: *Sikkim — At a Glance*, 1993, B.E.&S., GOS, p. 2.

The Sikkim Nationalised Transport (SNT), a State owned transport undertaking regulates total goods traffic and near-total passenger traffic too.

At the end of 1991-92, SNT is operating with 4 divisional offices, 16 depots and 975 persons. It has a fleet strength of 137 buses for passenger traffic and 181 trucks and tankers covering the total length of 3,727 Kms. It covers on an average 64 Kms. per route with gross earnings of Rs. 7.28 per Km. and spent Rs. 6.88 per Km. leaving a balance of Rs. 0.40 per Km. SNT carried 9.8 lakh persons and 235 lakh tonnes of goods during the year.[12] But in 1994-95 the cumulative loss stood at Rs. 7.7 Crore.[13]

The tax collected by the motor vehicle on SNT movement during 1991-92 was Rs. 37.5 lakh as compared to 1988-89's Rs. 22.0 lakh.

Power

Although Sikkim is endowed with immense potential for generation of Hydro-electric power, it could tap only 0.3 per cent of its water resources for electricity generation. As on 31.3.92, installed capacity was 18.7 MW and generation of electricity was 39.3 MKWH. All the 405 villages and 8 towns in the State were electrified in 1990-91. Despite the fact that cent per cent electrification of villages and towns has been achieved, the gap between the peak power load and the actual supply has been estimated at 12.4 MW. During 1991-92, 27.0 MKWH energy were purchased from outside the State to meet the domestic demand. A look into the pattern of distribution by type of its actual users indicates that during 1991-92 47.0 per cent were used in domestic sector, 38.0 per cent were used in the industrial and commercial sector and the remaining 15.0 per cent have been used for public lighting. There is no power plant in south district. Total transmission loss was 22.0 per cent. Revenue earned from power supply was Rs. 90.0 lakh. In 1979-80 which has risen to Rs. 291.0 lakh in 1991-92. The average charge per unit of energy was Re. 0.40 in 1979-80 and Re. 0.80 in 1991-92.[14]

The Power Sector has been suffering losses since 1979. In 1979-80 the loss was Rs. 2.4 Cr. During 1993-94, the loss was as high as Rs. 5.1 Crore.[15] This, however, is largely attributed to the cost of cent per cent electrification in the state and outlay on the ongoing power projects in the State.

Excise

The State generates excise mainly from liquor industry and liquor shops. Sikkim Distilleries Limited, and Yuksom Breweries Ltd., are the two most important excise duty payers to the exchequer.

During 1979-80 excise revenue collection was Rs. 1.2 crore which has gone up to Rs. 6.28 crore during 1991-92.[16]

Co-operative

Co-operative movement in Sikkim started with the establishment of 35 Multi purpose Co-operative Societies (MPCS) during Fifth Five year plan, mainly for the purpose of providing institutional credit to the Agricultural Sector. At present 252 Co-operatives are working in the State under 13 different types of activities. Table 2.24, depicts the number, capital and Reserve Fund of the major Co-operatives of the State. Out of 252 Co-operatives, 42 were MPCs, 80 each of Consumer Co-operatives and Milk Producing Co-operatives followed by 22 Agricultural Credit Co-operatives; the rest were of Transport, Industrial, Weavers, Marketing and Housing in nature.

TABLE 2.24

CAPITAL ENDOWMENT OF CO-OPERATIVE SOCIETIES ON 31.03.1992

(Rs. in Lakh)

Type	*No.*	*Paid Up Capital*	*Working Capital*	*Reserve Fund*
MPCS	42	13.0	161.0	2.0
Consumer Co-Ops.	80	11.2	34.8	15.6
Milk Producers Co-Op.	80	3.2	64.0	0.6

Source: Statistical Profile (1979-80 to 1991-92), B.E.& S., GOS, pp. 41-42.

The MPCS prossess largest paid up Capital of Rs. 13.0 lakh, working Capital of Rs. 161.0 lakh and Reserve Fund of Rs. 2.0 lakh as on 31.3.92. The Consumer Co-operatives maintains Reserve Fund of Rs. 15.6 lakh with a paid up Capital of Rs. 11.2 lakh.

In Table 2.25, comparative performance of Co-operative

sector is cited. The Short-term loan by the Co-operative has dwindled to a considerable extent from Rs. 40.2 lakh in 1979-80 to Rs. 0.7 lakh in 1991-92. However, retail sale of fertilisers and urban consumer goods has increased by Rs. 59.8 lakh and Rs. 27.9 lakh respectively during 1991-92. The marketing of agricultural produce by the Co-operatives was Rs. 15.7 lakh during 1991-92.

TABLE 2.25

PERFORMANCE OF THE CO-OPERATIVE SECTOR

(Rs. in Lakh)

	1979-80	*1991-92*
Short term loans	40.2	0.7
Medium term loans	8.1	—
Loan outstanding	—	35.4
Retail Sale of fertilisers	100.0	159.8
Retail sale of urban consumer co-ops.	60.0	87.9
Agricultural produce marketed	—	15.7

Source: *Statistical Profile (1979-80 to 1991-92)*, B.E.& S., GOS, p. 42.

For the Eighth Plan, the logistics of Co-operative movement aim to consolidate its structure further, extending its network towards agro-based industries, village industries and artisans like Blacksmith, Tailoring, Floriculture, Poultry, Piggery and Weavers' Co-operatives as well as reviving sick units. An integrated Co-operatives as well as reviving sick units. An integrated Co-operative Development Project is also initiated to give impetus to the overall co-operative movement in the State.

Banking

The Scheduled Commercial Bank started its operation in the State in 1966 with the branch of the State Bank of India (SBI). Till 31.3.93, total number of branches of Public Sector Banks registered as 38. The State Bank of Sikkim, which was established by the King has 21 branches and another Private Sector Bank, the Sikkim Bank Ltd., has 4 branches. Thus taking all banks (Public and Private), the total number of commercial Banks operating in the State till at 31.3.93 was 63. Besides, National Bank for Agricultural and Rural Development (NABARD) and Small Industries Development Bank of India (SIDBI) act as refinancing agencies in respective fields.

Total deposits mobilised by Public Sector Banks till 31.3.92, as evident in Table 2.26, stood at Rs. 11,326.7 lakh and advance provided for was Rs. 3,097.5 lakh. The Credit Deposit ratio was 1:3.6. Total advance to priority sector was Rs. 1,006.7 lakh, which was 32.5 per cent to the total advanced amount. In priority sector, both agriculture and industry shared an equal amount of Rs. 350.5 lakh and Rs. 354.2 lakh respectively.

TABLE 2.26

PERFORMANCE OF PUBLIC SECTOR BANKS ON 31.12.91

(Rs. in Lakh)

	Advance to Priority Sec.					
Districts	*Agri.*	*Ind.*	*Tertiary*	*Total Pr. Sec. Advance*	*Total Adv.*	*Total Deposit*
East	154.1 (43.9)	323.5 (93.7)	227.3 (73.1)	704.9 (70.0)	2771.3 (89.5)	10040.9 (88.7)
North	34.2 (9.8)	1.6 (0.4)	16.0 (5.1)	51.8 (5.1)	58.2 (1.9)	214.9 (1.9)
South	86.5 (24.6)	17.4 (5 .0)	36.8 (11.8)	140.7 (14.0)	132.6 (4.2)	716.1 (6.3)
West	75.7 (21.7)	2.7 (0.9)	30.9 (10.0)	109.3 (10.9)	135.4 (4.4)	354.8 (3.1)
	350.5 (100.0)	345.2 (100.0)	311.0 (100.0)	1006.7 (100.0)	3097.5 (100.0)	11326.7 (100.0)

Source: *Statistical Profile* (1979-80 to 1991-92), GOS, p. 137.

A look into the districtwise distribution of the total deposits and total advances of Public Sector banks reveals that the lion's share of both the deposits and advances originate and are distributed in the east district which accounts for 89.0 per cent of both the deposits and advances. In priority sector, this district shared 70.0 per cent of the total advance. In the total industrial allocation to all districts, the east occupies 93.7 per cent of the industrial advance.

In case of State Bank of Sikkim (SBS), till 31.3.94, total advance was Rs. 3,835.0 lakh and total deposits amounted to Rs. 2,594.5 lakh. About 98.0 per cent advance was provided to non-priority sector viz., House Construction and Loans to Govt. employees.[17] This bank is facing severe resource-crunch for maladministration.

The Sikkim Bank Ltd. (SBI) accumulated deposits of Rs. 66.4 lakh and provided advances of Rs. 112.2 lakh during 1993-94.[18]

Tourism

Keeping in view the salubrious climate in the State and the excellent natural scenic beauties, Sikkim has high potentials for development of tourism which may contribute substantially in the form of spin-off benefits to the overall health of the economy. Table 2.27 shows the number of tourist traffic since 1975-76.

During 1975-93, a total of 3,02,866 tourists visited the State. In this, 92.0 per cent is domestic tourists. During 1992-93, tourist influx was 77,725 registering a growth of 15.0 per cent over the previous year.

During 1975-76 to 1991-93, the number of tourists have shot up from 1,300 persons to 77,725 persons i.e., 60 times. The actual plan outlay on tourism was Rs. 24.3 lakh in 1979-80 and it rose to Rs. 139.1 lakh during 1991-92 i.e., about 5 times.[19]

TABLE 2.27

GROWTH IN TOURIST TRAFFIC

Year	*Domestic*	*Foreign*	*Total*
1975-76	800	500	1300
1979-80	12862	2572	15434
1984-85	31439	2119	33558
1989-90	44478	1939	46417
1990-91	56706	4179	60885
1991-92	61360	6187	67547
1992-93	70365	7360	77725
	278010	24856	302866

Source: *Economic Survey*, 1992 B.E.& S., GOS, p. 57, and *Sikkim—At a glance*, 1993, B.E. & S., GOS, p. 2.

Never since its inception, has the tourism department made any Profit. The losses incurred during 1991, 1992 and 1992-93 amounted to Rs. 0.9 crore, Rs. 0.9 crore and Rs. 1.7 crore respectively. The cumulative loss suffered upto 1994-95 amounted to Rs. 14.4 crore.[20]

Registration of Industries

In a state like Sikkim with thousands of hindrances to set up industries, the people of Sikkim have always tried to be industrious with indomitable pragmatism. As a result, in the last decade many industrialists set up industries and a few of them still exists in some business or other. With a population growth of 28.0 per cent in 1991 census, the State realised industrial development as its destiny. There are many industries with high potential which could come up in the State viz., Electronics, Assembling industries, Small Scale Industries related to plants and herbs.

During 1978-79, out of a total of 196 units, some important units were : 65 units of Carpet weaving Centres, 22 tailoring shops, 18 paddy dehusking units, 13 motor repairing centres and 10 bakery and confectionery. Other medium-scale industries in 1979 were, Sikkim Distillery Limited, Govt. Fruit Preservation factory, Industrial Jewels Factory, Watch-assembling Unit and Sikkim Tannery Ltd. Till 1979, 43 units were registered as Small Scale Unit and 94 units as Tiny Units. A total of 2,200 persons were employed in these industries.[21]

The registration of industries increased many times over the years (Table 2.28). As on 31.3.93, provisionally registered SSIs in the State stood at 1,403, of which only 243 units obtained permanent registration from the Directorate of Industries. Thus only 17.0 per cent of the provisionally registered units got permanent registration. This is because the units could not arrange requirements like buildings, power, machinery etc., necessary for permanent registration. This signifies the inability of the units to procure infrastructure and inputs which demolishes the prospect of a unit in its initial stage.

TABLE 2.28

REGISTRATION OF INDUSTRIES

	North	*East*	*South*	*West*	*Total*
Provisional Registration	274	797	201	131	1403
Permanent Registration	5	179	39	20	243

Source: *Sikkim — At a Glance* 1993, B.E.& S., GOS, p. 2.

In view of the huge tourist influx in the State since the late eighties, hotels and transport alongwith some other indirect activities started flourishing at a galloping speed. As per economic census of 1990, 659 enterprises were engaged in hotel and restaurant business and 192 enterprises were moving with transport business. Altogether they provide an employment of 2,845 persons. These sectors needed resource to develop infrastructure to attract and cater for more tourists to contribute to the State economy.[22]

Plan Outlay

In order to maintain a pace in industrial development, plan allocation has been made on small and medium scale industries, since merger. Table 2.29, shows the trend in plan outlay on industry since Fifth Five Year Plans. The outlay under Industry, however, registered a relatively small growth. The Total expenditure on Industry during the Seventh Plan stood at Rs. 1010.9 lakh against Rs. 284.7 lakh during the Fifth Plan. The average annual expenditure in the former period was Rs. 202.0 lakh as compared to Rs. 71.0 lakh in the latter — thus registering a growth of less than three times.

TABLE 2.29

TREND IN OUTLAY DURING THE FIFTH THROUGH SEVENTH PLAN

(Rs. in Lakh)

Sector	*Fifth Plan (1976-80)*	*Sixth Plan (1980-85)*	*Seventh Plan (1985-90)*	*Total (1976-90)*
Industries				
Village & Small Scale	83.4	133.7	360.5	577.6
Medium Scale	201.3	249.6	650.4	1101.3
Industry Total	284.7 (4.7)	383.3 (2.7)	1010.9 (2.7)	1678.9 (2.9)
Total Plan Expenditure	6100.0 (100.0)	14340.0 (100.0)	36830.0 (100.0)	57270.0 (100.0)

Note: Figs. in parentheses are percentages.

Source: Computed from different Plan documents and Sikkim Compendium of Achievement, 1987, Planning and Development, GOS.

Within industry, the expenditure on large and medium industries accounted for 70.5 per cent of the total during the Fifth Plan, 65.3 per cent during the Sixth Plan and 64.3 per cent during the Seventh Plan. The relative shares of

Village and Small Scale Industries were thus 29.5 per cent during the Fifth Plan, 34.7 per cent in the Sixth Plan and 35.7 per cent the Seventh Plan.

Achievement

In industrialisation, the achievement is very meagre. After 1991 census, Table 2.12, op. cit., only 0.8 per cent of the total workers are engaged in industrial activities, whereas 65.6 per cent are engaged in agriculture and 33.6 per cent in services, trade etc. The industrial occupation has come down to 0.8 per cent in 1991 from 1.07 per cent in 1981.

In 1983-84, there were only 190 Small Scale Industrial units functioning with a production value of Rs. 525.0 lakh employing 1,100 persons. In handicrafts, the value of production in that year was only Rs. 4.3 lakh with numbers employed at 120. The number of industrial estates functioning in 1983-84 was only 3 with total number of units operating in them being only 6. The value of production in them was Rs. 380.0 lakh and the number of persons employed was 240. The District Industries Centre (DIC) assisted only 24 units in 1983-84 and the number of artisans assisted was 85.[23]

These developments in the economy of Sikkim cannot on the whole be considered satisfactory. There are many problems in the way of a faster progress. Apart from the problem of availability of infrastructure, there is an acute scarcity of people with entrepreneurial and technical skill. The problem of financing the development is also a big one.

To overcome financial and developmental problems and especially to promote and assist small scale and medium scale industries in the State, a State-level Industrial Development and Investment agency was established in

1977 under the name of Sikkim Industrial Development and Investment Corporation Limited or SIDICO, (hereinafter called Corporation). The Corporation, over the years wove and nourished the industrial fabric of the State immensely.

REFERENCES

1. Government of Sikkim (GOS), *An Economic Survey. 1993-94*, p. 1.
2. *Ibid.*, p. 78 and *Sikkim Compendium of Achievement*, GOS, 1987, p. 2.
3. GOS, *Report on Economic Census*, 1990, Vol. 1, p. 16.
4. *Ibid.*, pp. 20-21.
5. *Ibid.*, p. 28.
6. *Ibid.*, p. 14.
7. *Ibid.*, p. 15.
8. *Ibid.*, p. 17.
9. *Ibid.*, p. 18.
10. GOS, *Economic Survey, 1991-92*, p. 11.
11. *Ibid.*
12. GOS, *Statistical Profile (1979-80 and 1991-92)*, pp. 12-13.
13. GOS, *Study of Financial Position of the GOS*, 1994. p. 19.
14. GOS, *Statistical Profile, op. cit.*, p. 58.
15. *Study on Financial Position, op. cit.*, pp. 17-18.
16. *Statistical Profile, op. cit.*, p. 104.
17. GOS, *An Economic Survey, 1993-94*, pp. 81-84.
18. *Ibid.*, pp. 81-84.
19. *Statistical Profile, op. cit.*, p. 158.
20. *Study on Financial Position, op. cit.*, p. 19.
21. GOS, *Industrial Development in Sikkim*, 1979, p. 30.
22. GOS, *Economic Census*, 1990, p. 52.
23. GOS, *District Industries Centre (Action Plan), 1983-84*, 1987-88, pp. 1-26.

3

Ecology of Sikkim and Importance of the Small Scale Industries

Environment has been conceived of as the total web of life and man enters this ecologic scene with his traditions, perceptions, means, resources and social organisations — in short his culture which affects and is affected by the total web of life. Adaptation in man is the process by which he makes effective use for productive end of the energy potential in his habitat.

Life in the mountains is hard. It is a constant struggle with the uncongenial physical environment. However, the hazards and hardships of life in the mountainous region has never overwhelmed man or curbed his initiative. As a matter of fact these very hardships and hazards have had the contrary effect of bringing out the best in man in terms of adaptive skills and vigour. These two qualities are largely responsible for the self-sufficient economy of the hilly region. The people in the hills and their adaptation to their environment in view of industrialisation and other avenues of employment is an important topic of the day.

The basic characteristic of all mountainous areas is that they present a series of altitudinal zones or niches that can be exploited in different ways. In mountains, human biological interaction is static and correlational rather than dynamic and creative. An inability to appreciate the role of human response to environmental constraints leads to a focus on the natural resource base, in particular the nature of land, as the major force of change.[1]

The Himalayas, as the abode of snow, is taken as a vast rampart bordering the Indo-Gangetic and Brahamaputra plains on the north-west, north and north-east of India. This vast chain of mountains of the Himalayas measuring more than 2500 kilometre along its central axial range (i.e. the Central Himalaya) possesses together a width ranging between 160 mt. and more than 400 kilometre.[2]

In the Sikkim Himalaya, the high hills of Darjeeling form a mountain cleft and the region itself is in effect all but an enclosed basin occupied by the mountain torrent of the Tista along the axis of an overturned anticline at the core of which lies Kanchanjunga, 8579 metre high, the 3rd highest point in the World and the highest in India. The Central Himalaya in Sikkim is characterised by open folding (rather than the intense homoclinal folding in Western Himalaya), the latter may be the topographic clue for the Chumbi Valley (through Nathu La) providing the easiest passage into Tibet from India across the Donkiya range (4570—5180 mt.) leading directly to Gyantse and Lhasa.[3]

The variation of altitude easily reveals the east west felts of soil that varies from north to south. In the extreme north, one can find mountainous skeletal soil with a very thin layer of top soil. In the foot-hill zone where the rivers debouch, one can notice a belt of gravelly and sandy soil on extreme south, some alluvial soil is found along the river beds.

The soil of this area is derived from shales, schists and conglomerates which form a more sandy soil on the upper part of the foothill zone and become progressively clayey in the lower reaches.

In the zone of the tropical forest (the Southern part), the soil is well leached but is rich in humus contents. The elevation of land[4] in Sikkim is as under:

	Type of Land	*Level of Elevation*
1.	Lower Hills	Altitude ranging from 270 mt. to 1500 mt.
2.	Mid hills	Altitude ranging from 1500 mt. to 2000 mt.
3.	Higher hills	Altitude ranging from 2000 mt. to 3000 mt.
4.	Alpine zone	Altitude above 3000 mt. with vegetation, and
5.	Snow Land	Very high mountains without vegetation and with perpetual snow cover upto 8580 mt.

As compared to Western Himalaya this part has a warmer and a more humid climate. To the north Sikkim, the area having been occupied by the greater Himalayan range has hardly anytime when the temperature is above freezing point. The maximum ever temperature recorded is 32.2° Celsius in 1957 and the minimum ever recorded –9.7° Celsius in 1961. Sikkim is the most humid place in the Himalayas because of its proximity to the Bay of Bengal and its exposure to the moisture-bearing South Western monsoon winds. The average, annual rainfall varies from 821.1 milimetre to 3494.5 milimetre.[5] Interestingly, the Capital Gangtok receives the highest annual rainfall of 3494.5 milimetre.

In tropical zone (upto 1500 metres) figs, fir, orchids and oaks are most common species.

Among minerals coal, copper and dolomite are important.

The mainstay of the economy of Sikkim is agriculture. Rice, maize, millet, cardamom, mandarin, orange, apple, potatoes, ginger and soyabean are the main products.

The ecological balance in Sikkim hills is lopsided, gradually. However, this environmental degradation is a global phenomenon. Increase in population, soil erosion, depletion of forest, over-stocking of cattle, destruction of valuable flora and fauna and lack of infrastructure have become perennial problems in this region.

The problem of over population in Sikkim causes concern alongwith the rest of the country. A sizeable number of people from plain land migrate regularly to Sikkim. Again huge number of tourist-influx causes concern during the tourist season because over population creates scarcity in water supply, electricity and weaken the soil by cutting trees and hills for housing.

Soil erosion results in lowering of the production capacity of the soil. It is estimated that it takes 500 to 1000 years to form an inch of top soil.[6] It is obvious that an enormous amount of soil from the mountains of Sikkim is being lost to the Teesta river every year and there is no effective means yet evolved to stop the outflow of this vital component of environment.

The main causes of soil erosion are traditional agricultural system, removal of forest cover whereby the soil is directly exposed to the effect of weathering. It is estimated that the forest area has diminished from over 60.0 percent original to 10.0 to 15.0 percent. It is estimated that about 22 million to 45 million cubic feet of soil are annually wahsed down through landslides and soil erosion associated with road construction.[7]

Denudation of forest is carried out for housing and

dishonest earning. It has severe effect on climate and rainfall in Sikkim. Overstocking of cattle leads to destruction of young seedlings thus impeding regeneration of forest. Destruction of scientifically unstudied and unused flora and fauna causes loss to the environmental study. A lot of medicinal plant could be effectively used for earning and employment with sound ecological management.

Lack of infrastructure has caused inaccessibility in many parts in Sikkim and hindered spread of economic and industrial activities. Thus ecological pressure is being mounted on certain places due to futility in infrastructural facilities all around.

Keeping in mind the above ecological hazards for such a mountainous terrain, improvements and modernisation cannot be easily achieved unless there is considerable investment for development of the infrastructure of better communication facilities and proper planning for education, health, unification and economic development.

In 1978, the Department of Industrial Development, Government of India and the All-India Financial Institutions i.e. IDBI, IFCI, ICICI and SISI conducted two separate studies and recommended not to establish large and medium scale industries for lack of infrastructure. They specified a number of SSIs and fixed some criteria for selecting viable projects.

These industries —

(i) Should not involve sophisticated technology;

(ii) Should not require transport of raw material of high volume;

(iii) Should have high value added part; and

(iv) Should have a low break-even point.

With the establishment of Directorate of Industries in 1976, a list of viable industries was made as under:

(A) *Agriculture, Horticulture, Animal husbandry and forestry based industries, viz.,*

1. Ginger dehydration and Ginger Oil extraction;
2. Cardamom drying;
3. Vegetable seed production;
4. Fruit Nurseries;
5. Fruit Processing and Preservation;
6. Integrated Wood Working;
7. Pencil, incense and agarbati manufacture;
8. Floriculture;
9. Cheese and Milk Products manufacture.

(B) *Engineering and Allied Industries, viz.,*

1. Tin containers manufacture;
2. Wooden electrical fittings;
3. Diesel nozzle unit;
4. Electronics complex (selected items);
5. Polythylene film and bag manufacture;
6. Soap based on non-edible oil;
7. Battery manufacturing and charging Unit.

(C) *Rural Industries, viz.,*

1. Handlooms;
2. Carpet weaving.
3. Tribal Jewellery;
4. Thanka drawing;

5. Wood carving;
6. Bamboo and cane work;
7. Sericulture;
8. Bee keeping;
9. Knitting wares.

The above mentioned industries were assumed to be environment-friendly. As time elapses and the situation warrants, the government has to materialise different avenues of development. In this Process, the future should also be considered with the present. The decision makers should create awareness and find out devices to control pollution, effluents etc.

The Department of Environment, Government of India, can take up the problems of the mountain environment which on account of the environmental conditions have specific problems of both physical and socio-economic environment. A.S. Paintal in his presidential address of the Indian Science Congress at Lucknow in 1985 had emphasised the need for developing a Department of Mountain Development apart from the existing Department of Environment.[8] The great variety of environment with the multiplicity of specific conditions requires to be assessed properly. Tourism, hydel generation and mineral exploitation, horticulture and plantations have tremendous potentialities but the response of the diverse Himalayan People with their own socio-economic traits is the most important factor.

REFERENCES

1. Bhasin, V., *Ecology, Culture and Change*: Tribals of *Sikkim Himalays*, Inter-India Publication, New Delhi, 1989, pp. 10-12.
2. Pal, A. (ed.), *The Himalaya — Environment, Economy and Society*, Vikas Publishing House, New Delhi, 1995, pp. 29-30.

3. *Ibid.*, p. 37.
4. GOS, *Statistical Profile (1979-80 and 1991-92)*, 1994, p. 15.
5. *Ibid*, pp. 9-12.
6. Sarkar, R.L. and Lama, M.P. (ed.), *Eastern Himalayas,* Atma Ram and Sons, New Delhi, 1986, p. 41.
7. *Ibid* p. 42.
8. Pal, A., *The Himalaya — Environment, Economy and Society, op. cit.*, p. 229.

4

Importance of Finance and Review of Literature

The Industrial sector plays a pivotal role in the rapid expansion and development of agriculture, generation of employment avenues, securing a sizeable amount of foreign exchange and improving the standard of living of the Indian people. The Planning Commission has recognised the basic fact that there is a strong and positive relationship between wealth and standard of living of people and the extent of industrialisation. The planners of the Indian Government have regarded industrialisation as the panacea for under development and poverty.

Gunnar Myrdal, in describing the relationship of industrialisation to economic development remarked that, "the manufacturing industry represents, in a sense, a higher stage of production in advanced countries. The development of manufacturing has been concomitant with these countries' spectacular economic progress and rise in the levels of living. Not least in the underdeveloped countries, the productivity in the industry tends to be considerably greater than in the traditional agricultural pursuits."[1]

Considering the importance, it cannot be denied that industrialisation can be the best means of achieving higher growth rate in the context of developing economies. Pandit

Jawaharlal Nehru regarded industry as the temple. This comparison is significant in realising the necessity of industries, similar to that of the temple in the life of Indian people.

The success of the Programme of industrialisation depends on the availability of capital. Judicious flow of credit towards capital investment need depends largely on a sound and conducive structure of the financial institutions. For sound financial management, the financial institutions should have a well knit organisation structure for mobilising more resources and their utilisation for generation and promotion of economic activities.

Since independence, India had chosen the path of planned economy in a mixed economic way where both private and public sectors grew side by side.

Building up of a structure for financial institutions began with the establishment of the Industrial Finance Corporation of India (IFCI) in 1948. It aimed at making medium and long term capital available to industrial concerns. In 1951, the Indian Parliament passed the State Financial Corporations Act. Till March, 1995, there are 18 State Financial Corporations (SFCs) operating in the country, 17 of which were set up under the SFCs Act, 1951. Tamil Nadu Industrial Investment Corporation Ltd., was established in 1949 under the Companies Act.[2]

During the 1950s, National Small Industries Corporation (NSIC), Industrial Credit and Investment Corporation of India (ICICI), Life Insurance Corporation (LIC) were established as the prominent financial institutions. ICICI was set up mainly to underwrite shares of private companies. It was constituted in 1955 as a joint stock company with support from the Government of India, the World Bank, the Commonwealth Development Finance Corporation and the other foreign institutions. Refinance Corporation for Industry Ltd. (RCIL) came into being in 1958 for providing refinance to SFCs and commercial banks against term loan granted by them to industrial concerns in the private sector.

During 1960s, Industrial Development Bank of India (IDBI) was established as the principal financial institution for industrial development in the country. IDBI, established in 1964, caters to the growing and diverse needs of medium and large-scale industries. Besides, Industrial Reconstruction Bank of India (IRBI) came into existence in 1985 for aiding sick and closed industrial units. However, IRBI now provides financial assistance to all industrial enterprises like any other financial institution. Small Industries Development Bank of India (SIDBI) became operational in 1990 after taking over IDBI's operations in respect of the small sector with special emphasis on village, cottage and tiny sector.

Roles of SIDCs

During 1964-90, that is, before the advent of SIDBI with an exclusive responsibility of the small sector, state-level agency was very much in operation in various states. Different state Governments with their frantic desire to accelerate the pace of industrial development in their territories, established State Industrial Development Corporations (SIDCs). However, from the viewpoint of legal status, some were set up as Corporations under special status and others as Public or Private Limited Companies. The SIDCs in the sixties and seventies were incorporated as wholly-owned state government undertakings under the Companies Act, 1956 or as autonomous Corporations under Specific State Acts attuned to the Directive Principles of State Policy, for Promotion and Development of medium and large industries. The SIDCs in Gujarat, Maharashtra and Goa, Daman and Diu were set up as Statutory Corporations and some others were incorporated as companies under the Companies Act. Sikkim Industrial Development and Investment Corporation Ltd. (SIDICO), however, was established in 1977 under the Registration of Companies Act, Sikkim, 1961.

The functions of the SIDCs embrace the entrepreneurs of the state, so as to enable them to take the load of ushering in industrialisation in a cherished pattern. Promotion of industries is the primary function and financing is the secondary function of SIDCs. In case of SFCs it is the opposite. In general, in the states having both SFCs and SIDCs, the fomer takes care of the small sector and the latter medium industries. In areas with distinct function by the SIDCs and SFCs, their activities complement each other and ensure the development of all areas with distributive justice. To effect this, functions of the SIDCs are incidental to and allied with a wide range of activities for industrial development. SIDCs functions are different in different states, though promotion of small scale industries is the common area of operation. These operations play an effective role in promoting dispersed yet viable industrial growth, especially in backward areas.

As the catalytic agent for industrial development, SIDCs aim at providing a thrust to investment in their respective states. Assistance provided by SIDCs is in the form of term loan, underwriting, direct subscription to shares, debentures and guarantees. They undertake a variety of promotional activities which include preparation of feasibility reports, conducting industrial potential surveys, entrepreneurship development programmes and developing industrial areas and estates. Some SIDCs offer a package of developmental services which include technical guidance, assistance in plant location and co-ordination with other agencies. SIDCs are also involved in setting up of medium and large industrial projects in the joint sector and assisted sector in collaboration with private entrepreneurs or as wholly-owned subsidiaries. Moreover, SIDCs act as agents of IDBI and SIDBI for operating their seed capital scheme and as agent for passing on tax benefit under the State Government's incentive scheme. In line with the changing environment, many SIDCs are making efforts to diversify and enter into the fields of equipment leasing, merchant banking, venture capital and mutual funds.

There are 28 SIDCs in the country, 11 of them functioning also as SFCs to provide assistance to small scale sector. Such twin-function SIDCs are in Andaman and Nicobar, Arunachal Pradesh, Daman and Diu and Dadra and Nagar Haveli, Manipur, Meghalaya, Mizoram, Nagaland, Tripura, Goa, Pondicherry and Sikkim. Seven SIDCs including Sikkim are involved in infrastructure development and other extension services for the small sector.[3]

Operation of Financial Institutions

All Financial Institutions (AFIs) viz. IDBI, IFCI, ICICI, SIDBI, IRBI, SCICI, RCTC, TDICI, TFCI, LIC, UTI, GIC, SFCs and SIDCs together sanctioned assistance aggregating Rs. 61,555 crore during 1994-95 registering a growth of 49.0 per cent over the previous year. Overall disbursement increased by Rs. 33,560 crore in 1994-95 registering a growth of 26.0 per cent. The All-India Development Banks (AIDBs) viz. IDBI, IFCI, ICICI, SIDBI, IRBI and SCICI sanctioned a total assistance of Rs. 49,815 crore which was higher by 65.0 per cent as compared to the previous year. The sanction of investment institutions was lower by about 6.0 per cent at Rs. 10,156 crore. The sanction of Specialised Financial Institutions rose by 85.0 per cent amounting to Rs. 364.0 crore. Assistance sanctioned by SFCs during 1994-95 was Rs. 2,760 crore which was higher by about 45.0 per cent and assistance by SIDCs was Rs. 1,511 crore which was higher by about 65.0 per cent, as compared to the previous year.[4]

Table 4.1, shows figures related to the sanction and disbursement by AFIs. It is apparent from the table that, the sanction of SIDCs to IDBI's sanction accounted for 10.2 per cent and that of disbursement as 10.8 per cent whereas in state-wise assistance sanctioned and disbursement by the IDBI, Sikkim's share was very meagre with 0.02 and 0.03 per cent respectively.[5]

TABLE 4.1

ASSISTANCE SANCTIONED AND DISBURSED BY THE AFIs TILL 31.03.1995

(Rs. in Crore)

Institutions	*Sanction*	*Disbursement*	*Disbursement as % to Sanction*
All-India Development Banks			
IDBI	95810.9	65779.5	68.6
IFCI	24598.5	15387.1	62.5
ICICI	53307.0	30594.7	57.4
SIDBI	16216.4	12068.2	74.4
IRBI	2761.0	1874.4	67.9
SCICI	7696.5	3695.6	48.0
Specialised Financial Institutions			
RCTC	78.4	70.5	89.9
TDICI	225.0	188.1	83.6
TFCI	754.7	376.0	49.8
Investment Institutions			
LIC	11563.0	8932.0	77.2
UTI	39641.8	29284.9	73.9
GIC	4437.2	2886.1	65.0
Others			
SFCs	19349.5	15337.0	79.3
SIDCs	9774.2	7125.8	72.9

Source: Report on Development Banking in India, 1994-95, IDBI, p. 7.

SIDCs act as a catalyst of term-lending institutions in most of the backward states in the country. Especially, SIDCs in North-East Region of the country and Sikkim are working with manifold activities. It is observed in Table 4.2.

TABLE 4.2

ASSISTANCE SANCTIONED BY AFIs AND SIDCs IN BACKWARD STATES TILL 31.03.1995

(Rs. in Crore)

State	*1990-91*	*1991-92*	*1992-93*	*1993-94*	*1994-95*	*Cumulative 31.3.95*
1. Arunachal Pradesh						
AFIs	4.4	0.9	1.1	0.4	4.0	26.0
SIDCs	1.8	1.0	0.5	0.1	0.5	6.6
2. Goa						
AFIs	77.9	132.5	107.2	242.0	205.7	1447.6
SIDCs	20.5	21.3	20.7	32.9	36.6	251.8
3. Manipur						
AFIs	2.3	3.1	1.5	1.1	0.2	52.8
SIDCs	1.0	0.2	—	—	—	26.3
4. Meghalaya						
AFIs	5.0	8.1	1.9	4.1	5.6	104.8
SIDCs	1.1	1.0	0.9	2.8	1.9	31.0
5. Mizoram						
AFIs	3.9	1.6	2.6	2.1	1.8	47.3
SIDCs	3.0	1.2	1.5	2.1	1.7	35.8
6. Nagaland						
AFIs	5.0	5.4	2.5	0.4	1.9	49.6
SIDCs	2.7	0.7	1.1	—	0.4	22.1
7. Pondicherry						
AFIs	85.3	67.4	64.8	31.2	164.8	680.6
SIDCs	7.8	5.1	7.7	7.1	11.3	97.1

State	*1990-91*	*1991-92*	*1992-93*	*1993-94*	*1994-95*	*Cumulative 31.3.95*
8. Sikkim						
AFIs	2.3	4.4	0.6	2.9	1.1	43.3
SIDCs	2.1	4.1	0.2	2.5	0.4	31.9
9. Tripura						
AFIs	3.6	1.3	3.4	0.7	3.2	44.8
SIDCs	2.8	0.2	3.1	0.6	3.2	13.9
10. Assam						
AFIs	71.8	70.1	86.9	72.5	126.9	986.1
SIDCs	3.1	4.9	—	2.7	1.8	51.2
11. Himachal Pradesh						
AFIs	273.1	311.6	252.5	97.7	853.5	2471.8
SIDCs	6.8	9.1	7.1	7.3	10.2	106.1

Source: Report on Development Banking in India, 1994-95, IDBI, pp. 106-220.

I. SIDCs were the Premier lending institution in backward areas.

II. In Sikkim and North-Eastern region, SIDCs alone provided about 75.0 per cent of the financial assistance by All Financial Institutions.

SIDCs, since their inception, have been playing a pivotal role in setting up of Small and village industries to generate employment avenues. The necessity of Small and Village industries in India is ever-increasing. Small Scale industries employ crores of people in their varied activities. In a country like ours, labour-intensive industries should be set up widely to cater for large chunks of society.

Besides, as foreign-exchange earner the SSIs play a vital role. On the Export front, Village and Small Scale Industries (VSI) occupy 65.0 per cent in 1994-95 with an average annual growth of 29.0 per cent during the quinquennium. Exports of SSI increased from Rs. 9,664 crore in 1990-91 to Rs. 25,308 crore in 1993-94 resulting in a growth of 162.0 per cent.[6]

The production of modern SSIs increased from Rs. 1,55,340 crore in 1990-91 to Rs. 2,41,648 crore in 1993-94, registering a growth of 55.6 per cent.

TABLE 4.3

PERFORMANCE OF VILLAGE AND SMALL SCALE INDUSTRIES

	Production (Rs. Cr.)		*Export (Rs. Cr.)*		*Employment (Lakh No.)*	
	1990-91	*1993-94*	*1990-91*	*1993-94*	*1990-91*	*1993-94*
A. MODERN SSIs						
SSIs	155340	241648	9664	25308	125	139
Powerlooms	14306	25520	662	1854	52	64
SUB TOTAL A	169646	267168	10326	27162	177	203
B. TRADITIONAL INDUSTRIES						
Khadi	286	357	Neg.	Neg.	14	14
Village Inds.	1994	2877	6	18	34	39
Handlooms	3974	4754	407	1297	92	125
Sericulture	866	1060	441	791	52	59
Handicrafts	11325	18255	8100	16303	44	58
Coir	279	521	48	129	5	5
SUB TOTAL B	18724	27824	9002	18538	241	300
TOTAL (A+B)	188370	294992	19328	45700	418	503

Source: Annual Report, 1995 SIDBI, p. 14.

The net addition to employment with the VSI sector

was 85 lakh persons during 1990-91 to 1993-94. The SSIs, however, added only 14 lakh persons during the same period. (Table 4.3)

Small Scale Units and Small Road Transport Operators avail themselves of financial assistance from (1) SFCs; (2) Banks (Commercial, Co-operative both regional and rural); and (3) SIDCs which seek refinance from SIDBI. The relative share of these institutions in refinance during 1994-95 was 66.0 per cent, 27.0 per cent and 7.0 per cent respectively.[7]

During the five year period commencing from 1990-91 to 1994-95, the share of SFCs rose gradually from 52.0 per cent to 66.0 per cent and that of SIDCs from 4.0 per cent to 7.0 per cent. In the case of banks, the share has, however, come down from 44.0 per cent to 27.0 per cent during 1990-91 to 1994-95.[8]

Thus, SIDCs are not only instrumental in backward states but perform complementary roles with SFCs in other states too. Besides being an agent in developmental process, SIDCs contributed to foreign-exchange earning of the country.

In topographically difficult states, SIDCs performed righteous duties in favour of state government in consonance with the directives and policies of the refinancing agency. In such states, SIDCs helped preserve and nourish traditional art, crafts and industries as constant source of capital and guidance till other all-India financial institutions trod in those areas and avenues.

Let us determine the locus standi of the Corporation in similar types of institution in north-eastern states.

The annual sanction and disbursement of assistance by the SIDCs since 1977 is enlisted in Table 4.4. The sanction

TABLE 4.4

ANNUAL SANCTION AND DISBURSEMENT OF SIDCs

(Rs. in Crore)

Year	*Sanction*	*Disbursement*	*% of Disbursement to Sanction*
1977-78	87.9	44.8	51.0
1978-79	98.3	60.1	61.1
1979-80	157.7	85.3	54.1
1980-81	216.4	124.6	57.6
1981-82	299.6	191.1	63.8
1982-83	296.6	208.0	70.1
1983-84	364.6	236.5	64.9
1984-85	477.9	297.6	62.3
1985-86	527.0	364.0	69.1
1986-87	570.3	425.5	74.6
1987-88	641.5	448.6	69.9
1988-89	722.1	472.1	65.4
1989-90	691.0	545.2	78.9
1990-91	823.7	598.3	72.6
1991-92	1009.0	678.7	67.3
1992-93	973.1	694.7	71.4
1993-94	917.9	700.8	76.4
1994-95	1511.3	984.4	65.1
Compound Growth Rate	17.1	18.7	

Source: Report on Development Banking in India, 1994-95, IDBI, p. 75.

was Rs. 87.9 crore in 1977-78 which had risen to Rs. 1,511.3 crore in 1994-95 i.e. more than 17 times. Disbursement, on the other, increased from Rs. 44.8 crore in 1977-78 to Rs.

984.4 crore during 1994-95 registering a growth of about 22 times. The compound growth rate accounted for 17.1 per cent for sanction and 18.7 per cent for disbursement; whereas the compound growth in sanction and disbursement of the Corporation accounted for 12.6 per cent and 32.4 per cent respectively, Table 10.7.

In terms of assistance sanctioned and disbursed as evident in Table 4.5, SIDICO occupied a key position amongst the SIDCs in the north-eastern region. Its rate of disbursement is higher compared to the rate of sanction. Despite being the smallest populated state in the country, Sikkim has adhered to a large quantum of loan through its SIDC i.e. SIDICO and the assistance is higher than many other SIDCs in north-east region.

The per capita assistance sanction and disbursement by SIDICO is the highest among all north-eastern SIDCs. As evident in Table 4.6 the per capita assistance of SIDICO is Rs. 695.0, ZIDCO's Rs. 457.2, MIDC's Rs. 159.9, NIDC's Rs. 159.2 and so on.

In the foregoing discussion, it is transparent that in the north-east hilly region, SIDICO appeared as an important development agency. The need for industrial activities made its role imperative. It is observed that :

I. SIDICO's growth in disbursement is much higher than the all India SIDC's growth.
II. SIDICO is in operation in the smallest state in terms of area and population in the eastern zone.
III. SIDICO is the highest per capita assistance provider in any state in the eastern zone.

Besides its performance in the region, the Corporation possesses some outstanding merit inside Sikkim. Firstly, the Corporation was entrusted with the post-merger

TABLE 4.5

ASSISTANCE SANCTIONED AND DISBURSED IN BACKWARD AREAS TILL 31.03.1995

(Rs. in Crore)

	SIDCs	*Sanction*	*Disburse—ment*	*% of Disbursement to Sanction*
1.	APIDFC	6.6 (0.1)	6:1 (0.2)	92.4
2.	IDC, GOA	251.8 (5.0)	164.6 (4.2)	65.4
3.	MANIDCO	26.3 (0.6)	19.6 (0.5)	74.5
4.	MIDC	31.0 (0.6)	25.6 (0.6)	82.6
5.	ZIDCO	35.8 (0.8)	30.9 (0.8)	86.3
6.	NIDC	22.1 (0.4)	19.4 (0.5)	87.8
7.	PIPDIC	97.1 (2.0)	87.2 (2.2)	89.8
8.	SIDICO	31.9 (0.6)	27.8 (0.7)	87.1
9.	TIDC	13.9 (0.3)	9.3 (0.2)	66.9
10.	WBIDC	247.8 (4.9)	203.9 (5.2)	82.3
11.	OTHERS	4235.8 (84.7)	3348.0 (84.9)	79.0
	ALL SIDCs	5000.1 (100.0)	3942.4 (100.0)	78.8

Note: Figures in parentheses indicate percentages.

Source: Report on Development Banking, 1994-95, IDBI, pp. 220-221.

TABLE 4.6

PER-CAPITA ASSISTANCE SANCTION AND DISBURSEMENT TILL 31.3.94

(in Rs.)

SIDCs		*Sanction*	*Disbursement*
1.	APIDFC	69.7	64.4
2.	IDC, GOA	2000.0	1307.4
3.	MANIDCO	133.0	99.1
4.	MIDC	159.9	132.0
5.	ZIDCO	457.2	394.6
6.	NIDC	159.2	139.8
7.	PIPDIC	1125.1	1010.4
8.	SIDICO	695.0	605.7
9.	TIDC	46.8	31.7
10.	WBIDC	45.8	35.1
	ALL INDIA	107.7	78.5

Source: Report on Development Banking in India, 1994-95, IDBI, p. 222.

economic development in Sikkim. Secondly, it inculcated awareness among the people regarding the national policies which was extremely needed to surmount ascendency of monarchism. Thirdly, till the end of March, 1993, 38 Public Sector commercial banks in Sikkim provided loan amounting to Rs. 3097.5 lakh mainly in retail trade business and other trade;[9] IDICO on the other, till that period enhanced loan of Rs. 2,453.1 lakh to SSIs, small trader, hotels, taxi owners and others.[10] Thus, the Corporation with the help of refinancing agencies laid a strong industrial base with welfare motive at par with the Government. Last but not least, the Corporation with the people-oriented policies of the government, established a nexus between the people and financial corporations to uplift the downtrodden and help industrious entrepreneurs in socio-economic development of the state.

Review of Literature

No significant attempt has been undertaken so far to study the performance of SIDICO. The Corporation itself published a few brochures, pamphlets depicting various schemes etc. However, there have been some attempts to identify the trend of operation in Sikkim's economy. IDBI, as refinancing agency conducted study every year to evaluate the performance of the corporation.

Just after accession to India, a study was conducted by Datey Committee appointed by the Government of India in 1976 on the 'Institutional Arrangements for Agricultural Credit in Sikkim'. That was the first attempt to provide 'institutional finance' to a sector. In 1978, the Govt. of India published a report on the Industrial Development in Sikkim.

The report contained information of a few important studies, viz.,

1. Prospects of New Industries in Sikkim by the Ministry of Industry, New Delhi, 1974-75;
2. On Small Scale Industries by the Development Commissioner New Delhi, 1975-76;
3. Study on the prospect of Industries in Sikkim by IDBI, 1977-78;
4. Survey on Industries by High Powered team of the Ministry of Industry, 1977-78; and
5. Problems and Prospect of handloom industry by the Commissioner of Handloom, New Delhi, 1977-78.

Besides, some potential surveys on specific projects

were conducted during 1975-77 on high quality insulation, paper and paper pulp; watch-assembling by the Hindustan Machine Tools Limited; on Powerloom and Roller Flour Mill by the National Industrial Development Corporation.

In 1983 the Government of India constituted a Standing Committee on the Development of Industries in the North-Eastern region comprising five states viz. Assam, Manipur, Tripura, Nagaland, Sikkim and Union Territories of Andaman and Nicobar Islands. They dealt with the main resources of the states and also identified the major constraints of Sikkim's economy. The techno-economic survey team identified certain 'candidate industries' for the region based on the resources and demand.

A survey on Sikkim was conducted by the lead bank i.e., State Bank of India in 1985 which entails resource position and achievement by various sectors in tapping resource potentials.

An Economic Survey on Sikkim was conducted by the Bureau of Statistics and Economics for the first time during 1991-92 comprising the economic state of affairs of the state. However, the bureau published a report on the industrial economy of Sikkim in 1990. This was also the maiden effort to explore industrial activities in the state.

Some research publications revealed Sikkim's economy from time to time, researches on Sociological Perspective being the maximum. Prof. J.C. Debnath undertook research on the economy of Sikkim till 1971. The book entitled 'Problems and Prospects in Sikkim' by Prof. M. Dasgupta was also a publication of substance.

In recent times, the corporation i.e., SIDICO alongwith the IDBI, in an effort to find out laxities and revive activities, conducted a study through the West Bengal Consultancy

Limited (WEBCON) named 'Organisation Study' on the SIDICO. The study reviewed the present organisation structure and departmentalisation of the corporation. These reports and studies made earlier provided a broad picture of Sikkim's economy and suggested different types of industries to be established for the state's industrial development.

Considering the above points, to fill the gap of study of financial institutions in the state, the researcher has chosen to study the performance of Sikkim Industrial Development and Investment Corporation Limited, which is one of the leading financial institutions set up for industrial growth in the state.

Methodology

The study was based mainly on secondary data collected from the SIDICO, the IDBI, and the SIDBI. In particular, the annual reports and studies made by them were consulted. Data was also collected from the concerned Government Departments with provision of infrastructure and other facilities to industrial units. Returns submitted by the assisted units to the SIDICO were the main source for evaluating the performance of those units. Due to laxity of proper maintenance of records in maximum cases, questionnaire were used to obtain certain information from small scale units and hoteliers. Personal interviews with the top level executives like Managing Director, Deputy General Managers and other departmental heads were taken to gather off-the-record information.

The data were processed and interpreted in terms of the objectives of the study. Statistical methods were applied wherever necessary in order to draw meaningful conclusions.

Objective of the Study

This study examines the objective of the corporation in the economic arena of the state. This objective has been evaluated through:

(i) the examination of the extent of assistance provided by the corporation for different industrial projects;
(ii) the evaluation of the performance of SIDICO as Small Industries Development Corporation;
(iii) the study of corporation's recovery performance of loan disbursed; and
(iv) the suggestion for remedial measures based on findings of the study.

Limitation of the Study

The paucity of the literature for review is one of the limitations of the present study. No overall investigation of the SIDICO has been done. Especially, laxity in maintenance of accounts and records has compelled the researcher to assimilate data from other reliable sources to derive a meaningful conclusion. Due to non-availability of returns from the assisted units, the Corporation had to concentrate on the instalment payment to judge the performance of Village and Small Scale units to a large extent. The present researcher is also handicapped because of the dearth of the primary report of those concerns. However, care has been taken to guard against such limitations in arriving at better conclusion.

Period of Analysis

The study covers a period of Eighteen years i.e., since commencement in 1977-78 to 1994-95.

Rationale of the Study

This analytical study is of great importance and

relevance to the present day problem of financing industries by the financial institutions in general and the SIDICO in particular as these institutions are the most useful tools of the country, in attaining the goal of increased production on the industrial front. The urge of financing is acute in the land-locked state of Sikkim. In the light of the fast changing industrial-techno-conditions and the changing role of the SIDCs, a revision and identification of constraints in flow of capital to industrial sector, which needs a different look, is needed. In the absence of such a competent and adequate evaluation of the functioning of the SIDCs, they may be identified as mere reservoir for pumping finance. The importance of any institution must correspond to the constraints coming in the way of financing industries. In view of the growing importance of the SIDCs functioning, the need for a detailed investigation of the corporation i.e., SIDICO is more obvious and relevant.

Contribution to Knowledge

The investigation conducted on the problem of activities of the corporation and the findings of the study would aid in decision-making to the management and would also fill gaps in the literature on the functioning of the Corporation.

REFERENCES

1. Myrdal, Gunar, *An International Economy*, Harper and Brothers, New York, 1956, p. 226.
2. IDBI, *Report on Development Banking*, 1994-95, p. 70.
3. *Ibid.*, p. 75.
4. *Ibid.*, p. 7.
5. *Ibid.*, pp. 132-33.
6. SIDBI, *Annual Report*, 1995, p. 13.
7. IDBI, *Report on Development Banking*, 1994-95, p. 155.
8. *Ibid.*
9. Government of Sikkim, *Sikkim-At a Glance, 1993*, p. 2.
10. SIDICO, *Annual Report*, 1992-93, p. 34.

5

Role of SIDICO

The Sikkim Industrial Development and Investment Corporation Limited (SIDICO) was established on 13 March, 1977. The Corporation was registered under the Registration of Companies Act, Sikkim 1961.[1] Among the total of eleven twin-function State Industrial Development Corporations (SIDC) in the country, SIDICO is the only Organisation not registered under the Companies Act, 1956. The Corporation was incorporated as a wholly-owned undertaking of the Government of Sikkim.

The Corporation is working as a catalyst for the industrial development of the State. Sikkim was merged in India in 1975 and the Corporation started functioning in 1977. Thus, the Corporation covers almost entire Post-merger period of Sikkim's economy. The corporation enhanced financial assistance to more than 90.0 per cent of the industrial units in the State including hotels and taxis.

The Corporation undertake activities as per the guidelines of the IDBI, the State Government and the top-level management i.e., Board of Directors.

The Corporation provide assistance to medium and small scale industries, tiny sector, hotels and small road transport operators mainly taxis in the form of term loan, bridge loan, direct subscription to shares and supply scarce raw-materials to small scale units, reimburse investment and transport subsidies. It has executed wide range of promotional activities such as preparation of feasibility report, conducting industrial potential survey, entrepreneurship development programmes and developing industrial areas and estates. The Corporation is also involved in setting up of medium and large industrial projects in the joint sector, assisted sector in collaboration with private entrepreneurs or as wholly-owned subsidiaries.

In this chapter, performance of relevant objectives and activities have been discussed.

The Corporation enlisted elaborate objectives in the Memorandum of Association. The clauses of Memorandum are divided into three different type of objectives. These are main objectives, ancillary objectives and all other objectives not included in main or ancillary objectives.[2] The SIDICO attains a large extent of these objectives. It formulate policies to achieve the desired goal of industrialisation. In course, the Corporation has designed many secondary objectives to reach out main objective. Thus, in practice, SIDICO could not perform even all the provisions in all the objectives. For instance, in one objective of buying, underwriting and investment in stocks and shares, SIDICO has accomplished buying and investment portion but could not underwrite so far.

The Corporation, as per Memorandum deals with the following important objects.

1. to work for the industrial development of the State of Sikkim by promoting industries in the Corporate Sector or otherwise, by purchasing the existing industrial units in the Corporate Sector or otherwise, by developing the existing units in the Corporate Sector or otherwise and

by investing or financing the industrial enterprises in the State, whether for starting, running, expanding, modernising or otherwise howsoever;

2. to encourage and promote the expansion of investment markets in the State of Sikkim;
3. to buy, underwrite, invest in and acquire and hold shares, stocks, debentures, debenture-stock, bonds, obligations and securities issued or guaranteed by any Company or body incorporate or unincorporated or by a person or association;
4. to acquire any shares, stock, debenture, debenture-stock, bonds, obligation or securities... by original subscription, participation in Syndicates, Tender, purchase, Exchange or otherwise and to subscribe for the name either conditionally or otherwise and to guarantee the subscription thereof and to exercise and enforce all rights and powers conferred by or incidental to the ownership thereof;
5. to borrow money by way of refinance from the IDBI;
6. to lend money with or without security and to make advances upon, hold in trust, issue, buy, sell or otherwise acquire or dispose of, on commission or otherwise any of the securities or investments or to act as agent for the like purposes.
7. to grant or guarantee or recommend the grant of loans to industries to which such sub-contracts are given or orders are issued as specified, in order to enable them in carrying out the sub-contracts or orders, to finance plant constructions, conversion or expansion, including the acquisition of land, or to finance the acquisition of equipment, facilities, machinery, supplies or materials or to

supply such concerns with working capital to be used in the manufacture of articles, equipment, supplies or materials under contract to Govt. or to this company[3] to provide them with such financial, technical, managerial and other assistance as may be deemed necessary for the purpose of enabling them to execute and carry out the sub-contracts and orders satisfactorily and to organise production and manufacture for meeting such contract and sub-contract and orders adequately and according to specification and to ensure satisfactory production by all necessary instruction, assistance, inspection and supervision;

8. to procure capital for financial assistance or accommodation for or provide managerial equipment, technical and managerial assistance, information instruction, supervision and other facilities to any Company, person or association for the purpose of carrying into effect of its objects;
9. to promote and establish companies, firms, establishments, concerns, undertakings and associations for the prosecution or execution of industrial undertakings, works, projects, and enterprises of any description whether of a private or public character, which in the opinion of the Company would contribute to the industrial development of the State of Sikkim and to acquire and dispose of shares and interest in such companies or associations or any undertaking thereof or for any purpose calculated to benefit the Company;
10. to promote, improve, establish and execute industries, projects or enterprises for manufacture

and production of goods, plant and machinery, tools, implements, material or substances of any description whatsoever which in the opinion of the Company are likely to promote or advance the industrial development of the State of Sikkim;

11. to acquire by lease, grant, assignment, transfer or otherwise, any grants or concessions of any minerals, field, mines, mineral and mine contracts, works and premises from any person, corporation, company, Government or local authority in the State of Sikkim or elsewhere and to perform and fulfil the conditions thereof;
12. to enter into any partnership or arrangements for joint working in business, sharing of profits of any industrial undertakings, joint or reciprocal or amalgamation with any other company, firm or person or co-ordination or engage in any manufacture or business within the objects of the company or similar thereto;
13. to establish, promote, subsidise and otherwise assist, any company or companies, syndicate or other concern for the purpose of setting up any industry or running industrial undertaking acquiring any property or furthering in all of the objects of this company;
14. to aid, counsel, assist, finance, protect and promote the interests of industries in Sikkim whether owned or run by Government, statutory body, company, firm or individuals and to provide them with capital, credit, means, resources, technical and managerial assistance for the prosecution of their work and business, to enable them to develop and improve their methods of manufacture, management and marketing and their technique of production;

Among Ancillary or Incidental Objectives

15. to invest any money of the company not required for the purpose of its business in such investment or securities as may be thought expedient;
16. to create any depreciation fund, reserve fund, insurance fund, sinking fund or any other special fund whether for depreciation or replacement, improving, expanding, or maintaining of the property of the company or for any other purposes conducive to the interest of the company;
17. to the financing of long or medium term loans to any concern which is engaged or proposes to engage in the business of manufacturing, processing or refrigeration of goods, wares and merchandise or the exploitation of mineral resources or in the generation or distribution of electricity or any other form of power or the business of shipping or shipping transport or any business the shipping companies normally transact in or in the hotel industry or the business of transport or transport services or in the field studies for purchase of sophisticated equipment and construction of buildings or in the rural medical profession for purchase of clinical and surgical instruments and nursing home requirements;
18. to encourage and promote participation of capital in industrial enterprises in the State of Sikkim;
19. to receive grants, loans, advances or other moneys, or deposit, or otherwise from State or Central Government (including Union Territory Government, Banks, Companies, Trusts or individuals), with or without allowance of interest thereon.

20. to purchase, take on lease or in exchange, hire or otherwise acquire any immovable or movable property, patents, licences, rights or privileges which the Company may think necessary or convenient for the purpose of its business and to construct, maintain and alter any building or work necessary or convenient for the purpose of the company;
21. to sell, dispose of, let on lease or on hire or transfer the business, property and undertaking of the company, or any part thereof, for cash, stock, or shares of any other company or for any other consideration which the company may see fit to accept;
22. to consult and to cooperate with the appropriate officers of Government of Sikkim and of India having necessary powers in order to utilise the potential productive capacity of plants operated by industrial concerns;
23. to form, or organise and assist or aid in any forming or promoting, subsidising, organising or aiding companies, syndicates or partnership of all kinds for the purpose of acquiring and undertaking any property and liabilities of this Company or any other company or of advancing directly or indirectly the objects thereof or for any other purpose which the company may think expedient and to take or otherwise acquire, dispose of shares, debentures and other securities in or of any such company and to subsidise or otherwise assist any such company;
24. to employ or pay experts, foreign consultants etc., in connection with the planning and development of all or any of the business connected with the company's operations;

25. to carry on the business of engineers and manufacturers of agricultural and other machinery, plants, implements and tools, equipments, apparatus and accessories, rolling stock and other like goods and the production and working of metals and minerals of all kinds and the production, manufacture and preparation of any other materials which may be usefully or conveniently combined with the engineering or manufacturing business of the company;
26. to obtain from any Government, Ministry, Department, establishment or agency such reports concerning the giving of contracts and sub-contracts and making of loans to business concerns as may be deemed necessary for carrying out the main objects;
27. to promote and operate schemes for development of industries in the country and for that purpose to prepare reports, blue prints, statistics and other information;
28. to amalgamate with or enter into partnership or any joint pursuit or profit sharing or arrangement with or co-operate with or subsidise or assist in any way any company, association or person;
29. to obtain any provisional order or Act of State Legislature for enabling the Company to carry any of its objects into effect or for effecting any modification of the company's constitution or for any other purpose which may seem expedient and to oppose by lawful means any proceedings or applications which may seem calculated directly or indirectly to prejudice the company's interest;
30. to empower the company to apply for any Act of Parliament or of the State Legislature either

of the State of Sikkim or any other State or Union Territory in the Indian Union for any purpose which may seem expedient to the company;

31. to take suitable steps to enable the company to carry any of its objects into effect or for effecting any modification of the company's constitution, or for any other purpose which may seem expedient;
32. to manufacture, buy, sell, import, export, instal, work and generally deal in, any plant, machinery, substances, tools, materials, goods or things of any description, which in the opinion of the company may be conveniently dealt with by the company in connection with any of its objects;

Other objectives

33. to sell, mortgage, exchange, lease, grant licences, easements and other rights over, improve, manage, develop and turn to account and in any other manner deal with or dispose of the undertaking, investments, property, assets, rights and effects of the company or any part thereof for such consideration as may be thought fit including any stocks, shares or securities of any other company, whether partly or fully paid up;
34. to transact or carry on agency business and in particular in relation to the investment of money, the sale of property and the collection and receipt of money;
35. to employ experts to investigate and examine into the conditions, prospects, value, character and circumstances of any business concern and undertaking and generally of any asset, concession and property or rights; and

36. to communicate with Chambers of Commerce and other mercantile and public bodies in India and elsewhere and concert and promote measures for the protection and advancement of trade, industry and commerce and other facilities;

Alteration in any objective of the Memorandum can be done by three-fourth majority of the Board of Directors. In practice, majority of the Directors attend the meeting of the corporation.

Scope and Limit of Assistance

The Corporation envisaged wide range of activities in its periphery. The scope of the corporation's assistance depend on the IDBI, State Govt. and as per the decisions of the Board which changes from time to time.

A maximum and minimum loaning limit is fixed by the Corporation. Again, for specific demarcation, assistance limits have been fixed for Board, Executive Committee and Managing Director.

The maximum limit of assistance by the Corporation is Rs. 90.0 lakh for Private and Public limited Companies and Registered Co-operatives. In case of Proprietorship and Partnership the maximum limit is Rs. 30.0 lakh.[4]

The minimum loan provided by the Corporation is Rs. 10,000. However loan upto Rs. 10,000 is available from the Directorate of Industries or Sikkim Khadi and Village Industries Board and Commercial Banks.[5]

Competent Authority

The financial assistance to industrialists is provided by different competent authorities of the Corporation. The assistance limit is entrusted to three different levels of management.

The Managing Director of the Corporation is empowered to sanction a loan of Rs. 1.0 lakh. The Executive Committee comprises five members including Managing Director. This Committee is authorised to sanction loan above Rs. 1.0 lakh and upto Rs. 7.5 lakh . The top-most management level i.e., Board of Directors are entitled to sanction loan above Rs. 7.5 lakhs.[6]

An Ad-hoc Committee for scrutinising loan proposal of more than Rs. 1.0 lakh was established in 1990. But the first meeting of this Committee was held Only in December, 1994. The Committee is comprised of four members including the Managing Director.[7]

Function

In the functional aspect, the SIDICO is different from other SIDCs in India. SIDICO has been engaged in quadruple functions of State Financial Corporation (SFC), State Industrial Development Corporation (SIDC), State Small Industries Development Corporation (SSIDC), and Industrial Infrastructure Development Corporation (IIDC) in the State of Sikkim, whereas in most of the states different institutions have been established for different functions.

As a SFC, the SIDICO meets the term loan requirement of small scale and medium scale industries for acquisition of fixed assets like land, buildings, machinery and equipment; and also implemented Seed Capital Assistance Scheme specially for technocrats and professionals.

As a SIDC, the Corporation has been looking after the financial requirements of large and medium scale industries by way of providing share capital assistance, loans and guarantees. Since SIDC's primary function is to promote industrial enterprise, SIDICO set up joint sector projects in the State.

As a SSIDC, it looks after all aspects of indenting for procuring, warehousing and distribution of scarce and other selected raw materials to the Small Scale units in the State.

As an IIDC, the Corporation has established industrial estates in other districts in the State.

The SIDICO has framed certain rules to make the industrial units eligible for assistance.

(i) Concerns which are engaged in or to be engaged in manufacture, processing, mining, hotel industry, transport i.e., taxis, maintenance, repair, testing or servicing of machinery or any description or vehicles or vessels, assembling, repairing or packing any article with the aid of machinery or power are eligible for financial assistance;

(ii) Nursing Homes are also eligible for assistance.

(iii) Artisans and Small industrial activities utilising locally available natural resources and human skills are given composite loans not exceeding Rs. 50,000.

(iv) Industrial concerns whose constitution is proprietory, partnership, private or public limited company and registered Co-operative Societies are eligible to get financial assistance from the Corporation.

Schemes Implemented

For overall industrial development in the State, with the active support extended by the IDBI, the SIDICO has taken it as a challenge and implemented various schemes to meet the requirements of all categories of entrepreneurs and to encourage the establishment of Small Scale units. A few notable among them are:

1. General Loan Scheme.
2. Integrated Term Loan Scheme.
3. Composite Loan Scheme.
4. Seed Capital Assistance Scheme.
5. Scheme for assistance to SC/ST entrepreneurs and physically handicapped.
6. Modernisation Scheme.
7. Assistance for setting up Nursing Home.
8. Scheme for setting up X-Ray Clinics.
9. Assistance for Generator Sets.
10. Single Window Scheme.
11. Scheme for Self-Employment of Ex-Servicemen (SEMFEX).
12. Scheme for assistance to Women entrepreneurs.
13. Scheme for Rehabilitation of Sick Units.
14. Equity Participation Scheme.

Activities

The loan assistance provided by the Corporation is the largest segment of its activity. Total sanction till 31 March, 1995, was Rs. 2,948.2 lakh , of which disbursement figured at Rs. 2,540.9 lakh i.e., 86.2 per cent of the total sanction. In this the Corporation sanctioned Rs. 2,430.6 lakh as term loan in which disbursement was Rs. 2,159.3 lakh. , which is 88.8 per cent of the sanctioned amount. For the same period, bridge loan and other soft loan sanctioned was Rs. 517.6 lakh in which disbursement was Rs. 381.7 lakh . Total number of assisted units were 1302.[8]

In the total loan assistance of Rs. 2,948.2 lakh, Small Scale Industries (SSI) received the highest amount. Till 31 March, 1995, SSIs received Rs. 1,673.2 lakh i.e., 56.7 per cent. The number of SSI units assisted till that date was 205. The largest number of beneficiaries were in Composite

Loan Scheme. Till March, 1995, 646 units, mainly in the tiny sector, were assisted with Rs. 165.2 lakh . Hotel loans also accounted for a significant share. 206 units were assisted with Rs. 673.4 lakh. Another important category was taxi loan (S.V.O.), where 245 loans with a total amount of Rs. 236.4 lakh were provided till March, 1995. Among other schemes, Equity participation was made in six units with an investment of Rs. 242.2 lakh.[9] Many Schemes are yet to be implemented.

Recovery

The recovery position of the Corporation is dwindling sharply in recent years. The rate of recovery has come down to single digit of 5.4 per cent in 1994-95, compared to 35.4 per cent in 1989-90 as evident from Table-9.1. This dismal picture is attributed by multiple factors.

The quantum of repayment of Principal by the Corporation to the IDBI and SIDBI was meagre Rs. 23.2 lakh in 1994-95. This futile repayment by the Corporation for the last few years accumulated huge outstanding to the IDBI and SIDBI. The outstanding of the Corporation to these institutions raised to Rs. 400.0 lakh . Consequently, these institutions stopped providing refinance to the Corporation. These institutions insisted at least 50.0 per cent payment of this backlog.[10]

In a desperate attempt, the Corporation took recovery action on chronic defaulters in accordance with the provisions of Sikkim Public Demand Recovery Act, 1988. The total number of cases filed in the Certificate Officer's Court and in the Court of District Judge is 121 accounts involving an amount of Rs. 7.2 crore.[11] The Corporation is making all concerned efforts for recovery of dues on a case to case basis.

In an overall assessment on the role of the Corporation, it can be said that with a span of eighteen years of working the Corporation has provided sizeable amount of fund mainly to the tiny and Small Scale industries in the State. This is more significant in relation to the inclusion of the State in Indian Economy only twenty years back. The utilisation of the fund was also phenomenal because more than 88.0 per cent of the sanctioned amount was disbursed to the entrepreneurs. Despite topographical barriers, the Corporation has contributed immensely in setting up of industrial background to the infant state and befit her in the process of self-reliance.

REFERENCES

1. Registered under Item No. 10, Vol. No. 1 dated 13.3.77 with the *Land Revenue Department*, GOS.
2. SIDICO, Memorandum of Association, Clause 3A contains 32 main objectives; Clause 3B comprises 62 ancillary objectives and Clause 3C incorporates 15 other objectives.
3. 'Company' denote 'the Corporation', i.e., SIDICO.
4. SIDICO, Scope of Financing and Guidelines for Entrepreneurs, p. 3.
5. *Ibid.*, p. 4.
6. *Ibid.*, p. 4 and *Annual Report,* SIDICO, 1991-92, p. 3.
7. SIDICO, *Annual Report*, 1993-94, p. 8.
8. SIDICO, *Annual Report*, 1994-95, p. 22.
9. *Ibid.*, pp. 5-23.
10. *Ibid,* p. 26 and as information received from the Manager, SIDBI, Gangtok.
11. SIDICO, *Annual Report*, 1994-95, p. 5.

6

Organisation and Management

SIDICO has been following a "line organisation" structure consisting of the Chairman, Board of Directors (BOD) Managing Director (MD) and other divisional heads. All divisional heads have direct links with the Managing Director. Initially, the Corporation had Planning, Raw materials and Accounts section. Now, the Corporation has Appraisal, Administration and Finance & Accounts Section under one Deputy General Manager (DGM)-I and loan disbursement, refinance and recovery under another Deputy General Manager (DGM)-II. DGM-I has Computer and Management Information System (MIS) Wing in control. The Legal cell is within the ambit of DGM-II. The Corporation has had no General Manager (GM) since 1991-92. All sections are supervised and controlled by the MD. Though the Corporation follows line organisation for efficient management, it is also supported by other Advisory Committees in line of staff organisation.

The chapter entails the evolution of the organisation structure since inception. In this process, constitution and working of the BOD and MD have been discussed. Moreover, functions of all the committees have been reviewed. The hierarchy of management is adorned by the induction of new personnel over the years. Many new departments have been augmented and training and development is undertaken to accommodate improved structure. A brief account of manpower development has also been drawn. In an overall review, lacunae in the structure and recommendations for development are proclaimed.

EVOLUTION

The Corporation envisaged many changes in the structural set up of the organisation, since its inception. The size of the organisation varied and enlarged with the increase in the business of the Corporation.

The Corporation started functioning with an-MD and Manager on deputation from the Directorate of Industries of the State. Thus, till 30.11.80, there were only four members on the pay-roll of the Corporation, as evident in Table-6.1. The induction of managerial personnel was mainly done during 1981-82. The Manager, for personnel, Finance and Accounts and Secretary were made available to help various sections. An advocate on a retainer basis was appointed to look after the legal affairs. All these were made to participate in joint venture projects.

The year 1986-87 inducted a GM in the Corporation. He was the Co-ordinator and In-charge of all managerial heads. More managers for Recovery, Refinance etc. were appointed in the same year. The Corporation appointed an Executive Director from the IDBI which was in existence only for two years. Till that year, excluding the MD and Executive Director, the Staff strength was 36.

The Corporation created the post of DGM during 1987-88. But, in practice the DGM-I and II started functioning after the voluntary retirement of the GM during 1991-92.[1] Meanwhile, the Corporation opened a Branch office at Jorethang, South district of Sikkim. The Branch covers both South and West districts. The Branch is in charge of a Manager, one assistant and two subordinate staff. The Branch is mainly entrusted with recovery and developmental activities. Till 31 December, 1994, the Corporation had a total of 39 employees including Managerial Personnel for Computer and Legal Affairs.

TABLE 6.1

ORGANISATION STRUCTURE OF SIDICO AS ON 30.11.80

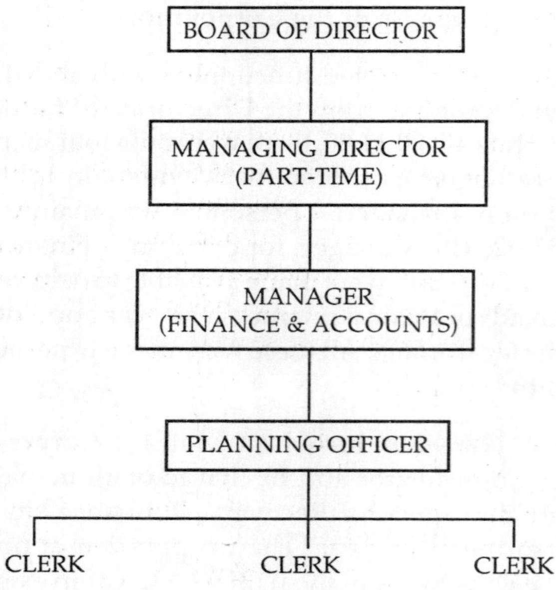

Source: Performance Evaluation Study Report, 1979-80, IDBI, p. 8

The latest change in the organisational hierarchy came into effect in the last quarter of 1994. The organisation structure as on 31 December 1994 has been depicted in Table-6.2. The day to day working of the Corporation is co-ordinated and managed by a full time MD flanked by two DGMs. DGM-I is in charge of two Deputy Managers

TABLE 6.2

ORGANISATION STRUCTURE OF SIDICO AS ON 31.12.94

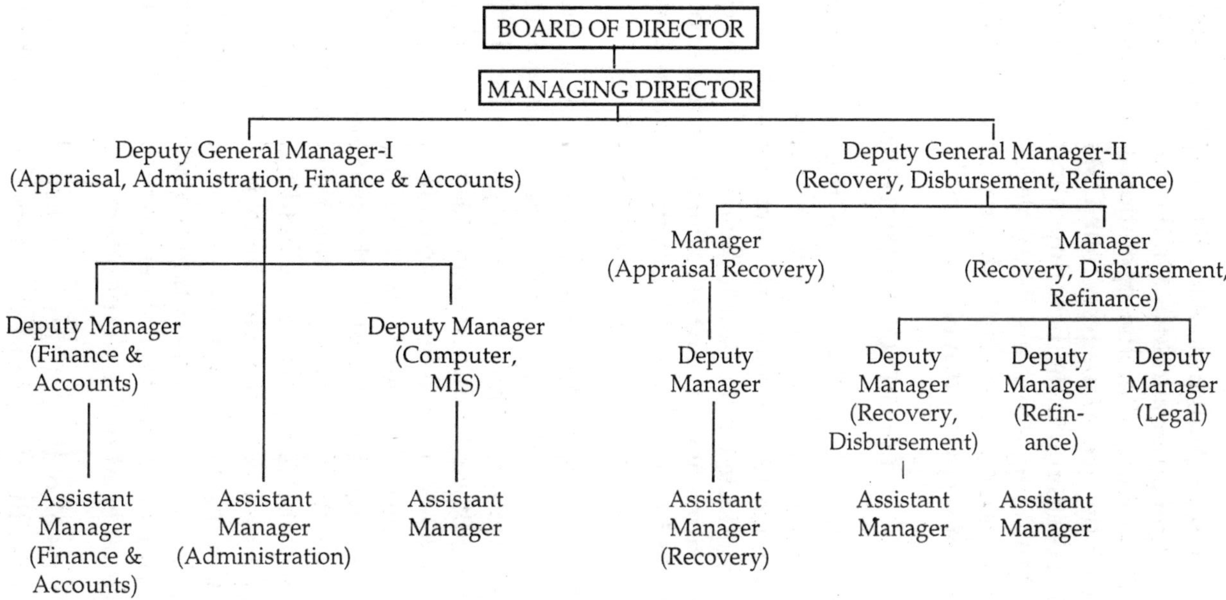

Source: As received from the official records of SIDICO.

(DM) and four Assistant Managers (AM) of which one DM is for computer and MIS. On the other hand, DGM-II is mostly looking after the operational activities and is supported by two Managers, four DMs and three AMs. The Corporation, for the first time allotted Legal matters to a DM fulfilling a long cherished necessity for the same. This, however, is required to look after increased litigations in course of recovery drive.

BOARD OF DIRECTORS

The number of directors on the board increased gradually. The Corporation started with five directors and reached ten in 1994. Top officials from various institutions are being inducted in the Board. Table-6.3 shows the changes in composition in the Board over the years. It is to be noted that the induction of an MLA in the Board as Chairman took place in 1984-85, i.e., after seven years of its working.

As new institutions came into existence in the State, the Corporation took full advantage of the experts from those institutions. Thus the incharge of the IDBI, SISI, SIDBI and SBI were inducted in the Board of the Corporation. During 1993-94, for the first time an industrialist has been selected in the Board. The clause of the Articles of Association has been altered to facilitate the maximum number of directors. Initially, the Corporation failed to satisfy clause 79 of the Articles regarding the holding of meetings. But, the problem was settled with the increase in the activities of the Corporation. The Board as the top most decision-making body of the Corporation is made instrumental by another top level managerial personnel i.e., MD. MD is the managerial head of the Corporation.

Clause 67 of the Articles of Association, was amended to increase the number of directors from eight to ten to include SIDBI nominee and one industrialist.[2]

TABLE 6.3

COMPOSITION OF BOARD OF DIRECTORS

Year		*Comosition*
1977-78	1.	Director of Industries, Government of Sikkim (GOS), also of the Managing Director of the SIDICO (Part-time), Chairman;
	2.	Finance Secretary, GOS;
	3.	Establishment Secretary, GOS;
	4.	Managing Director of the State Bank of Sikkim;
	5.	Development Commissioner, GOS.
1994-95.	1.	One Member of Legislative Assembly of Sikkim, Ex-officio Chairman;
	2.	Managing Director of the SIDICO;
	3.	Finance Secretary, GOS;
	4.	Managing Director of the State Bank of Sikkim;
	5.	Industry Secretary, GOS;
	6.	Deputy Director, SISI, Government of India;
	7.	Manager, SIDBI, Gangtok;
	8.	Assistant General Manager, State Bank of India, Gangtok;
	9.	Manager, IDBI, Calcutta; and
	10.	Managing Director of the Yoksom Breweries Limited, Sikkim.

Source: Annual Reports of the SIDICO, 1977-95.

Appointment and Removal

Clause 68 of the Articles stated that the directors shall, unless otherwise determined by the Governor from time to time, be appointed by the Governor. The Governor has the power to remove any Director, including the Chairman and the Vice-Chairman at any time in his absolute discretion. The Governor holds the right to fill any vacancy in the office of a director caused by retirement, removal, resignation, death or otherwise.

Remuneration

The remuneration of Director is determined by the Governor, subject to the provision of the Act. Any reasonable additional remuneration may be paid to any one or more of the directors for extra or special services rendered by him or them or otherwise. The directors may be paid all travelling, hotel and other expenses properly incurred by them in attending and returning from meetings of the Board or any Committee thereof or in connection with the business of the company according to the rates to be prescribed by the Company in General Meeting.

The clause 69 also states that, the IDBI is entitled to nominate two directors to the Board as 'Special Director.'[3] Such directors will get normal fees like other directors and travelling allowances for attending meeting and business activities. The non-IAS directors are eligible for sitting fees @ Rs. 100 per sitting.

Powers

The clause 70 of the Articles laid down the power vested in the Board. The Board of the Company shall be entitled to exercise all such powers and to do all such acts and things as the company is authorised to exercise and do. It is stipulated by sub-clause 2 that no regulation made by the Company in General Meeting shall invalidate any prior act of the Board, which would have been validated if that regulation had not been made.

Art 71 includes, in addition to general powers, some specific power entrusted to the Board as:

(a) to acquire property;
(b) to authorise the undertaking of works of a capital nature;
(c) to pay for property against debenture;

(d) to secure Contracts by mortgage;
(e) to appoint, remove, fix remuneration of the officers;
(f) to appoint trustees;
(g) to bring and defend action by or against the Company;
(h) to refer any claim or demand to arbitration;
(i) to authorise acceptance etc.;
(j) to invest in shares or scheduled banks;
(k) to sell or dispose of or transfer the business of property;
(l) to execute mortgage by way of indemnity;
(m) to give percentage of profit to related person with the approval of the Governor;
(n) to make, vary and repeal bye-laws;
(o) to establish local Board for managing any of the affairs of the Company in any specified locality in the State of Sikkim;
(p) to delegate powers.

Article 72 deals with the restriction on powers imposed by the IDBI by which the Board can not, without consultation with IDBI, exercise:

(i) the power to issue bonds and debentures;
(ii) the power to make any rules or regulations.

It is also provided that without the IDBI's approval, the Board shall not:

(i) borrow money from the Reserve Bank of India (R.B.I.);
(ii) borrow money from any financial institution notified in this behalf of the Centre or State Government.

General Meeting

Besides Annual General Meeting, all other meetings are in the name of 'Extra Ordinary General Meeting'. The Board can call an Extra Ordinary General Meeting whenever a requisition in writing is received in accordance with this Act.

Quorum

Article 43 stipulates that, three members present in person is the quorum for a General Meeting. Article 80, however, states that the quorum for a meeting of the Board of the Company shall be one-third of its strength or 3 Directors, whichever is higher.

Number of Meetings

Article 79 deals with the periodicity of the Board meetings. Accordingly, a meeting of the BOD is to be held to conduct the business of the Company at least once in every three months and at least four such meetings shall be held in every year.

Nominee Director

The Corporation has appointed director to some of its assisted units. These directors are known as nominee directors. Till 31 March, 1993, the Corporation has appointed 8 nominee directors in 15 assisted units.

In practice, assisted units hardly invite nominee directors from the SIDICO to their Board meetings. As a result, most of the nominee directors are not aware of the present status of units of which they are directors. In the process, the Corporation does not get any feedback from the nominee directors.

Managing Director

MD plays a pivotal role as the head of the Corporation.

MD is appointed by the State Government in consultation with the IDBI and BOD.

MD holds his office till the pleasure of the appointing authority. He is authorised by the Board to exercise such of the powers and discretion in relation to the affairs of the Corporation as are specifically delegated to him by the Board and are not required to be done by the Board at the General Meeting under the Act. He can sanction a loan upto Rs. 1.0 lakh.

The salary and allowances of the MD is fixed by the State Government. At present the salary is Rs. 4,000 per month, plus other allowances as per State Government. However, he is eligible to avail of full reimbursement of travelling and dearness allowances.

In the beginning, MDs were brought on a part-time basis from the Directorate of Industries. This convention persisted till 1982. In that year a full- time MD was appointed who continued in office for two years. It is a pity that till 31 March, 1992, the Corporation experienced full time MD discontinuously for four years only. Since 1992, the Corporation is being guided and administered by a full time MD. During 1995-96, a Joint Director from the Directorate of Industries assumed office as eighth MD of the Corporation. Table-6.4, depicted the account of MDs with background.

The Corporation's major shareholders i.e., the State Government and the IDBI are empowered under the Act to appoint a person to head the Corporation in mutual confidence. The Act does not specify qualifications or experience of assuming the office of MD. Experience of financial administration and commercial acumen for guiding the affairs of the Corporation is not dealt with in the Act. In the absence of the same, appointments are made in several cases where the appointee has sufficient merit in certain aspects but without having any experience and expertise in financial administration.

TABLE 6.4

MANAGING DIRECTORS OF SIDICO

Name	*Previous Occupation*	*Nature of Appointment as M.D.*	*Tenure*
1. K.C. Mathur	Director of Industries, GOS	Part-Time	1977-79
2. K.C. Pradhan	Industry Secretary, GOS	Part-Time	1979-80
3. P. Subba Rao	Director of Industries, GOS	Part-Time	1980-82
4. Sonam Gyamtso	Deputy Director, Industry, GOS	Full-Time	1982-84
5. Tashi Densapa	Additional Secretary, Culture Department, GOS	Part-Time	1984-89
6. Miss. C. Century	Secretary, Culture Department	Part-Time	1989-92
7. Sonam Topdan	Manager, Temi Tea Estate, Sikkim	Full-Time	1992-94
8. M.G. Kiran	Joint Secretary, Industry Department, GOS	Full-Time	1994-

Source: Performance Evaluation Study Report, relevant issues and through Personal Interview with the DGM-I, SIDICO.

The State Government having more power and authority over the Corporation sometimes overlooks or ignores the above aspect. Further, taking of prior advice and approval of the IDBI is also not followed in true perspective and consequently the consultation and approval of the IDBI have been reduced to mere formalities. The usual practice is not always followed. In a few cases, IDBI was not even consulted before appointing an MD by the State Government. It is felt that there may be much improvement in the working of the Corporation if the appointment is made on the basis of norms.

It is observed that the frequent change of MD within a short span of time jeopardizes the functioning of the Corporation. A new incumbent in this office needs sufficient time to have first-hand knowledge of the functioning of the Corporation and of the financial ability and integrity of the assisted concerns. The State Government may, after consulting the board, remove the MD from office but no MD should be so removed without reason. This is to satisfy natural justice common to all mercantile laws as well. Even, for all practical purposes, the post lies at the discretion of the State Government. Hence a new look should be given at the term of duration and contract, if any, for the highest office of the Corporation to implement its schemes. This office is also often subject to the policy of the ruling party and its Government in power in manning the post for the said office.

The Corporation has established different committees to gear up the working with expertise and vigour.

Executive Committee

The composition of the Executive Committee (EC) was made on the February 17, 1989 i.e., during 1988-89, with MD as the Chairman, two directors nominated by the State Government, one by the IDBI or SIDBI and one by the SISI. This was provided to expedite the process of day-to-day operations of the Corporation. Depending upon the importance and urgency of the matter certain items as allocated by the Board are left to be decided at the EC level. The Committee reduced the time gap involved in convening a Board meeting to discharge certain operations and also the cost involved therein. The Committee is empowered to deal with any matter within the competence of the Board and subject to such general or special directions as the Board may from time to time prescribe. Naturally, in pursuance of this spirit any action of the EC is within the purview of power delegated by the Board and hence the minutes of every meeting of the EC are placed before the next Board meeting for its information and record. On an average, the EC meets four times in a year.

In regard to the tenure of office of director, there prevails a distinction between a nominated director and an elected director. But as all the directors in SIDICO are nominated either by the State Government or other institutions, they hold the office at the pleasure of the authority nominating them.

Ad-hoc Committee

In 1991, the Corporation created one Ad-hoc Committee with four members. This Committee was meant to expedite the proposal faster than the EC. But the Committee met in December, 1994 for the first time since incorporation.

Default Review Committee

The Default Review Committee (DRC) emerged during 1987-88 from earlier Default Review Sub-Committee. The Sub-committee had been operating since 1985-86. But the actual operation started with the establishment of a full-fledged Default Review Committee. It comprised four members — two from the Finance and Industries department of the State, one from the SIDBI and the MD of the Corporation.

The Committee undertakes stupendous work on defaulting units. It invites promoters of such units to discuss problems to find out means to resolve them. The escalating default cases have activated the workings of the Committee. On an average, 50.0 per cent of the promoters appeared before the Committee.[4] The Committee met thrice to four times in a year.

Screening Committee

A considerable part of the population in the State hails from Defence Services. To cater for those retired persons at a comparatively early age, the Government stressed the need to start a programme for 'Self-Employment of Ex-Servicemen' (SEMFEX). Accordingly, during 1987-88, a Screening Committee for SEMFEX was established with three members including the Secretary of the Rajya Sainik Board, IDBI nominee and the MD of the SIDICO. The Committee met about three times in a year.

Other Committees

During 1984-85, the Corporation set up four sub-committees for considering pending cases in various fields.

These committees were Transport Loan Sub-Committee comprising four members; Hotel Loan Sub-Committee consisting of four members; Industrial Loan Sub-Committee again with four members and the Default Review Sub-Committee. All these Sub-Committees were very much operative for two financial years (FY) i.e., FY'86 and FY'87. Both Transport and Hotel Sub-Committees sanctioned an average of 25 cases per year. Industrial Sub-Committee cleared 8 cases per year.[5] Consequent upon the constitution of the EC, the Transport, Hotel and Industrial Sub-Committees ceased to function since February, 1989.

Delegation of Authority

The Corporation appears to be a highly centralised organisation and the intermediate level does not seem to have much contribution to the decision-making process because of inadequate delegation of authority. Even the MD can sanction only upto Rs. 1.0 lakh beyond which approval has to be obtained through the EC and the Board.

Administrative or Personnel Function

The Centralised hierarchy of the Corporation has restrained the development of manpower planning. It is observed that the personnel function of SIDICO involves activities like recruitment and other personnel administration e.g., personal records, increments, leave etc. Human Resource Development activity covering manpower planning and training is conspicuously absent. However, the Corporation gradually developed training facility sending mainly middle and top level managerial personnel to avail of such facility.

Training and Manpower Development

Since incorporation, the Corporation faced the problem of trained managerial personnel. Lack of adequate trained and experienced personnel affected the appraisal system of the Corporation. In view of limited staff, the Corporation found it difficult to avail of training facilities afforded by various institutions in the country. Till 31 March, 1981, the Corporation completely relied on the Directorate of Industries and SISI for technical appraisal of the projects.

Since 1981-82, the Corporation started deputing its managerial staff to IDBI and other institutions for training and development in various departments. So far, the Corporation has got its employees trained from the IDBI, National Institute of Small Industries Extension and Training (NSIET), Tamilnadu Industrial Investment Corporation (TIIC), Karnataka State Financial Corporation (KSFC), Management Development Institute (MDI), Gurgaon, Management Development Institute (MDI), Bangalore, Entrepreneurship Development Institute (EDI), Ahmedabad, and the Southern India Banks' Training College, Bangalore. A total of 40 staff were trained in various institutions, since 1985 to 1995, as shown in Table-6.5.

TABLE 6.5

MANPOWER DEVELOPMENT (TRAINING)

Year	*No. of Trainees*	*Place of Training*
1985-86	7	NA
1986-87	4	IDBI & others
1987-88	4	IDBI
1988-89	6	IDBI, TIIC & KSFC
1989-90	6	IDBI, MDI, NSIET
1990-91	3	NSIET, MDI, SIBST
1991-92	2	IDBI
1992-93	4	EDI, MDI, IDBI
1993-94	2	SIKKIM COMPUTER LTD.
1994-95	2	SIKKIM COMPUTER LTD.

Note: NA = Not Available.

Source: Performance Evaluation Study Report, relevant issues, IDBI, and Personal Interview with the DGM-I, SIDICO.

Staff-Officer Ratio

According to the organisational set-up on 31.12.94, the number of officers and staff was 15 and 24, respectively. The Staff-Officer ratio is about 1.6:1 which is not very ideal for qualitative aspect of the Corporation. Table-6.6 exhibited the position.

Review of Existing Structure

Reviewing the organisational structure, some of the inconsistencies noticed in the set up are as follows:

1. The important post of the GM has been lying vacant for the last few years. It certainly hampers administration in the Corporation.

TABLE 6.6

MANPOWER STRENGTH OF SIDICO AS ON 31.12.94

Designation	*No. of Personnel*
OFFICER	
1. Managing Director	1
2. Deputy General Manager	2
3. Manager	3
4. Deputy Manager	4
5. Assistant Manager	5
	15
STAFF	
1. Assistant	5
2. Junior Assistant	2
3. Personal Secretary to Managing Director	1
4. Stenographer	2
5. Typist	1
6. Driver	6
7. Peon	7
	24

Source: Official records and personal interview.

2. Most of the line function viz., disbursement, refinance and recovery have been kept under one operational wing i.e., DGM-II, except one important activity viz. Appraisal. The Appraisal Section has been put under DGM-I who in addition to this line function also looks after other important staff functions like Administration, Finance & Accounts. This

indicates overlapping of line and staff function in the organisation.

3. In the structure, there is no senior official responsible for appraisal of projects. Although Appraisal activity has been kept under DGM-I, interestingly the Manager for Appraisal and Recovery and DM of Appraisal and Recovery has been put under the DGM-II.
4. Although recovery has become the most vital area of activity of the Corporation, the Recovery Cell is under a Senior Official responsible for recovery performance. The cell is mainly confined to office work but there is no field officer for recovery and follow-up.
5. There is no technical officer in the Organisation which underlines the weakness of appraisal system. A DM is entrusted with the legal department since 1993.
6. There is no department responsible for dealing with Rehabilitation or Modernisation cases.
7. No one in the Corporation has any assigned responsibility for project identification and promotion activities.

Since its inception, the Corporation has been endeavouring to develop a strong industrial base in the hill-locked backward state of Sikkim. To this end, over the years, the Corporation has evolved an Organisation structure which helped it to accomplish the objective in a modest way, so far. However, detailed analysis of the existing Organisation structure reveals that there is further scope for improvement of the same.

Business Plan and Resource Forecasting (BPRF)

The existing Planning Process in SIDICO is essentially

a 'top down' exercise. Business Plan and Resource Forecasting (BPRF) is an important method of budgeting the prospective sanctions or lending activity by the Corporation for a year.

BPRF is necessary because of the requisition to be placed to the Refinancing institution for a certain amount of funds for a particular period. The Corporation considers all pending cases and viable cases to estimate yearly requirement. BPRF is prepared depending on the likely availability of resource support from the State Government and IDBI or SIDBI as appropriate to initiate in-house planning exercise which includes both the 'top down' and 'bottom up' processes.

Generally, current year resource forecasting is added with 10.0 to 15.0 per cent extra budget demand for next year. The IDBI in practice provided 65.0 per cent of the budgeted amount as refinance. Since 1992-93, the anticipated grant on total demand has been reduced to 55.0 per cent. Thus, the Corporation also prepares BPRF with such an amount for which even grant upto 55.0 per cent would suffice for the requirement. A study on the organisational structure[6] conducted by the West Bengal Consultancy Organisation Ltd. (WEBCON) in favour of the SIDICO reveals short-term and long-term organisational structure to redesign the existing structure to overcome existing lacunae.

In view of the poor recovery and tight liquidity position of the Corporation, it is thought prudent not to increase any manpower or even to fill up the vacant posts immediately. Therefore, an attempt has been made to redesign the existing structure in the short-term as far as possible within the existing manpower strength. Thus, two basic organisation structures (Table-6.7 and 6.8) have

TABLE 6.7

SUGGESTED ORGANISATION STRUCTURE OF SIDICO FOR SHORT TERM (2 YEARS)

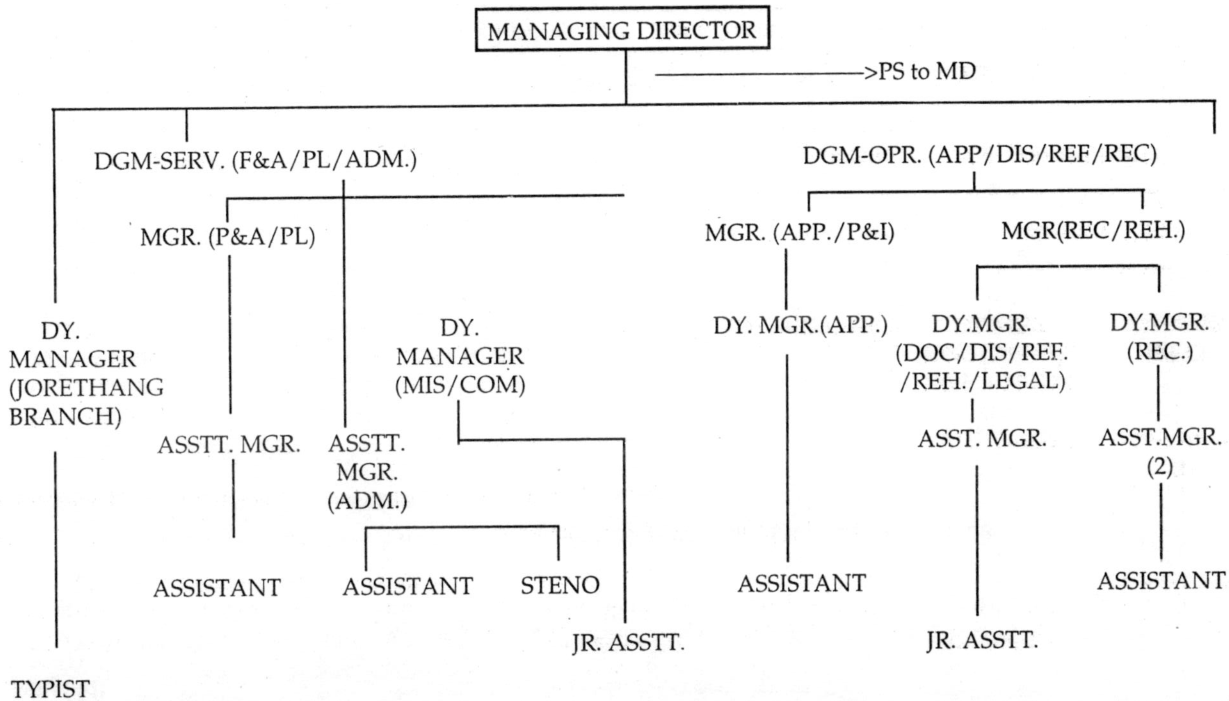

Note :

1. F&A=Finance & Accounts; PL=Planning; MIS=Management Information System; COMP=Computer ADM.=Administration; APP=Appraisal; DIS=Disbursement; REF=Refinance; REC=Recovery; PII=Project Promotion & Identification; REH=Rehabilitation; DOC=Documentation.
2. The position indicated in this chart do not represent the hierarchical status of the incumbent.

Source: Organisation Study of the SIDICO, 1993, WEBCON, p.57.

TABLE 6.8

SUGGESTED ORGANISATION STRUCTURE OF SIDICO FOR LONG TERM (AFTER 2 YEARS)

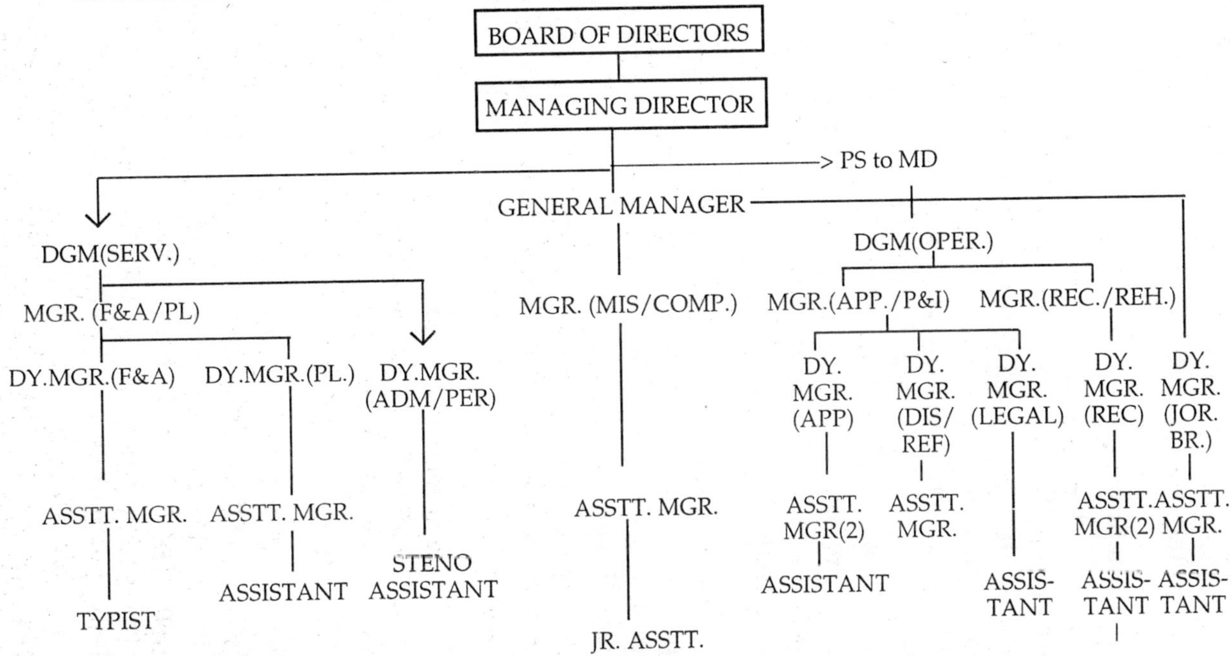

Note: The positions indicated in this chart do not represent the hierarchical status of the incumbent.

Source: Organisation Study of the SIDICO, 1993, WEBCON, p.58.

been proposed for 2 years and after 2 years, through the review of the organisation.

Short-Term Structure

1. In order to dilute the confusion in respect of overlapping of line and staff functions in the existing structure, it is proposed that there will be two separate operational wings each headed by the DGM. While the DGM (Operation) will look after the entire line functions of the Corporation viz. Appraisal, Disbursement, Refinance, Recovery, the responsibility of DGM (Services) has been fixed only for the staff functions like Finance and Accounts, Planning & Administration. Both the DGMs will report directly to the MD.

2. Since appraisal is one of the key functions of the Corporation, a separate section headed by a Manager (Appraisal & Promotion) has been created. The Manager concerned would directly report to the DGM (Operation) and would be supported by one DM and one Assistant. In addition to appraisal, this manager will also shoulder the responsibility of project promotion and identification.

3. There is immediate need to improve the recovery performance of the Corporation. Thus a strong and separate recovery cell has been conceived and headed by a senior level official in the rank of Manager.

4. In connection with recovery drive, the Manager (Recovery and Rehabilitation) will directly report to DGM (Operation). The Manager (Recovery & Rehabilitation) will be supported by one DM, two AM and one Assistant. Activities like documentation, disbursement, refinance and rehabilitation will be looked after by a DM (Legal) who will report directly to Manager (Recovery and Rehabilitation). The DM (Legal) will be flanked by one AM and one Junior Assistant.

The Administrative section has been put under AM (Administration) who will directly report to the DGM (Services). Apart from usual day-to-day work, the Assistant Manager (Administration) would be responsible for manpower planning of the organisation including arrangement for in-house and external training.

5. The Corporation has only one branch office at Jorethang. The branch which is headed by a Manager at present may be replaced by a DM as the function of the branch is mainly to follow-up Head Office instructions for recovery.

6. MIS has been proposed to put under a middle level official viz. DM (MIS & Computer). The responsibility of the DM (MIS & Comp.) will be not only to feed back necessary information in a structured format but also to arrange continuous environmental scanning so as to update the data bank of the Corporation.

7. For the time being the Corporation may continue with the system of utilising the services of legal professional on a retainer basis as and when the need arises. The services of DM (Legal) who is a law graduate may be utilised for general legal matters.

8. The Manager (Promotion & Appraisal) will be responsible for preparation of business performance plans related to the key area of activities of the Corporation in consultation with the DGM (Operation). Performance Review meeting is to be convened by DGM (Operation) in each quarter where all the departmental heads should be present. The MD may preside over such meetings.

9. In order to ensure the availability of technical and financial expertise, particularly for project cost of more than Rs. 20 lakh , a Statutory Advisory Committee may be

formed by the Corporation where outside experts from different disciplines or areas of industries may be invited. The MD may be the convener of the Committee.

10. The existing system of functional overlapping needs to be replaced by the concept of integral responsibility on a particular department or person. This is felt necessary to stop or eliminate buckpassing. For this purpose, an integral division under DGM (Operation) has been suggested. The DGM in consultation with MD may rationally balance all the key functions in order to minimise default cases.

11. In order to impart necessary professional expertise to the senior level officials, the Corporation may arrange to send them for suitable training programmes conducted by various professional agencies.

Long Term Organisation Structure

1. It is felt that through vigorous recovery drives, the Corporation would be able to overcome its severe liquidity crunch within the next two years. Consequently, the Corporation will not only be able to revamp its normal activities but also will be in a position to further expand and improve its activities. At that time there will be need for recruiting efficient personnel to fill up the vacant posts. Accordingly, in order to design a balanced structure, it has been suggested to fill up all the vacant posts. This apart, the total manpower strength has been suggested to increase to 50 persons against the sanctioned posts of 48 persons. Only 2 additional posts in the rank of DM have been created.

2. The span of control of the MD has been delegated down so as to enable him to concentrate more on policy, planning and external matters. A GM has been put under the MD so as to shoulder a part of this responsibility. All

detailed managerial functions have been distributed between the two GMs.

3. To avoid overlapping of line and staff functions, two clear wings each under one DGM (Services) and DGM (Operation) have been suggested. However, while DGM (Services) will be under the MD, DGM (Operation) will report to the GM who will be the overall incharge of the 'Operation' wing as well as MIS and Computer Section.

4. MIS and Computer have been put directly under the GM so as to make it more effective and meaningful.

5. The Appraisal and Project Identification and Promotion should be headed by a technical manager who should be an engineering graduate with 3-5 years experience. The Manager (Technical) will be flanked by DM (Appraisal), DM (Disbursement & Refinance) and DM (Legal). The induction of DM (Legal) is to improve the legal documentation system and for better follow-up of legal matters.

6. One senior official in the rank of DM has been suggested to head the Administrative department who will be assisted by one Assistant.

7. Planning activity has been given more importance and a separate cell headed by the DM has been proposed. The DM (Planning) will be assisted by one AM and one assistant. This cell must maintain close co-ordination with MIS and Computer Section so as to keep updated information about the internal as well as external changes that are continuously taking place. The change in the macro environment should have proper reflection in the planning documents of the Corporation.

8. A separate section for one of the most important

functions viz. Finance and Accounts has been formulated as Manager-in-Charge of Finance and Planning. He will be the head of the section flanked by one DM, one AM and one Assistant.

The study team has provided many propositions both for short-term and long-term perspective. It is observed that the Corporation has responded positively to some of the propositions. Induction of an industrialist in the Board, setting up of a Legal Cell under a Senior Official and effective Staff-Officer ratio are all the outcome of a long drawn demand fulfilled during 1993-94. However, changes in the structural framework in the Organisation of the Corporation will not pay enough if it cannot generate resources especially by satisfactory recovery position.

To sum up the details of Organisational hierarchy in SIDICO, it can be said that within a short span of time the Corporation has devised the set up as per requirement, though many a change is on the anvil. From the management point of view, the Corporation is well managed and administered by a sound internal management system.

The existing managerial personnel are insufficient for monitoring and guiding the assisted units. Educational and administrative background is also not sufficient for some of the posts. Two DGMs and two other managers are overburdened with more than one department. The most important department i.e. recovery is looked after by DGM and Manager alongwith other departments. Improper weightage is given to recovery department. In other SIDCs in the north-east, recovery alone is looked after by a Manager under direct supervision of the MD. In SIDICO, Recovery is exclusively to be entrusted to a DGM, who is well experienced in debt-recovery legislations. The Corporation can open a cell under a woman manager to boost woman entrepreneurs.

It is observed in the Corporation that a sluggish attitude in the Organisation has affected its effective working. . Selection and training must be properly adhered to. Work culture has to be improved with adequate and congenial Co-ordination amongst personnel. The concept of punctuality and sense of duty is not enough in the State as a whole. Similarly, the Corporation is also facing trouble in updating the work in due time. The entrepreneurs often complained about the excessive time taken by the Corporation in settling down filing work. This procedural delay, defects in appraisal, monitoring and follow-up must be eradicated with the imposition of accountability. The Organisation of the Corporation has to be revivified urgently. An effective and sound organisation can reduce the waste to bring back self-sufficiency for the Corporation in resource-generation and render adequate lending operation.

REFERENCES

1. The GM was an M.B.A. His resignation created a vacuum in the Corporation.
2. SIDICO, *Annual Report*, 1991-92, p. 2.
3. 'Special Director' is immune from holding Qualification Share and not liable to retire by rotation.
4. IDBI, *Performance Evaluation Study Report*, (PES), 1988-89, p. 4.
5. IDBI, PES, 1986-87, p. 3.
6. WEBCON, *Organisation Study of the SIDICO*, 1993, pp. 22-58.

7

Resource Position of SIDICO

The resources of the Corporation depend on the share capital and loans from the IDBI, SIDBI and the State Government. The sources can be divided into two categories viz. external and internal. The former consists of paid-up Share Capital, borrowings, grants etc., while the latter constitutes plough-back, repayment by the borrowers, interest and dividend received and disinvestment.

This chapter explores various sources of fund contributing to the Resource-mix with the objective of assessing the weightage of fund component since incorporation of the Corporation.

Share Capital

The Share Capital of the Corporation forms an integral part of the fund and helps in mobilising more funds from other institutions. The share capital of the Corporation is on regular accretion annually on matching basis by the State Government and the IDBI. The fund so raised in the form of accretion in Share Capital tends to get blocked in equity investments in assisted and promoted concerns.

The Corporation started functioning with an authorised capital of Rs.100.0 lakh and paid up capital of Rs.8.3 lakh. It accumulated paid up capital of Rs.69.3 lakh till 1982-83. The amount was provided by the State Government. The reason behind the non-availability of IDBI's contribution to Share Capital was due to limited activities of the Corporation. Moreover, the refinance by the IDBI since 1979-80 attributed the delay in the procurement of share capital from the IDBI. To strengthen the equity base first contribution of Rs.60.0 lakh received during 1983-84. The Corporation registered the highest growth of 118.8 per cent in share capital during 1983-84, because of IDBI's contribution. In the following years, the average growth in share capital stood at 25.0 per cent. The State Government is a constant contributor of share capital. But, the IDBI discontinued the contribution of share capital since 1991-92. The reason is ascribed to the non-repayment of the loan by the Corporation. However, in continuation of the contribution of Share Capital, the State Government has provided Rs.240.0 lakh since 1991-92 till March, 1995. In total, till March, 1995, the Corporation had share capital of Rs.1,043.3 lakh, where the contribution by the State Government was Rs.656.5 lakh and by the IDBI was Rs.386.8 lakh.[1]

Pursuant to the increase in share capital, the Corporation changed the limit of its authorised capital four times. Table-7.1 exhibited that the highest increase took place during 1985-88, where it rose from Rs.400.0 lakh to Rs.1,000.0 lakh registering a phenomenal growth of 2.5 times. The rate of growth in later years is more due to acceleration of activities.

TABLE 7.1

CHANGES IN AUTHORISED CAPITAL

(in lakhs)

Year	*Authorised Capital*
1977-78	100.0
1983-84	200.0
1985-86	400.0
1987-88	1000.0
1992-93	1500.0

Source: *Annual Reports*, 1977-93, SIDICO.

Borrowings

The borrowings of the Corporation are in the form of refinance from the IDBI and now SIDBI. Besides, State Government also contributed some soft loans and grants to the Corporation.

Till March, 1995, the Corporation received refinance from the IDBI and SIDBI to the tune of Rs. 1,747.4 lakh. The amount outstanding to these institutions was Rs.993.7 lakh i.e. 56.9 per cent of the borrowings is unpaid till March, 1995. The State Government adhered Rs.204.6 lakh as grants and soft loans, till March 1995. The Corporation repaid a meagre Rs. 1.7 lakh to the Government till that period. The Corporation received borrowings in the form of refinance from the IDBI during 1979-80. The first refinance amounted to Rs. 12.6 lakh.[2]

There are two types of refinance by the IDBI. These are Automatic Refinance Scheme (ARS) and Normal Refinance Scheme (NRS). Automatic Refinance Scheme covers all projects upto Rs.7.5 lakh except hotels. For ARS no project report needs to be sent to the SIDBI for approval. All other schemes outside the ARS comes under NRS.[3]

Normally, refinance facilities are available in respect of term loan granted to industrial concerns for financing acquisition of fixed assets, either for setting up a new project or for expansion or modernisation of an existing unit. The minimum period for loans eligible for refinance is three years. The maximum period in respect of loans given by the Corporation is upto ten years. Till 31 March, 1983, the Corporation was getting refinance to the extent of 90.0 per cent of the eligible loan i.e., term loan. Since 1983-84, the Corporation had been allowed refinance to the extent of 100.0 per cent as a special incentive for all industries located in 'No Industry District'.[4]

During 1985-86, IDBI reduced refinance limit to 85.0 per cent of the loan to SSI units and Single Road Transport Operators (SRTOs) under the Normal Refinance Scheme as compared to 90.0 per cent received previously; 75.0 per cent of loans to medium sized units and hotels as against 90.0 per cent earlier. Again within two years, changes were made in the refinance rate structure : for Composite Loan, SRTOs loan and other industrial loan upto Rs.7.5 lakh., the refinance made available was 100.0 per cent and for hotels and industrial loans above Rs.7.5 lakh refinance was to the extent of 90.0 per cent.[5]

During 1991-92, limit of the schemes for refinance was enhanced from Rs.7.5 lakh to Rs.10.0 lakh and more.[6]

Since 1992-93, the rate of refinance was brought down to 55.0 per cent.[7] The refinance repayments were delinked to recovery from the ultimate borrowers.

In case of Seed Capital assistance provided for only two cases, the refinance was to the extent of 100.0 per cent by the IDBI.[8]

In the process of refinance, the schedule for repayment is synchronised with the schedule for repayment of the corresponding loan and all repayments received from the borrowing concerns passed over the IDBI except in cases where partial refinance has been granted. The schedule for repayment of refinance as per agreement between the SIDICO and the IDBI is prepared on the lines of repayment schedule made by the SIDICO with its constituents.

The application for refinance is made by the Corporation soon after the sanction of the loan but not later than one year from the date of first disbursal of loan by them. The subsequent instalments are drawn by exchange of letters at the time of disbursement of the instalment to the concerns.

In practice, the Corporation's refinance deal is fluctuating in nature. This is obvious, as the requirement of refinance depends on sanctions and disbursement, repayment of loan by the loanees and repayment to the IDBI.

TABLE 7.2

BORROWINGS, REPAYMENT AND OUTSTANDING OF SIDICO

(Rs. in Lakh)

Year ending 31 March	*IDBI and SIDBI*			*State Government*	
	Amount Received	*Repaid*	*% of Repayment to Amt. Received*	*Amount Received*	*Repaid*
1978	—	—	—	4.6	—
1979	—	—	—	—	0.3
1980	12.6	—	—	—	0.3
1981	20.2	0.9	4.4	—	0.3
1982	8.0	3.8	47.5	—	0.3
1983	44.0	5.4	12.3	—	
1984	23.8	11.5	48.3	—	
1985	70.5	18.8	26.7	—	
1986	132.3	32.9	24.9	—	
1987	157.9	43.6	27.6	—	0.4
1988	330.8	51.1	15.4	—	
1989	145.3	87.8	60.4	—	
1990	242.3	104.4	43.1	—	
1991	213.5	128.7	60.3	—	
1992	272.5	166.1	60.9	—	
1993	73.7	73.4	99.6	200.0	—
1994	—	2.1	—	—	—
1995	—	23.2	—	—	—
TOTAL	1747.4	753.7	43.1	204.6	1.6

Source: *Annual Report*, 1995. SIDICO. p.28.

As evident from Table-7.2, during the first five years from 1981-86 on the average, refinance availed of by the Corporation amounted to Rs.55.7 lakh. In the last five years, during 1988-93, the average refinance amounted to Rs.189.4 lakh, i.e., a more than 3 times increase between 1981-86 and 1988-93.

New Debt Instrument

Besides IDBI's regular financing system, another Special Loan was provided by the IDBI. The scheme was New Debt Instrument (NDI) Scheme for supplementing resources of SFCs and SIDCs as a special loan repayable in 4 equal annual instalments after an initial moratorium of 4 years. The loan was of 11.0 per cent interest per annum and the ceiling was 10.0 per cent of the projected disbursement of the term loan. During 1987-88, the Corporation availed for the first time of a sum of Rs.35.0 lakh. Since then the Corporation has not taken any further amount under the scheme.[9]

In addition to equity and borrowings, the Corporation generates its own funds through reserves and recoveries.

Reserves

The State Financial Corporation Act, 1951, prescribes the creation of General and Special reserves. Further, the financial Corporation must create a reserve fund before any other appropriation. The rate of such reserves is left to the discretion of the Corporation. As SIDICO is not governed either by the SFC Act or Companies Act, 1956, the Corporation has discretionary power regarding the creation of reserve fund and declaration of dividends.

The Corporation has generated a satisfactory surplus. The percentage of general reserve to paid-up Capital as indicated in Table 7.3 shows the reserve position of the Corporation. It ploughed back reserves to raise financial resources. The creation of General Reserve is dependent upon the quantum of available free profit. Thus, the greater the amount of General reserve, the better the financial position of the Corporation.

TABLE 7.3

RESERVE POSITION OF THE SIDICO

(Rs. in Lakh)

Year Ended 31 March	*General Reserve*	*Cumulative*	*% of Cumulative General Reserve to Paid-up Capital*
1978	0.3	0.3	3.3
1979	0.9	1.2	7.5
1980	2.0	3.2	10.2
1981	2.4	5.6	13.4
1982	2.9	8.5	16.5
1983	14.0	22.5	32.4
1984	3.4	25.9	17.1
1985	3.5	29.4	15.4
1986	3.9	33.3	12.9
1987	4.7	38.0	12.2
1988	5.7	43.7	10.0
1989	7.9	51.6	9.6
1990	(-)2.5	49.1	—
1991	(-)64.2	—	—

Source: Annual Reports, 1977-91, SIDICO.

Till 1989, the average annual General reserve was 4.3 per cent. However, on an average, the percentage of General reserve compared to paid up capital stood as high as 13.3 per cent. No dividend has, so far, been declared by the Corporation. Dividend accruing to the State Government and the IDBI has been retained as General reserve. However, no guidance still exists, for the utilisation of money from the said fund. Nor does it reveal to what extent it has helped development and expansion of business and generation of additional flow of income.

On annual observation, the year 1982-83 accounted for the largest amount of reserve creation for which the cumulative general reserve as percentage of paid up capital stood a record high.

The Corporation has been incurring sustained losses since 1990-91. The main reason was the change in accounting system from accrual to cash basis since 1989-90. To neutralise the losses, the State Government provided grants in the form of reserve which is accounted as Rs.60.7 lakh till 1994-95.[10] Such incentives, however, could not ameliorate the reserve generation capacity of the Corporation.

Repayment by Units

Recovery of loan is as important as providing loan itself to any financial institution. Poor recovery affects adversely the future planning of the financial institutions and thereby responsibilities and it also chokes the credit plan which in turn may impede the development programme of industries. Therefore, prompt recovery of loan is one of the essential factors for the success of operations of the Corporation.

The Corporation's recovery performance over the years is not satisfactory. It is gauged further from Table-7.4, that the recovery of principal amount to total demand of Principal has been dwindling for the last few years. The recovery from the unit was only one-fourth of the amount disbursed to those units. Till March, 1995, total repayment made by the units amounted to Rs.617.7 lakh. Till March, 1995, the Corporation repaid the refinance received, to the IDBI and SIDBI worth Rs.753.7 lakh. Thus, deficit arose persistently resulting in the discontinuation of refinance since 1993-94.

TABLE 7.4

REPAYMENT OF LOAN BY ASSISTED UNITS

(Rs. in Lakh)

Year ending 31 March	*Term Loan*	*Bridge Loan and Soft Loan*	*Total*
1978	N.A.	N.A.	N.A.
1979	N.A.	N.A.	N.A.
1980	0.1	—	0.1
1981	0.1	—	0.1
1982	2.3	—	2.3
1983	5.2	3.1	8.3
1984	8.0	5.4	13.4
1985	11.9	6.2	18.1
1986	11.1	2.0	13.1
1987	23.3	32.0	55.3
1988	36.5	26.7	63.2
1989	46.0	12.6	58.6
1990	73.1	43.7	116.8
1991	59.3	—	59.3
1992	56.6	—	56.6
1993	46.4	0.4	46.8
1994	53.2	—	53.2
1995	46.1	—	46.1
TOTAL	485.4	132.3	617.6

Note: N.A. signifies data not available.
Source: Annual Report, 1995, SIDICO, p. 22.

The ever-falling trend in recovery causes concern to the Corporation. This has to be revamped for sustenance and growth. In recent years, poor recovery performance led to poor repayment to the refinance by the IDBI. This, again compels the IDBI to discontinue matching grants and refinance in previous tune. Thus, recovery constraints caused a vicious cycle or debt-trap to the Corporation.

It is observed that the resource position of the Corporation has been crunched over the years. Especially, the Corporation had no dearth of funds till contribution in Share Capital and refinance from IDBI continued. At that time, the top officials of the Corporation opined in favour of the new applicant. They wanted to invest in projects to mobilise more funds. Suddenly, the position changed. This is because investment by the Corporation in a big project proved bad. The Corporation was used as an institution to channelise political mandate. Loanees were not dealt with properly. All these factors dwindled resource position resulting in default in the repayment of refinance to the IDBI and SIDBI.

Lack of Professionalism and judicious use of resources of the Corporation was largely due to interference by the ruling party of the State. Often, viable projects were not given proper attention due to some unknown reason. However, interference by the representatives of the People in getting any work done from any institution directly or indirectly controlled by the Government, is a common phenomenon in our country. To some extent honest endeavour by the politicians might prove well but mostly such acts admonish morale of the majority of the people. In recent years i.e., 1992-93, the then Government granted soft loan of Rs.2.0 crore to Sikkim Vanaspati Limited, a sick and non-viable project. The amount was provided to businessman to enter into partnership with the Corporation to make Vanaspati Limited Operative.

The resource position of the Corporation is mainly contributed by the IDBI and SIDBI in the form of refinance. The State Government confines its activity mainly to the contribution of Share Capital. Thus the main stake in total resources was of IDBI's. Obviously, IDBI is in a commanding position. IDBI formulates policies in consultation with the Central Government and RBI and communicates to the primary lending institutions and respective State Governments. The State Government cannot change but adjust the position as per IDBI's guidelines.

In Sikkim, the State Government allocates resources to the SIDICO through plan expenditure. It segregates annual contribution from Annual Plan Outlay on the head of SIDICO.

Sikkim contemplates a development expenditure for the Eighth Five Year Plan in the order of Rs.550.0 crore. The approved annual plan outlay in 1994-95 is Rs.135.0 crore. The annual budget of Sikkim for 1994-95[11] shows an estimated expenditure of Rs.299.9 crore which is 8.6 per cent more than the previous year level. The revenue receipt in the budget estimated at Rs.263.7 crore in 1994-95. The total internal revenue of the State Government amounts to Rs.58.1 crore, which is only 38.7 per cent of the total non-plan expenditure of the State Government. The major sources of collection of revenue are

(a) income tax under state law 7.9 percent;
(b) State excise 15.5 percent; and
(c) Sales Tax 6.9 per cent.

Out of every three rupees collected as tax revenue, two rupees come from State's Share in centrally collected taxes and one rupee from the taxes collected by the State. In the revenue receipt of Rs.263.7 crore, non-tax revenue occupied 11.7 per cent and Grants-in-Aid by the Central Government accounted for 47.8 per cent. It is clear that of the total budgetary provision of Rs. 301.0 crore for 1994-95, total plan and non-plan expenditure amounted to

Rs.285.0 crore. Besides, about 47.8 per cent of the total revenue receipt of the budget is provided by the Central Government as grant-in-aid.[12]

The infusion in share capital is being done by the State Government alone since 1991-92 as the IDBI stopped contributing share capital since then. This obviously squeezed the source to some extent. The internal generation and ploughing back of profits were also not possible due to sustained loss since 1989-90 with the inception of cash basis of accounting. Thus the Corporation's dependence on other sources increased gradually. The repayment of loans by the borrowers has not at all been encouraging. Increased reliance is, therefore, being placed on refinance through the IDBI. Borrowings however is costlier than internal-generation.

Borrowings by way of refinance may be resorted to as and when required by the Corporation and hence the said amount need not be kept idle in the hand of the Corporation. In case of deposit, the amount may not come as and when it is required. Till recently borrowing by way of refinance was cheaper than public deposit. The IDBI used to give refinance for this region at the rate of 11.00 to 13.5 per cent for various ceiling. The IDBI is of the opinion that in view of the weak financial position of most of the SIDCs, the Corporation should raise its funds through share capital.

REFERENCES

1. Vide, Appendix No.1.
2. SIDICO, *Annual Report, 1979-80*, p.6.
3. SIDICO, *Annual Report, 1985-86*, p.5.
4. SIDICO, *Annual Report, 1984-85*, p.2.
5. SIDICO, *Annual Report, 1987-88*, pp. 7-8, *Annual Report*, 1985-86, *op.cit.*

6. SIDICO, *Annual Report, 1991-92,* p.8.
7. SIDICO, *Annual Report, 1992-93,* p.7.
8. SIDICO, *Annual Report, 1985-86,* p.3.
9. SIDICO, *Annual Report, 1987-88,* p.8.
10. SIDICO, *Annual Report, 1994-95,* p.13.
11. Government of Sikkim, *Annual Budget, 1994-95,* pp. 2-8.
12. *Ibid.*

8

Lending Policies and Procedures

STATE GOVERNMENT AND THE POLICY MATTER

The operational pattern of the corporation is well guided by certain pre-planned policies. The State Government direct the policy matters within the parameter of IDBI guidelines. Policies expressed in general statements or understanding guide or channel thinking and action in decision-making of subordiantes. In discharge of its functions the Board of Directors is guided by such instructions on question of policy as may be given to it by the State Government within the policy of IDBI. In practice the policy cannot be formulated without the prior approval and advice of the IDBI. The spirit of enactment is not only to transform the matter into mere official consultation but practically it also means seeking of consent and approval of the IDBI in favour of certain actions. In most of the provisions of the Act the term 'Consultation with' has not been properly elaborated. In this respect, the general regulation of the corporation may elaborate on the practice and manner of consultation. The provision of the Act implies, by consultation, taking of favourable consent and prior approvals which is virtually done for all practical purposes. In case of any dispute between the State Government and the Board as to whether a given question is related to policy matters, the decision of the State Government will be final. For State Financial Corporations, the statute has authorised the IDBI to carry out inspection of the workings of the corporation. The IDBI may inspect the workings of the State Industrial Development Corporation also as per power given to them by the respective SIDCs. It is not a statutory power but derivative power conferred upon it by the SIDCs for their mutual interest and benefit.

The policy decision of a development banking agency like SFCs and SIDCs is always subjective, qualitative and its policy is always dynamic, flexible and innovative. It has been kept flexible to meet the requirements of a specific case on the merits of each unit.

The State Government in policy matters, is conceived to be above the Board of Directors and the Boards jurisdiction has been restricted within the policy structure of the State Government. This indicates the dual character of both State and Central level organisations enjoyed by the Corporation. Hence, the Act does not give a free hand to the State Government in the formation of policy matters.

This Chapter critically analyses various Plans and Policies adopted by the Corporation in the process of loan sanction and monitoring.

The Corporation is basically a term-lending institution. It provides loans on various schemes of the IDBI and now SIDBI to mitigate dearth of assistance. Besides loan assistance, various subsidies and incentives are also provided to eradicate backwardness of the entrepreneurs. Some of the important schemes and incentives are discussed below.

General Scheme

The Corporation advances loans to small and medium scale industries which are technically and financially viable. The project for loan assistance should be in accordance with the Industrial policy of the Government of Sikkim.

Loan assistance was provided for creation of fixed assets such as purchase of land, construction of building thereon, purchase of plant and machinery, pre-operative expenses and other assets. Besides this, loans are also provided for setting up a new industrial project, renovation of existing plant and machinery, expansion or diversification and shifting of existing unit from non-conforming to conforming areas. The repayment period was 7½ years with a moratorium of 18 months.[1]

Composite Loan Scheme

This scheme was intended to meet the complete financial requirements of both equipment finance and working capital of artisans, village and cottage industries and small scale industries in the tiny sector. The maximum amount of loan available under this scheme was Rs. 50,000. The ceiling of Rs. 50,000 was not related to the project cost but to the amount of loan assistance needed by artisans. The repayment period of such loans were 5 to 8 years with an 'initial' moratorium period of 12 to 18 months. No promoter's contribution is needed in this scheme.[2]

Single Vehicle Operator Scheme

Under this scheme the Corporation provides financial assistance for purchase of cars to be used as local taxis or trucks or mini trucks or tankers or buses or tourist coaches. Clearance from the Motor Vehicle department and Sikkim Nationalised Transport is necessary. The loan is available for purchase of new vehicles. Some conditions are as follows:

(1) It should be ensured that the vehicle was used as Public Transport Carrier or Contract Carrier;

(2) Preference was given to applicants with driving licence or possessing experience in the transport line as a driver, employee in transport firm or transport agent.

In practice, loan in this scheme was provided for purchase of vehicles to be used as local taxis. Educated unemployed persons were the recipients of this loan. The repayment period was 3 to 5 years with a moratorium period of 6 months. The promoter's minimum contribution was 20.0 present of the cost of the vehicle.[3]

Hotel Loans

The Corporation provides financial assistance for establishing hotels to cater to the needs of tourists. The hotel as a loanee should have boarding, lodging and restaurant facilities and should have been planned on modern life. The hotels should also be approved by and enlisted with the appropriate authorities like the Municipality, Local Self Government, Tourism etc. Loans to hotels are sanctioned under the General Scheme. Thus, the procedure and moratorium period is the same as provided for in the General Scheme.

Seed Capital Scheme

The scheme aims at assisting new entrepreneurs who do not have adequate resources of their own to contribute as promoter. To be eligible for assistance under the scheme, the entrepreneur should be technically or professionally qualified or possess experience or skills either in industry, business or trade and should have the traits of an entrepreneur for setting up and running the enterprise successfully. Basically, the applicant should be a new entrepreneur. The seed capital assistance can not in any case be more than the promoters' contribution.

Single Window Scheme for Fixed Assets and Working Capital

New tiny and small-scale industrial units whose project cost (excluding working capital margin) does not exceed Rs. 5.0 lakh and the total working capital requirement at the normal level of operation is upto Rs. 2.5 lakh are eligible for assistance under the single window scheme. Industrial units seeking additional assistance for expansion, modernisation, diversification are not eligible for working capital assistance. In this scheme financial assistance is eligible upto Rs. 15.0 lakh. Term loans and working capital loans are sanctioned simultaneously to meet the initial working capital requirement of tiny and SSI units. The moratorium upto 3 years is given for repayment of loans depending upon the cash generation of the unit. The loan component has to be repaid with a maximum period of 10 years including the moratorium period.[4]

Rehabilitation Scheme

The units which are considered to be potentially viable but sick, are taken up for rehabilitation with relief packages to overcome its sickness. Maximum limit of loan is Rs. 90.0 lakh with at least 10.0 per cent promoters' contribution.

In conformity with the policy of the Government of India, the State Government from time to time introduced various subsidies and incentive schemes to harness industrial activity. These are:

1. Central Investment Subsidy (CIS);
2. Central Transport Subsidy (CTS);
3. Subsidy on Power;
4. Subsidy on Interest on Working Capital;
5. Subsidy to Artisan-oriented Units;
6. Subsidy to beneficiaries under Differential Rate of Interest (DRI) Scheme.
7. Price Preference for marketing assistance;
8. Concessions on Sales Tax;
9. Subsidy on Publicity and Advertisement;
10. Subsidy on Power Generation and Connexion;

11. Subsidy on Registration fee of Promotion Council, Indian Standard Institute (ISI), Commodity Board and Chamber of Commerce;
12. Deferment of Excise Duty;
13. Grant on Pre-Operative Expenses;
14. Special incentive for 'High Value Low Volume' production units and units utilising local raw-materials.

The Corporation, however, adopts any such scheme, subsidies or incentives formulated by the SIDBI as the activities of the Corporation are circumscribed by it.

Amongst subsidies, central investment and transport subsidies are considered a major relief to the investors and producers in the state.

Central Investment Subsidy

All the four districts of the state have been classified as 'No Industry Districts' and hence were eligible for investment subsidy @ 25.0 per cent in the cost of fixed assets subject to a maximum of Rs. 25.0 lakh and Rs. 50.0 lakh for electronic projects[5].

A state level committee comprising government nominees, representatives of the Corporation and banks, was formed to sanction such subsidy. This was an outright grant and need not be refunded. In Sikkim, the SIDICO was empowered to the sanctioned amount of central subsidy. Against the subsidy, the Corporation provided bridge-loan tc expedite the need for funds. Such bridge-loan was adjusted on receipt of the subsidy amount from the Central Government.

Table 8.1 shows that the Corporation received investment subsidy since 1980-81. Till 1992-93, the amount of subsidies sanctioned was Rs. 497.5 lakh and disbursement was also upto the sanction i.e. Rs. 489.8 lakh. However, some units became sick even before receiving the subsidies.

TABLE 8.1

CENTRAL SUBSIDIES

(Rs. in Lakh)

Year	*Central Investment Subsidies*		*Central Transport Subsidies*	
	Sanction	*Disbursement*	*Sanction*	*Disbursement*
1980-81	2.0	0.9	—	—
1981-82	—	1.2	—	—
1982-83	12.5	17.5	—	—
1983-84	21.5	34.1	—	—
1984-85	33.4	18.6	1.4	0.9
1985-86	53.8	28.2	—	8.9
1986-87	130.2	137.1	—	
1987-88	125.1	61.4	7.8	4.3
1988-89	—	73.8	—	—
1989-90	97.8	117.0	39.3	61.4
1990-91	21.2		60.8	39.1
1991-92	—	—	125.2	120.0
1992-93	—	—	2.2	2.1
1993-94	—	—	55.5	55.5
TOTAL	497.5	489.8	292.2	292.2

Source: Annual Reports and Official Records of the SIDICO, 1980-94, SIDICO.

The Central Government, however, discontinued investment subsidy during 1988-89. This seizure caused wide gap in the means of project finance as the CIS contributed to a large extent to the equity of the project.

The promoters of projects have been adversely affected as the equity contribution required to be raised has increased to that extent and hence have had to resort to unsecured borrowings at high interest.

Central Transport Subsidy

Another important subsidy provided by the Central Government was central transport subsidy.

The CTS was provided on the following criteria:[6]

1. Reimbursement to the extent of 90.0 per cent of the transport cost incurred on transportation of basic raw materials from the nearest railhead to the factory site and for transportation of finished goods from the factory site to the rail head. For this purpose, Siliguri or New Jalpaiguri was considered to be the nearest railhead.
2. Reimbursement to the extent of 75.0 per cent of air freight incurred for transportation of raw materials and finished products in between the nearest designated airport. Here, Bagdogra and Calcutta were treated as nearest designated airports.

The first sanction and disbursement of CTS took place during 1984-85 (Tab. 8.1). Till 1993-94, the total amount of CTS availed of and disbursed was Rs. 292.2 lakh.

Among other subsidies and incentives, some of the important are as follows[7]:

a) **Subsidy on Power:** The entrepreneurs were given free use of power upto Rs. 25,000/- per annum.

b) **Subsidy on Raw Material:** A subsidy of 25.0 per cent of the invoice value, subject to a ceiling of Rs. 5,000 per annum was provided to the industrial units procuring woollen and cotton yarn from SIDICO for carpet making.

c) **Subsidy on interest on Working Capital:** The entrepreneurs were given subsidy on the interest exceeding 13.0 per cent on the working capital, to the non-defaulting unit in respect of interest payment, subject to a maximum of Rs. 25,000.

d) **Price preference:** The price preference not exceeding 15.0 per cent was provided to the units in Sikkim.

e) **Concession on Sales Tax:** The units were exempted from Sales Tax upto five years from the commencement of production.

The industrial interest of the state is being served by the following agencies:

1. Directorate of Industries;
2. District Industries Centre (East & North);
3. District Industries Centre (South & West);
4. District Industries Office, District Administration Centre;
5. Sikkim Industrial Development & Investment Corporation Limited;
6. Small Industries Service Institute, Government of India;
7. The Development Commissioner (Handicrafts), Ministry of Textiles, Government of India;
8. Sikkim Khadi and Village Industries Board;
9. Small Industries Development Bank of India;[8]
10. Sikkim Consultancy Centre;
11. National Small Industries Corporation Limited;
12. Directorate of Handlooms & Handicrafts;
13. Lead Bank i.e., State Bank of India;

14. State Bank of India (Main Branch);
15. United Commercial Bank (Main Branch);
16. Central Bank of India (Main Branch).

Processing of Loan Applications

The Corporation generally follows the guidelines as prescribed by the IDBI in respect of procedural affairs including processing of loan applications. Accordingly, the intending loanee applicant submits the application in the prescribed form, prepared on the basis of guidelines framed by the Corporation in collaboration with the IDBI.

Scrutiny of applications is done in two cells of the Corporation, namely, financial and technical. The financial cell looks after the financial aspect of the scheme and the technical cell studies the technical feasibility of the scheme. If both the cells are satisfied about the viability, a joint discussion is held by them with the Managing Director, General Manager, Deputy General Manager or Manager, whose views are also considered. The memorandum of consensus on the loan proposal is then placed before the Managing Director for his approval and comment. The same in turn, is circulated among other members of the Board and Executive Committee for their perusal and consideration in the ensuing meeting. Finally, the Board or Executive Board accords approval to the proposal with or without certain special terms and conditions, including the amount of sanction, rate of interest, period of loan and mode of repayment etc.

To expedite the process of approval, sanctioning power has been bifurcated between the Managing Director and the Executive Committee. However, the cancellation power, to make it more judicious, unbiased and rational, has been vested in the Board only. Sometimes, a pre-sanction inspection is carried out jointly by Technical and Appraisal

& Financial wing in order to get first hand knowledge about the feasibility of the project.

The SIDICO started maintaining accounts of application received, sanctions, rejected and pending in the Annual Reports since 1982-83. Unitwise, the number of sanctions has increased gradually over the years. Table 8.2 exhibits that, during 1982-83, 19 out of 32 applications were sanctioned constituting 59.4 per cent of the total. During 1991-92, 223 out of 236 applications were sanctioned, recording the highest ever 94.5 per cent of the total. Again, in 1992-93 the percentage of the sanctioned application to the total applications came down to the lowest at 42.9 per cent. This sharp decline, however, was due to scarcity of funds of the Corporation. The situation of sanctions improved during 1994-95, but the pending rate also deteriorated.

Amountwise, the year 1982-83 witnessed sanction of Rs. 42.2 lakh of the total of Rs. 108.3 lakh, which accounted for 38.9 per cent. The year 1989-90 registered a sanction of Rs. 324.4 lakh as against the total of Rs. 432.2 lakh i.e. 75.0 per cent of the total, the highest since 1982-83. Unfortunately, the year 1992-93 could sanction only 16.0 per cent i.e. Rs. 20.9 lakh of the total amount of Rs. 130.6 lakh. for consideration. This was the lowest rate of sanction since 1982-83.

Applications were rejected, cancelled or withdrawn for various reasons. Both parties were responsible for such rejection. During 1991-92, rejection was the lowest. Only 3 cases out of 236 were rejected, which accounted for 1.3 per cent. The very next year 1992-93 experienced the highest rejection—of 19 cases out of 70 cases, i.e., 27.1 per cent. The year, amountwise also recorded the highest rejection of Rs. 95.9 lakh of the total Rs. 130.6 lakh which was 73.4 per cent of the total.

TABLE 8.2

APPLICATIONS RECEIVED AND DISPOSED

(Rs. in Lakh.)

Year	Sanctioned		Rejected/ Withdrawn		Pending at the end of yr.		Total for consideration	
	No.	Amt.	No.	Amt.	No.	Amt.	No.	Amt.
1982-83	19	42.2	—	—	13	66.1	32	108.3
	(59.4)	(38.9)			(40.6)	(61.1)	(100.0)	(100.0)
1983-84	61	99.1	7	15.5	17	71.5	85	186.1
	(71.8)	(53.2)	(8.2)	(8.3)	(20.0)	(38.4)	(100.0)	(100.0)
1984-85	148	179.4	19	22.8	51	304.3	218	506.5
	(67.9)	(35.4)	(8.7)	(4.5)	(23.4)	(60.1)	(100.0)	(100.0)
1985-86	140	257.9	15	104.0	67	331.2	222	693.1
	(63.1)	(37.2)	(6.8)	(15.0)	(30.1)	(47.8)	(100.0)	(100.0)
1986-87	152	392.5	39	284.7	51	228.9	242	906.1
	(62.8)	(43.3)	(16.1)	(31.4)	(21.1)	(25.3)	(100.0)	(100.0)
1987-88	139	402.3	49	189.3	11	24.8	199	616.4
	(69.8)	(65.3)	(24.6)	(30.7)	(5.6)	(4.0)	(100.0)	(100.0)
1988-89	83	363.0	8	471.7	24	114.7	121	949.4
	(73.6)	(38.2)	(6.6)	(49.7)	(19.8)	(12.1)	(100.0)	(100.0)

1989-90	97 (78.9)	324.4 (75.0)	16 (13.0)	29.3 (6.9)	10 (8.1)	78.5 (18.1)	123 (100.0)	432.2 (100.0)
1990-91	82 (86.5)	213.4 (70.9)	8 (8.3)	46.8 (15.6)	5 (5.2)	40.6 (13.5)	96 (100.0)	300.9 (100.0)
1991-92	223 (94.5)	369.3 (63.6)	3 (1.3)	126.2 (21.7)	10 (4.2)	85.1 (14.7)	236 (100.0)	580.6 (100.0)
1992-93	30 (42.9)	20.9 (16.0)	19 (27.1)	95.9 (73.4)	21 (30.0)	13.8 (10.6)	70 (100.0)	130.6 (100.0)
1993-94	27 (49.1)	51.7 (49.7)	21 (38.2)	23.9 (23.0)	7 (12.7)	28.4 (27.3)	55 (100.0)	104.0 (100.0)
1994-95	28 (62.2)	43.6 (37.3)	7 (15.5)	28.7 (24.6)	10 (22.3)	44.5 (38.1)	45 (100.0)	116.8 (100.0)

N.B. Fiugre in brackets indicates percentages.

Source: Annual Reports, 1982-95, SIDICO.

Pendency in application process was resultant of sanction and rejection. Amountwise, the early eighties saw a comparatively high rate of pendency.

Many reasons are assigned for the rejection, cancellation and withdrawal of applications. Non-availability of Market Survey Report, inadequate managerial capability and failure to produce assurance letter of the State Government were lacunae from the borrowers side. The government assurance letter was necessary as the government departments were the major purchaser of the local product. By assurance, the respective department ensures the willingness to purchase the borrowers service.

Appraisal and Finance

The process of considering the proposal of a project is governed by two factors viz, financing and appraisal. The guidelines of the Central Government, RBI and IDBI are taken into account while financing the project. The appraisal exercise involves pre-sanction inspection and verification of facts and figures given by the applicant and the prescription of suitable terms and conditions too. The appraisal of the proposal leads to the sanction of the loan after documentation of securities.

The appraisal of term loan is the most crucial job of the lending institutions because the term loan has to be liquidated from the surplus created out of the earnings of the project. It has to be liquidated by the realisation of asset given as security. Loan is serviced in future, not out of present assets. The term loans are not intended to be repaid out of the sale proceeds of the fixed assets which are given as security for the loan.

Assessment of earning potential and generation of cash surplus to repay the loan is a vital ingredient in the appraisal of term loans. Thus, the unit should produce goods of more economic value, both in quantity and quality, acceptable to the market which results in surplus earnings.

With a shift from "security oriented" lending to "purpose oriented landing", the study of viability of projects has become more vital while financing a project. A project should satisfy the tests of technical, commercial, financial and managerial feasibilities.

I. Technical Appraisal

Technical feasibility analysis of a project is an attempt to determine how well technical requirements of the industry can be met.

Technical study includes the following aspects:

1. Technical Process or Technology: The selection of process depends on quantity of production required, quality of product, its end use, availability of particular raw material and cost of process. Available technology-banks are Technology Data Bank by Government of India, venture Capital Fund by IDBI, Risk Capital and Technology Finance Corporation provided by the IFCI etc.

2. Arrangement for Technical Know-how: It may be ensured that satisfactory arrangements have been made to obtain necessary technical know-how required for the proposed manufacturing process.

3. Size of the Plant: The size of the plant or its capacity can be expressed by the input or output or with respect to the number of machines.

4. Product Mix or Product Range: product-mix or Product-range may be decided according to market requirements.

5. Selection of Plant and Machinery: Selection of plant and machinery should be done according to manufacturing process and size of the unit.

6. Procurement of Plant and Machinery.

7. Plant Layout: Layout can be done by Line, Functional and Group Layout.

8. Location of Project: Study of the location includes selection of general location and also a particular site without the general location.

9. Schedule of Project Implementation: The Project Evaluation and Review Technique (PERT) or Critical Path Method (CPM) helps the promoters in proper planning, scheduling and controlling various activities essential for the execution of a project.

To sum up, it would be prudent on the part of the Corporation if it ensures that the project has been prepared with an eye ever open to the technical feasibility of the project.

II. Commercial Appraisal

Commercial Appraisal is the appraisal by the Corporation of the demand forecast made by the borrowers. The information is required on:

1. Demand;
2. Supply;
3. Distribution;
4. Pricing; and
5. External forces.

The various techniques used for forecasting aggregate demand are:

a) Import Substitution: In case the project intends to substitute import, past trend, cost, price of such a product has to be obtained;

b) Past Trend Method;

c) End Use Method;

d) Correlation and Regression; and

e) Export Market.

III. Financial Appraisal

Financial Appraisal means how much and to what extent finance is required to materialise the project which is otherwise well-planned and sound. The Corporation is to determine whether the cost of project as envisaged is realistic. It involves the following aspects:

1. Estimation of the cost of project;
2. Sources of finance;
3. Projection of future profitability, cash flow, debt-service coverage, debt-equity and break-even analysis;
4. In case of expansion, modernisation and shifting of existing units from non-conforming to conforming areas, an analysis of the working results of the existing units, balance sheets and cash flow for the last 3 years.

Promoters' Contribution

A certain percentage of the capital cost of a project should be met by the promoters to have their stake in the project. Such contribution can be in the form of share capital, internal generation during the period of implementation of the project, additional capital or unsecured deposits or loans brought or arranged by the promoter. The extent of the promoters' contribution is determined keeping in view the nature of the industry, size of the project, location of the project and background of the promoters.

In case of a project having capital cost above Rs. 5.0 crore, the minimum level of promoters' contribution is generally kept at 25.0 to 30.0 per cent of the project cost. In case of small and medium projects having capital cost upto Rs. 5.0 crore; eligible for refinance from IDBI or SIDBI, the norms for minimum promoters' contribution[9] stipulated by the refinance agency are as follows:

	Category	*Minimum Promoters' Contribution as Percentage of Project Cost*
1. a.	Loans upto Rs. 50,000	
i.	Under the composite loan scheme to Artisans, village and Cottage Industries and tiny units	
ii.	To SC and ST entrepreneurs	
iii.	To physically handicapped Entrepreneur.	
b.	Loans for financing, quality control, facilities by SSI units upto Rs. 7.5 Lakh	NIL
c.	Loans to Small Road Transport Operators holding national permits.	
2.	Projects set up in 'A' category backward districts (All districts of Sikkim)	12.5 per cent
3.	a. Projects in SSI Sector set-up by women entrepreneurs in 'A' category backward districts.	12.5 per cent
	b. Projects in SSI sector set-up by women entrepreneurs other than 'A' Category districts.	15.0 per cent

4.	Projects promoted by technician entrepreneurs.	17.5 per cent
5.	Equipment Refinance Scheme	22.5 per cent
6.	SRTOs owning upto six vehicles	15.0 per cent
7.	Modernisation Assistance	Flexible No fixed
8.	Rehabilitation assistance	norms
9.	National Equity Fund Scheme	10.0 per cent
10.	Scheme for assistance to Ex-Servicemen	10.0 per cent
11.	All other cases not indicated above.	22.5 per cent

Central or State subsidy is treated as equity for debt-equity ratio. However, it is not counted as promoters' contribution because the finance does not come from promoters.

Seed capital assistance is provided on soft term to new entrepreneurs for promoting small and medium projects having capital cost upto Rs. 5.0 crore to meet the gap between the normal expected level of promoters' contribution and the actual amount that the promoters could bring from their own resources. The seed capital assistance can be given upto 10.0 per cent of the project cost to a ceiling of Rs. 15.0 lakh.

IV. Economic Appraisal

Economic appraisal of the project is the examination of the economic viability of the project in the following aspects:

1. Market potential, sales promotion;
2. Employment potential of the project; and

3. Various permission from the Government and other authorities.

The Corporation follows the appraisal in parlance with the broader government policies. The contribution of the project towards employment and society as a whole, *is* well evaluated by the Corporation.

In general, banks and financial institutions in India prefer to follow guidelines issued by the Government regarding priorities for financing instead of calculating economic rate of returns based on shadow-pricing. A project in backward areas gets preference. The Corporation calculates labour-capital employed ratio to give more importance to labour-intensive projects.

V. Appraisal of Management

Manpower as an input is not only a factor but an actor, meaning thereby that utilisation of input factors of an enterprise or a firm depends upon how effectively it could organise the phenomena involved in production process. The one input factor that could make the others as productive as human power is, managerial activity. Therefore, the effectiveness of an industrial project hinges on the managerial functions for survival and prosperity. The appraisal of management is the touch stone of term capital analysis.

The appraisal mainly consists of the following:

1. Professional qualification of the promoters;
2. Promoters' past industrial business experience;
3. Availability of skilled manpower requirement; and
4. Proposed Organisational patterns.

On the successful completion of all the appraisal methods the Corporation evaluates other implications of term loan as under.

Time Required for Loan Sanction

The time taken by the Corporation to sanction loan assistance is largely dependent on whether the applicant has furnished complete and precise information. Normally, the Corporation takes about one month for sanctioning small loans and a little longer for larger amounts.

Security

Business operations of an enterprise depend on exogenous and endogenous factors. Hence, an amount of risk is to be calculated in view of the uncertainty. To be on the safeside the Corporation stresses security for the recovery of loans. Security considerations include physical security and personal guarantee.

Till 31 March, 1991, the Corporation accepted English or Registered mortgage. The following were the procedures.

(i) Registered mortgage (first charge) of fixed assets viz, land, building, plant and machinery etc.

In regard to hypothecation and personal surety;

(ii) Security of collateral assets.

It is to be noted that, in case of lease-hold land and premises, permission to mortgage from the competent authority in favour of the Corporation is required. All assets subsequently acquired with the loan or otherwise and added to the mortgaged premises during the currency of the loan, shall automatically stand mortgaged to the Corporation and no such assets should be disposed of or alienated without prior written approval from the Corporation. However, regular inspection has not been carried out to assess the physical existence of mortgaged or hypothecated assets.

Margin Money

The security margin is the difference between the value of assets offered as security and the amount of loan sanctioned against the secured assets. The Corporation normally stipulates 10.0 per cent to 25.0 per cent security margin on fixed assets in the project and not to the cost of project.

Documentation

The credit facilities often extended by the Corporation are under statutory obligation and administrative convenience.

The Corporation was accepting simple [English] mortgage which involved Registration charges and stamp duty. The corporation fixed the Registration charge @ 2.0 per cent on the loan and stamp duty @ 1.0 on the amount of loan. However, as a policy matter, the Corporation incurred 2.0 per cent out of total 3.0 per cent i.e. Registration plus Stamp duty as an incentive towards entrepreneurs. During 1991-92, the amount incurred for such incentive by the Corporation stood at Rs. 16.8 lakh. The amount is to be realised from the State Government.

Compliance with Certain Obligatory Requirements

At any time during investigation of the application or during the currency of loan the borrower shall be bound to:

(i) Comply with any general or special requirement of the Corporation, in regard to inspection of the premises, plant or stock in hand;

(ii) Permit the inspection of all accounts, relating to the enterprise;

(iii) Maintain all accounts or to furnish such statements as the Corporation may require, from time to time;

(iv) Submit the accounts of the enterprise to such scrutiny or audit as the Corporation may require and bear the cost of such scrutiny or audit, if such cost is required to be borne by him;

(v) Submit half-yearly and annual progress report in the forms prescribed by the Corporation; and

(vi) Furnish any information required by the Corporation in the interest of promotion and development of industries in the state.

Recalling the Loan in Full

The entire loan may be recalled in case of:

(i) Misuse of funds;

(ii) Misapplication of funds;

(iii) Proceed misrepresentation, for detaining loan assistance;

(iv) Undue delay in the implementation of the project;

(v) Any act done by the borrowing concern which is prejudicial to the interest of the Corporation or the state, such as involvement in an economic offence;

(vi) A deliberate default in repayment of dues;

(vii) Failure to properly maintain and safeguard the secured property;

(viii) Breach of the agreement entered into at the time of sanction of loan.

Repayment Period

The Corporation fixes the repayment schedule taking into consideration the profitability, estimated cash-generation and debt-servicing capacity of the proposed industry. In respect of certain categories, the IDBI has prescribed repayment norms.

The Corporation accepts premature repayment of any instalment or even full repayment of any instalment or even full repayment of a loan. The Corporation considers granting reschedulement of principal amount on the merits of each case with the approval of SIDBI. In any case, interest on loans should be paid regularly.

In general, the repayment period of the Corporation is fixed by the IDBI. Likewise, the Corporation also fixes the repayment period of loanees at par with their repayment schedule. Thus the repayment period of the Corporation and borrowers is almost the same.

In taxi (SVO) loan, the repayment is fixed within 4 years. In other cases repayment period ranges between 5 and 10 years.

Disbursement Procedure

The Corporation provides liquid cash disbursement for hotel and construction of factory sheds. Generally, loans are provided on short-term basis except two cases of long-term loans. Disbursement is generally made on the purchase and installation of machinery or for construction of building. The release of instalment depends on the progress of work as per the satisfaction of the Corporation. The Corporation disburses the amount direct to the supplier for delivery of machines or to the bank against presentation of documents.

The SIDICO stipulated an important criterion whereby the entrepreneur is required to raise 50.0 per cent of equity as detailed in the Appraisal note, before first disbursement.[10] However, this is not being implemented in most of the cases. The remaining amount is released proportionately with the term loan.

Generally, a loanee has to avail of the loan within 18 months from the date of sanction. In some cases, fulfilment of certain conditions attached to sanction becomes difficult within the period of 18 months.

Disbursement Elasticity

The efficiency of fund management of the Corporation can be judged by 'Elasticity Co-efficient'.[11] This ratio indicates the relationship with the scale of operation i.e., inflow of fund.

The Co-efficient is calcualted as:

$$D_e = (dD/D)/(dS/S),$$

where D_e = Disbursement Elasticity Co-efficient,
D = Disbursement,
S = Sources of Fund,
dD and dS Signifies changes.

Disbursement Elasticity has been calculated in Table-8.3. It is evident that, over the years, the Corporation experienced D_e of various degrees.

Since the source of fund and disbursement is positively related, any reverse trend in the growth of source or disbursement resulted in negative elasticity co-efficient.

In the earlier period i.e., in 1980-81, the co-efficient was the highest at 8.8 and in later period in 1993-94, it reached 7.6. In the remaining years, the range of co-efficient lies between 2.1 and 4.9.

The co-efficient reveals that since 1990 to 1995, negative trends persisted. Although, 1993-94 shows positive signs, this was the result of two negative growth i.e., in source of fund and disbursement. Recent trends visualise lesser utilisation of funds for disbursement. This, coupled with other exogenous factors, fettered the growth of disbursement.

TABLE 8.3

DISBURSEMENT ELASTICITY

Year	*Disbursement Elasticity* (D_e)
1979-80	1.1
1980-81	8.8
1981-82	1.1
1982-83	0.8
1983-84	0.4
1984-85	4.9
1985-86	0.2
1986-87	1.0
1987-88	1.3
1988-89	1.4
1989-90	0.3
1990-91	–0.2
1991-92	–0.6
1992-93	–0.3
1993-94	7.6
1994-95	–2.1

Source: Annual Reports, 1979-95, SIDICO.

Interest

The rate of interest charged by the Corporation is subject to the rate of interest fixed by the Reserve Bank of India from time to time. Normally, the rate of interest for term loans should be higher than that for working capital facilities.

Since 1984 to 25 October, 1994, the Corporation has changed its interest rates four times. Table-8.4 exhibited the change in rate structure. The Corporation maintained the same rate for the longest period from 1984-90. Since then the rate became volatile, as it changed every year. Even on a few occasions, the rate changed more than once in a year. The Corporation's rate of interest on the units was 3.5 per cent more than the IDBI's rate of interest. It means the Corporation charged 3.5 per cent more in the interest rate as compared to the rate charged by the IDBI on the Corporation. During 1990-91, the Corporation changed the difference and the rate was lowered by 0.5 per cent. Since 1990-91, the Corporation maintains a spread of 3.0 per cent over the above refinance interest rate being charged by the SIDBI or IDBI.[12] The Corporation had to charge a few per cent more to earn for its survival and growth.

TABLE 8.4

CHANGES IN INTEREST STRUCTURE
(IN PER CENT PER ANNUM)

Category	*1984-85*	*1990-91*	*1991-92*	*1992-93*	*1993-94*	*1994-95*
1. SSIs	12.5	13.5	18.5	19.0	17.0	—
2. Hotels	12.5	13.5	18.5	19.0	17.0	—
3. SRTOs	12.5	15.0	20.0	19.0	18.0	—
4. Single window Scheme						
i. Block Capital	—	13.0	15.5	16.5	—	—
ii. Working Capital	—	15.0 to 16.5	19.0	19.0	—	—
5. i. Upto Rs. 25000.0	10.0	11.0	13.5	13.5	12.0	12.0
ii. Rs. 25000.0 to Rs. 2.0 Lakh.	10.0 (upto Rs. 50000)	11.0	14.0 to 15.0	15.0	14.0	13.5
iii. Above Rs. 2.0 Lakh	—	—	18.0	19.0	18.0	17.5

Source: Annual Reports, 1984-95, SIDICO.

In relation to the new economic policy, the government has simplified and reduced the interest rate structure during 1994-95. Only three categories have been formulated. These are not on the basis of industries but on the basis of quantum of loan. Interest rate varies from 12.0 per cent to 17.5 per cent. The spread of interest also varies from 1.0 per cent to 3.0 per cent. Now, the highest rate 17.5 per cent is lower than the highest rate of 19.0 per cent during 1992-93. The Corporation is entitled to fix interest rates over and above SIDBI's rate, as practicable. The rate of interest by the Corporation is maintained with the rate followed by other financial institutions of the state.

Follow-up

The follow-up and supervision is as important as lending loans. The progress of the project and its workings are continuously supervised and measures are taken to correct the errors, if any, by the lending institutions.

To ensure the sustainability and growth of the project, proper supervision and follow-up is necessary during and after project implementation. The Corporation generally adopts the following methods to follow up the units:

(i) Scrutiny of progress reports;
(ii) Analysis of annual financial statements;
(iii) Visit and Inspection;
(iv) Appointment of Nominee directors;
(v) Regulatory control; and
(vi) Discussion with management.

The Corporation mainly confined the activity of follow-up and supervision to the assisted units through inspection. Other tools have been applied in a few cases only.

The inspection was undertaken annually on an average

of less than 50.0 per cent of the total unit. The scrutiny process was conducted for a negligible number e.g. 13 units of the total. The Corporation appointed director to a total of 15 companies.

The Corporation started evaluation of project reports through format since early 90s. During 1992-93, out of 876 units in the loan portfolio, 418 units were inspected. Only in respect of 13 units, SIDICO was getting progress reports regularly. The Corporation nominated 8 officers to the Board of 15 companies. The assisted units hardly invite nominee director from SIDICO to their Board meetings. As a result, most of the nominee directors are not aware of the present status of the units of which they are directors. In the process, the Corporation does not get any feedback from the nominees. There is, therefore, considerable scope for improvement in all these areas.

Review

In a review of policies and procedures it is observed that the Corporation has to follow many modus operandi from the receipt of application till disbursement of loan amounts. Both the Corporation and loanee are responsible in this formidable process.

The Corporation shows relaxation in Appraisal method. However, in a state like Sikkim, where barring a few medium scale industries all others have been established at the tiny and small scale level, strict appraisal is not necessary. The Corporation in consonance with the Government's policy, enhanced loans, more with the intention of employment generation and as a source of resource generation than to adhere strictly to profit earning capacity of the unit. The Corporation guides and advises at every stage the entrepreneurs, most of whom are of first generation, till the loan is repaid i.e., upto four and five years of successful operation of the unit.

The Corporation is faced with a lot of anomalies regarding Application Procedures, sanction and disbursement. The policies and practices noticed a phenomenal gap resulting in difficulties in the operation of the Corporation. A discussion on the difficulties, reasons for delays in sanction and disbursement and measures to be taken can be summarised below.

In general, a loanee has to avail of the loan within 18 months from the date of sanction. In some cases, fulfilment of certain conditions attached to sanction becomes difficult within the period of 18 months.

It has been observed that on certain occasions loan granted by the Corporation was diverted by the entrepreneurs to personal consumption expenditure. Under the SFC Act, in case of diversion of loan amount for other purposes, the Corporation may recall the entire loan money from the loanee. To avert diversion that may arise from the influential quarters, the Corporation had simply to insist upon the borrower to clear the dues at the earliest. The IDBI may be authorised to conduct such informal investigation into the affairs of assisted units to check this undesirable drainage of resources. Table 8.2, op.cit., exhibited the trend of activities of the Corporation, as reflected in the amount of loan sanctioned and disbursed by it during the past years and also loan availed of by various units. The spurt in the number of applications in 1984-85 is due to coverage of a large number of artisans and similar village and cottage industries i.e., tiny sector under the composite loan scheme. The same trend is also followed during 1991-92 and this time also it is due to huge applications from the tiny sector.

It may be mentioned in this connection that loan sanction is always made during the year. Loan disbursement may be done in respect of previous sanctions also. This is because non-fulfilment of conditions often delays disbursement. Thus, in some years disbursal is higher than the sanction because of the disbursement of previous sanctions in the following years. The Corporation has no system of segregating the amount disbursed since disbursement procedure automatically necessitates that disbursement will be made in various instalments from time to time which may linger from one year to the next year and so on. Similarly, in the next year some additional new loans may be sanctioned. It is a chain system based on cyclical process.

The coefficient of correlation between loan applied for (X) and loan sanctioned (Y).

r_{xy} = 0.57 and

The coefficient of correlation between sanction (Y) and disbursement (Z).

r_{yz} =0.71

Testing the significance of the coefficients with the help of 'student t',

t^{13} = 2.30; t = 4.03.

Tabulated value of

t.05, 11= 1.80
t.01, 11= 2.72; and
t.05,16 = 1.75
t.01,16 = 2.58

Since the calculated value of t for r_{xy} is greater than the tabulated value at 5% level, the value of correlation coefficient is significant thereby implying the closest positive relation between the loan applied and the amount of loan sanctioned. But, at 1% level, the calculated value is less than the tabulated value indicating the non-significance of correlation coefficient at that level. Again, as the calculated value of t for r_{yz} is higher than the tabulated value at both levels, the correlation coefficient is significant.

The Corporation had to adopt a liberal lending policy and sometimes norms of financing had to be relaxed in the initial stages in order to generate an atmosphere of industrial growth. As a result, within a few years, the Corporation became burdened with a backlog of arrear dues, when many such industrial units approached the Corporation for extension of time to repay their dues. It is worth mentioning that the Corporation being a development agency for a backward region, it has to give due consideration for development of industries in remote and backward areas often by relaxing usual norms of term lending. Instances are not rare when the corporation had to come to the assistance of some sick units even by ignoring their default, to help them revive their position.

It may be mentioned that disbursement is made as per the disbursement schedule to be furnished by the borrower to the Corporation. It was stipulated that the loans should be availed of within 18 months from the date of sanction. The borrower may submit the disbursement schedule immediately before or after the sanction of the loan but invariably before the execution of mortgage deed. It is presumed that after the sanctioning of loans it is incumbent upon the borrowers to avail themselves of the sanctioned amount at the earliest convenience for their own benefit. The periodicity of availing of loan varies from 2 months to 2 years. Here, the Board can extend the period on, the specific request from the concerned borrower. If the party fails to avail of the loan within the specified period mentioned in the Board's resolution of sanctioning the loan and if no proper request for extension is made to the Corporation, the sanctioned amount will be treated as automatically lapsed. The Board's resolution usually carries the term of availing of loans varying from Rs. 7.5 lakh and above. It is observed that due to inability and delay in utilisation of the amount by the loanee, the whole amount sanctioned cannot be disbursed.

Reasons for Difference

The reasons for difference in the amount sanctioned and disbursed was due to inadequate information, improper maintenance of accounts, legal formalities and complications, unsatisfactory functioning of the applicant in the past, scanty financial position, inability to arrange for working capital, insufficient security, doubtful title to the property offered as security. Sometimes, the property offered as security does not stand in the name of the promoters but rather in the name of partners or others. In such cases necessary legal formalities have to be complied with. Execution of mortgage deed and other ancillary papers requires enough time. The Title deed of the mortgaged property has to be examined thoroughly and legal formalities have to be fulfilled. Often, the applicants fail to furnish full particulars and then further information is called for clarification which causes some delay in disbursement.

Besides the value of security, the earning capacity of the proposed project, efficiency of its plant and machinery, soundness of management, availability of raw materials, viability and profitability of the project, certification of antecedents by other related agencies like bank etc. about the financial stability and integrity of the applicant concerned are also to be assessed before any proposal is finalised. It has been observed in the SIDICO that time and again an applicant applies for loan with the intention of starting a business but in the midway gives up the plan to carry out

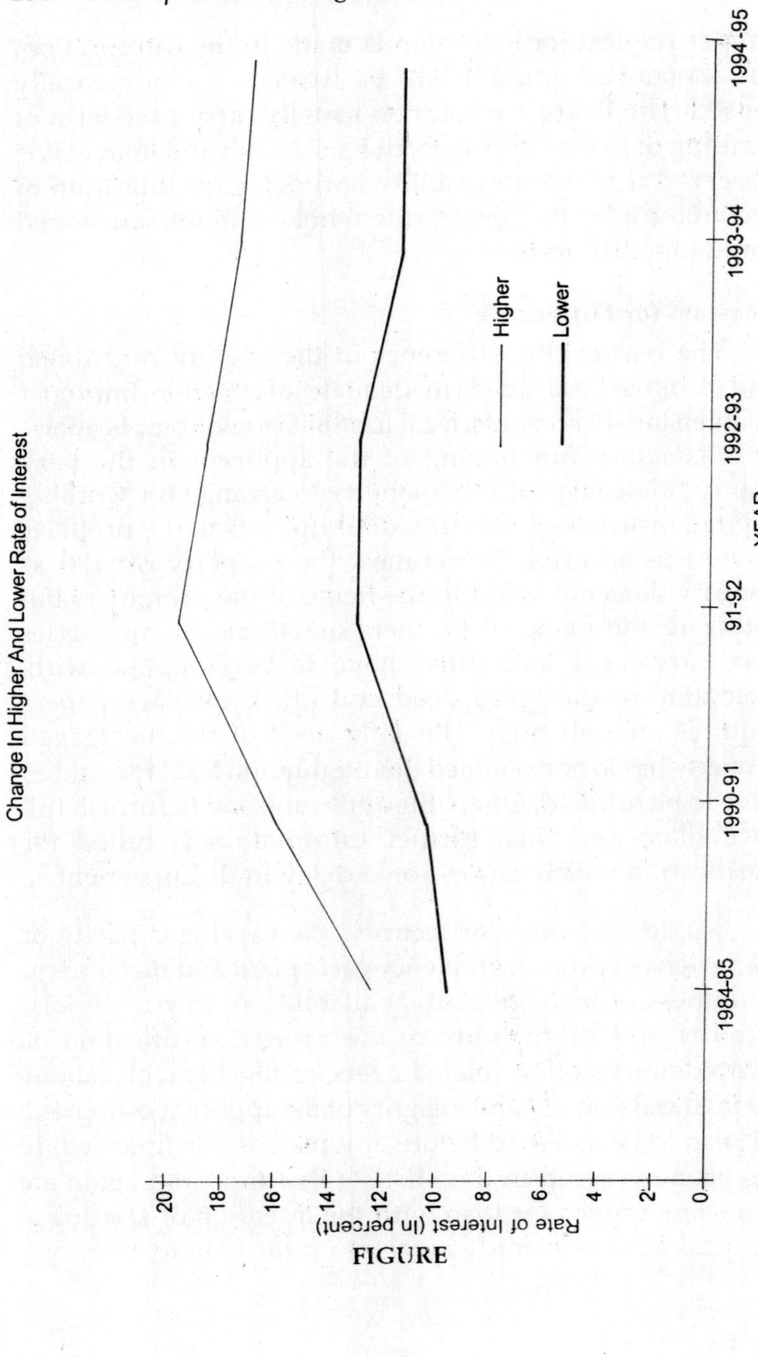
Change In Higher And Lower Rate of Interest
Higher
Lower
Rate of Interest (in percent)
0
2
4
6
8
10
12
14
16
18
20
1984-85
1990-91
91-92
1992-93
1993-94
1994-95
YEAR

FIGURE

the business for various reasons and keeps the loan money idle in his hand and hence liquidity of the Corporation is reduced to that extent. All these factors taken together cause the delay in sanctioning and disbursing loans and also account for the difference between loan sanctioned and loan disbursed. The various other reasons as per priority attributed to delay in disbursement of loan are as follows:

1. Gradual loss of interest in the projects undertaken by the promoters for adopting other occupations cause delay in disbursement.
2. Getting the requisite machinery from the supplies either for distance and delayed despatch or transport bottleneck creates setback for the project.
3. Absence of industrial background, technical know-how and first generation entrepreneurship cause delay in proper utilisation of the disbursement.
4. Inability of promoters to bring in their contribution in time, insistence on bringing the same in full or on pro-rata basis before disbursement have also caused delay in disbursement.
5. Excessive time taken by commercial banks to sanction working capital required by units causes delay in disbursement of term loan.
6. Delay due to non-fulfilment of conditions made in sanctions prior to availing of loans by the entrepreneurs.
7. Poor quality of documentation submitted by promoters due to lack of knowledge about pre-requisites also results in delay in disbursement of sanctioned amount.

Last but not least, the delay occurs due to lack of

infrastructural facilities, power shortages and non-availability of raw materials. In cases where disbursement was delayed due to fund constraints of the Corporation, very often a concern had to face overrun. In that case the Corporation was to some extent responsible for the delay.

REFERENCES

1. SIDICO, *Scope of Financing and Guidelines for Entrepreneurs*, 1991, p. 15.
2. *Ibid*, p. 18.
3. *Ibid*, pp. 15-31.
4. *Ibid*, pp. 21-22.
5. *Ibid*, p. 10.
6. GOS, *Assistance to Industrial Entrepreneurs*, 1991, p. 36.
7. SIDICO, *Scope of Financing, op.cit.*, pp. 8-10.
8. SIDBI opened its branch at Gangtok during 1991-92.
9. SIDICO, *Scope of Financing, op.cit.*, pp. 17-31.
10. *Ibid*, p. 14.
11. Reddy, C.R. Model on Finance function in the Management of Co-operative Banks, 'Indian Management'. Vol.XVIII, No. 4, April, 1978, p. 26, quoted by P. Kallu Rao, 'Development Banking - SIDCs in India', Anmol Publication', New Delhi, 1993, p. 48.
12. SIDICO, *Annual Report*, 1990-91, p. 6.
13. $t = \dfrac{r}{\sqrt{1-r^2}} \times \sqrt{n-2}$

9

Recovery Performance

The recovery performance of the Corporation is not satisfactory. The rate of recovery has receded over the years. Feeble recovery is causing serious threat to the Corporation squeezing the repayment obligation.

In this chapter, discussion have been made on the recovery of Principal and interest. The reasons for poor recovery, and their remedies have also been evolved in the chapter.

It is transparent from Table 9.1, that the rate of recovery to demand diminishes continuously. During 1980-85, on an average the rate of recovery was more than 40.0 per cent. In 1982, the recovery rate was as high as 72.0 per cent. But since 1990 onwards the rate descended sharply and in 1995 the rate reduced to only 5.4 per cent. The compound growth in demand stood at 73.7 per cent while in recovery it is 55.1 per cent. This exhibits the disparity in the growth of demand for recovery and actual recovery.

The analysis of 'Principal recovery', as per Table 9.2, shows higher recovery rate as compared to the combined recovery rate of Principal and interest, Table 9.1. The annual recovery in earlier years was good. In later period, both annual and cumulative rate of Principal recovery is downturn.

TABLE 9.1

TOTAL DEMAND AND RECOVERY OF PRINCIPAL AND INTEREST

(Rs. in Lakh)

Year ended 31 March	*Demand*	*Recovery*	*Recovery as % of Demand*
1980	0.3	0.1	33.3
1981	2.4	0.8	33.3
1982	3.2	2.3	72.0
1983	19.9	8.2	41.2
1984	50.5	16.3	32.3
1985	81.2	23.0	28.3
1986	134.6	40.6	30.2
1987	199.3	80.0	40.2
1988	336.5	85.9	25.5
1989	502.1	117.2	23.3
1990	623.6	219.3	35.2
1991	719.1	105.6	14.7
1992	1173.8	137.3	11.7
1993	1379.2	109.3	7.9
1994	1760.7	118.9	6.7
1995	2070.3	111.9	5.4
Compound growth rate	73.7	55.1	

Source: *Annual Reports*, 1979-95, SIDICO.

In realisation of interest, the Corporation shows very slow progress. As per Table-9.3, out of total demand of Rs. 956.9 lakh only a total of Rs. 65.8 lakh could be realised. This sluggish recovery accumulated huge interest arrear causing inefficiency in resource administration.

Both in the recovery of Principal and interest, the Corporation failed to exert any improvement. Its recovery performance is so dismal that the Corporation is entering into a vicious cycle of credibility and inefficiency. This has affected the repayment of borrowings to the IDBI and SIDBI. These two all-India financial institutes always insist upon the Corporation to repay in time.

TABLE 9.2

RECOVERY OF PRINCIPAL

(Rs. in Lakh)

	Demand		*Recovery*		*% of Recovery to Demand*	
Year	*Amount*	*Cumu-lative*	*Amount*	*Cumu-lative*	*% Annual*	*% Cumu-lative*
1977-78	—	—	—	—	—	—
1978-79	—	—	—	—	—	—
1979-80	0.3	0.3	0.1	0.1	33.3	33.3
1980-81	2.4	2.7	0.1	0.2	4.2	7.4
1981-82	3.2	5.9	2.3	2.5	71.9	42.4
1982-83	10.5	16.4	8.2	10.7	78.1	65.2
1983-84	.16.7	33.1	13.4	24.1	80.2	72.8
1984-85	23.4	56.5	18.1	42.2	77.3	74.7
1985-86	43.9	100.4	19.1	61.3	43.5	61.0
1986-87	47.1	147.5	55.4	116.7	117.6	79.1
1987-88	70.8	218.3	63.2	179.9	89.3	40.9
1988-89	138.4	356.7	58.6	238.5	42.3	66.9
1989-90	118.0	474.7	116.9	355.4	99.0	74.9
1990-91	135.7	610.4	59.3	414.7	43.7	67.9
1991-92	360.0	970.4	56.6	471.3	15.7	48.6
1992-93	225.9	1196.3	46.8	518.1	20.7	43.3
1993-94	261.7	1458.0	53.2	571.3	20.3	39.2
1994-95	181.5	1639.5	46.1	617.4	25.4	37.6

Source: *Annual Reports*, 1977-95, SIDICO.

TABLE 9.3

RECOVERY OF INTEREST

(Rs. in Lakh)

Year	*Demand*		*Recovery*		*Recovery as % of Demand*	
	Annual	*Total*	*Annual*	*Total*	% *Annual*	% *Total*
1984-85	21.4	37.8	6.3	11.3.	29.4	29.4
1985-86	32.5	59.2	9.0	21.5	27.7	36.3
1986-87	58.1	95.8	12.3	25.5	21.2	26.6
1987-88	115.2	185.6	23.7	49.3	20.6	26.6
1988-89	112.5	248.8	28.2	60.7	25.1	24.4
1989-90	111.4	282.3	40.1	102.4	36.0	36.3
1990-91	170.3	350.5	20.3	54.8	11.9	15.6
1991-92	181.8	477.6	65.7	80.6	36.1	16.9
1992-93	212.0	608.9	53.1	62.5	25.0	10.3
1993-94	229.6	776.0	—	67.2	—	8.6
1994-95	247.1	956.9	—	65.8	—	6.9

Note: Total of Demand and Recovery includes the respective arrear of Previous Year.

Source: Annual Reports, 1984-95, SIDICO.

The repayment by the Corporation is much better than the repayment by assisted units, as evident in Table-9.4. Despite less recovery from the units, the Corporation repaid at an increased rate till 1992. This was possible due to the increase in the capital, borrowings etc. in the fund of the Corporation, during that period.

The factors responsible for the repayment by the units and Corporation are different from each other. The Corporation's repaying capacity depend on its resource-generation capacity whereas assisted units repayment capacity hinges upon the profitability of the concern. The loan assisted units seldom provide return to the Corporation. Most of the units are sick and such widely dispersed that frequent inspection and persuation is not possible by the Corporation. The Corporation expressed inability to provide profit and loss figure to the present researcher which prevented the scope of profit analysis of assisted units.

TABLE 9.4

RECOVERY AND REPAYMENT OF PRINCIPAL BY SIDICO

(Rs. in Lakh)

Year ended 31 March	*Recovery from Units*	*Repayment to IDBI*	*Repayment as % of Recovery*
1981	0.1	0.9	900.0
1982	2.3	3.8	165.2
1983	8.2	5.4	65.8
1984	13.4	11.5	85.8
1985	18.1	18.8	103.9
1986	19.1	32.9	172.2
1987	55.4	43.6	78.7
1988	63.2	51.1	80.8
1989	58.6	87.8	149.8
1990	116.9	104.4	89.3
1991	59.3	128.7	217.0
1992	56.6	166.1	293.5
1993	46.8	73.4	156.8
1994	53.2	2.1	3.9
1995	46.1	23.2	50.3

Source : Annual Report, 1995, SIDICO, pp. 22-28.

Arrears of Loan

The loan portfolio of the Corporation consists of term loan, bridge and soft loan against subsidies. Term loan, thus, accumulates major arrears in principal and interest.

Till 31 March, 1995, total principal outstanding amounted to Rs. 1,922.9 lakh, as depicted in Table-9.5. Till 31 March, 1994, secured loan from IDBI as refinance was Rs. 271.3 lakh and from SIDBI was Rs. 745.6 lakh. The interest on loans due to IDBI and SIDBI amounted to Rs. 116.2 lakh till March, 1994.[1]

TABLE 9.5

PRINCIPAL OUTSTANDING (CUMULATIVE)

(Rs. in Lakh)

Years ending 31 March	*Term Loan*	*Bridge & Other Loan*	*Total*
1978	0.6	—	0.6
1979	4.3	—	4.3
1980	21.6	—	21.6
1981	48.3	5.1	53.4
1982	68.8	6.1	74.9
1983	103.8	5.8	109.6
1984	136.0	11.4	147.4
1985	241.5	18.0	259.5
1986	348.8	30.4	379.2
1987	486.7	47.3	534.0
1988	791.6	48.3	839.9
1989	953.1	75.2	1028.3
1990	1137.9	43.3	1181.2
1991	1357.2	46.2	1403.4
1992	1554.9	49.8	1604.7
1993	1630.2	249.3	1879.5
1994	1625.1	249.3	1874.4
1995	1673.6	249.3	1922.9

Source: *Annual Report 1995*, SIDICO, p. 22

The arrears of loan in the Corporation was mounting because of poor recovery performance. In the total outstanding of Rs. 1,874.4 lakh for 1274 units, arrears affected principal outstanding was of Rs. 1,635.5 lakh for 710 units i.e. 87.2 per cent to the total (Table 9.6). The growth of principal outstanding from 1977 to 1994 was more than 2725 times.

TABLE 9.6

DISTRICT-WISE ARREARS OF LOAN

(Rs. in Lakh)

District	*No. of Units*	*Outstanding Principal*	*Arrears (A)*	*Interest Arrears on Arrears(B)*	*Total (A+B)*
East	418	1132.5	679.1	460.1	1139.2
West	49	107.7	49.9	44.9	94.8
North	156	47.6	41.7	30.7	72.4
South	77	347.7	161.3	146.8	308.1
	710	1635.5	932.0	682.5	1614.5

Source: Arrear-wise analysis of Loan, 1994, SIDICO, pp.3-12.

The arrears-wise analysis of total loan amount shows that, the east district is responsible for highest amount of arrears of loans. Among total principal outstanding of Rs. 1,635.5 lakh, east district occupy Rs. 1,132.5 lakh. i.e. 69.2 per cent. The south district had an outstanding of 21.3 per cent of the total principal outstanding. In the arrears of principal and interest, the east district held 73.0 per cent arrear in principal and 67.4 per centof the interest arrears of the corresponding total.

Table 9.7 exhibited hotels with largest amount of principal outstanding followed by food and food product and metal and metal product industry. However, unitwise, textiles and textile products industry counted highest followed by hotels and SVOs.

TABLE 9.7

INDUSTRY-WISE ARREARS OF LOAN

(Rs. in Lakh)

Type	*Units*	*Outstanding Principal*	*Arrears (A)*	*Interest Arrears on Arrears(B)*	*Total (A+B)*
1. Food & Food Products	35	204.7	96.3	70.2	166.5
2. Textile & Textile Products	182	48.0	28.2	20.5	48.7
3. Wood & Wood based	98	18.1	13.3	9.5	22.8
4. Metal & Metal Products	19	179.7	116.8	85.9	202.7
5. Paper & Paper Products	14	67.6	67.6	49.8	117.4
6. Electric & Electronics	12	17.9	17.3	12.4	29.7
7. Leather & Leather Products	7	2.1	2.1	1.5	3.6
8. Chemical based	4	57.5	24.1	17.6	41.7
9. Plastic & Plastic based	3	131.1	104.6	76.2	180.8
10. Hotels	111	299.4	140.5	120.3	260.8
11. S.V.O.	104	83.2	59.5	33.4	93.1
12. Services	80	57.4	44.3	32.2	76.5
13. Others	41	468.8	217.4	153.0	370.1
	710	1635.5	932.0	682.5	1614.4

Source: Arrear-wise analysis of Loan, 1994, SIDICO pp.3-8.

Arrears in principal and interest made responsible the hotel industry with maximum arrears followed by metal industry and plastic industry.

Constitutionwise, private and public enterprises accounted 709 units and 1 unit respectively. The share in the outstanding principal of the former was Rs. 1,541.7 lakh and of the later was Rs. 93.8 lakh. In the arrears of principal and interest, almost same amount stood for private and public enterprises.[2]

Sectorwise, the Small Scale Units constitute total principal outstanding and arrears of principal and interest.

In terms of age, about 60.0 per cent of the principal outstanding was due for more than 36 months. Same is the rate per cent for arrears in principal and interest due for more than 36 months.[3]

Sizewise, out of total 695 units, 669 units i.e. 96.0 per cent were upto the bracket of Rs. 10.0 lakh. Amountwise, principal and interest arrears of Rs. 644.0 lakh were in between Rs. 50.0 lakh and Rs. 100.0 lakh.[4]

As time elapsed, fresh default committed in each year raised the magnitude of arrears. Again, the amount of arrears loan recovered in one year has been annulled by the corresponding default committed afresh in that year. With a view to abate the incidence of default, the Corporation has been adopting a noble policy to help the assisted units which are in financial difficulties, either by rescheduling repayment of instalments of loan or by granting them extended time or more gestation period in order to enable defaulters to recover or even by sanctioning additional loan when there is considerable overrun in the cost of projects.

The Corporation has rescheduled the loan and rate of interest for Scan Industries Private Limited, Labott Private Limited, Agarwal Wire (Private) Limited, Metalex Industries (Private) Limited etc. A total of Rs. 121.2 lakh—Rs.25.9

lakh during 1989-90 and Rs. 95.3 lakh during 1992-93, was rescheduled to help respective loanees.[5]

Capitalisation of Interest

In a dismal condition with massive outstanding the Corporation is unable to restrict the Commitment of default. As a remedial measure, interest can eventually be capitalised in certain cases. Accrued interest on loan sanctioned may be capitalised and merged with principal loan amount, thereby principal loan amount will be enhanced to the extent of accrued interest and a new repayment schedule will be made on new principal amount. The process help reviving sick units clubbing their arrears of interest with principal. The financial and banking institutions cannot remain indifferent to the hardships of the small borrowers caused by the economic environment, and laxity in the recovery would be self defeating. It has been suggested that the state government should pass suitable legislation on the basis of the Talwar Committee recommendation to help the financial institutions in the matter of recovery.

CAUSAL EFFECT

The State envisaged a number of hurdles in the process of industrialisation which in turn affected recovery position, too. Following are the obstacles in the process of industrialisation.

1. The risk factor for investment in industries is high, in view of competition, lower grade of expertise etc.
2. The investment is low and central investment subsidy is stopped.
3. Often assistance for industries are diverted to satisfy self-esteem need.

4. Lack of financial planning and control restrained many units to close-down in the mid-operation.
5. Marketing problem hindered the growth of industries. However, Price preference was given to Sikkim-made product. But still, local products were replaced by outside-products.
6. Shortage of Working Capital led to the closure of many units.
7. Escalating transportation cost caused hike in prices.

Besides the above distinct features which led to poor performance of industries resulting very low rate of recovery, other common factors are wilful default, scarcity of raw materials, working capital shortage etc.

It has been noticed that loan sanction based on project viability and feasibility concept has not been properly adhered to. The said missing link connected with sanction, can reduce the magnitude of arrears dues.

Generalising the reasons for huge chronic default in the Corporation, following are the observations for feeble recovery:

1. Low standard of project feasibility study;
2. Over-enthusiasm by the Corporation to sanction and disbursement of the loan;
3. Liberal attitude for project evaluation;
4. Lesser insistence on clearance of arrear dues; and
5. Inability to reconcile quantitative and qualitative parameter of loan sanction.

The causal impact may be also due to external pressure to increase the quantity of assistance. The efficacy of assistance can be assumed to be the best where quantity and quality can be brought at an ideal level. The maintenance of such ideal relation is also connected with pace of industrialisation of the respective state concerned. It has been suggested that the relationship between SFCs and SIDCs and management of assisted units must be on a continuous basis, dependent on healthy principles. So far observation over SIDICO is concerned, it has been a practice with the Corporation to contact the assisted units casually on certain specific occasion. The follow up was looked after by the Manager-II now been promoted to DGM-II. During 1992-93, 418 units were inspected and of them 13 progress reports were scrutinised.[6]

On account of total 1247 assited units till 1992-93, inspection for 418 was not sufficient. A casual inspection cannot improve the functioning nor the causes of default and other difficulties experienced but can bring them into light. Very often, though the causes are pointed out in the inspection report the remedial measures are beyond control of the Corporation and the assisted units. Such regular causes are related to scarcity of raw material, competitiveness, non-availability of subsidy, extension of moratorium period, non-contiguity of market, heavy transportation cost and other terrain and infrastructural difficulties and so on.

A close liaison need be set up with the assisted units and they may be advised from time to time as how to overcome the hurdles cropped up in the process of operation. In order to render expert service it may be suggested for setting up of a pool of experts in respective field like the IFCI. The services of experts of the pool may be availed of by other similar sister concerns operating in the same region.

As practiced in the IFCI, in case of inspection of assisted units by its officials, the incidental cost of inspection shall be borne by the assisted units concerned. This step keeps the assisted concerns cautious of incurring additional cost in the form of inspection fees in case of commitment of default. This type of psychological and financial pressure should be imposed by the Corporation upon the assisted units. If the recovery of such inspection expenses can be stipulated in the loan agreement and followed properly it will certainly be worthy to combat the tendency of default.

Under the constant pressure of arrear dues, the Corporation had no other way but to file law suits for recovery. Till the end of March, 1995, the Corporation registered 121 cases involving an amount of Rs. 7.2 crore.[7] To expedite litigation process, a Certificate officer under the Act was appointed. The Certificate officer with magisterial power expedite cases since mid 1993. The cases were also referred to the Court of District Judges.

Section 29 of the SFC act empowers the Corporation direct sale of mortgaged property. As the SIDICO is established under Sikkim Companies Act, 1961, there is a technical difficulty in adopting the said section.

In Sikkim even Court's verdict to attach property was not welcomed because of social, environmental and economic background and lack of co-operation of public as well as civil authorities in acquiring the possession of mortgaged property by the Corporation. There is an example of such resistance in the Capital of Sikkim i.e. in Gangtok itself. The Corporation in recourse of an auction of acquired building, could not sell the same due to non-availability of bidders.

In litigation process, defaulters plead through some of the King's law which still prevails in the State. For example, according to one Debt Law of Chogyal's time, total interest could never exceed the Principal.

In practice, non-payment of instalments made the interest much more than the principal amount. Due to the provision of such law, recovery-drive has been hampered for many units.

In the light of a judgement, the loanee had to bear the cost of suit as ordered by the court.[8] It is observed that the defaulter is willing to bear the litigation expenses, legal cost of the petition but reluctant to repay the instalment of Principal and interest of the Corporation. A person having the ability to bear all such cost, time, patience for litigation has not the ability to repay the loan is unbelievable. This indicates the attitude of the loanee towards the Corporation's loan which is common to almost all the Corporations especially government level agencies. This attitude creates blockage of public resources and hinders the cyclical flow of scarce funds.

The appointment of nominee director to the Board of assisted units is restricted only to limited companies. Such appointments could not help check the growth of default in respect of non-corporate sector which also constitutes substantial portion of default. Any type of nomination in the management or external surveillance for non-corporate sector should be stipulated for future guidance and effectiveness.

The inspection procedure should be made elaborative and informative. The response of the loanees for non-repayment of dues etc. should be recorded on spot, leaving little chance of framing biased opinion later on in the report. This will lead to improve the existing follow-up and recovery methods.

In evaluating different practices as resorted to by the Corporation from time to time is to be viewed from the angle of economic environment of the state. Default by some of the units are mainly attributed by two sets of factors: one relates to market constraints, higher cost of inputs, non-availability of raw materials, working capital shortage etc., the other relates to internal lapses and deficiencies like delay in implementation of projects causing overrun, weak and inadequate management, with deleterious effect on the performance of assisted concerns. These factors act either individually or in combination. The recovery procedure has to be framed paying due regard to the rehabilitation of sick units having fair chance for revival. For maintaining congenial relationship, dues should be settled outside the Court. The Corporation, to prevent recurrence of default incident, should insist upon additional guarantee at the time of settlement to ensure regular payments.

The analogy comes out from above discussion that industrial development of a State like Sikkim is dependent not only on money alone but also on the manpower, expertise and entrepreneurial ability to bear risk of industrial venture. In Sikkim, industrial environment and business culture have not developed as yet to make promising entrepreneurs mostly of first-generation entrepreneurs capable of bearing the risk of their investment.

The Corporation with all possible measures must overcome the situation for its survival. It may be suggested to create some social and legal pressure upon the borrowers to repay their dues, keeping in mind the urgency of growth of small scale sector in the backward region to fulfil the aspiration and objects of the Corporation. Further, continuous cyclical and quantitative flow of credit should be maintained to ensure flow of funds from the lender to the borrower and vice versa and thereby bringing maximum number of needy industrial units under the coverage of financial accommodation to help total growth of the economy of Sikkim.

REFERENCES

1. SIDICO, *Annual Report, 1993-94*, pp. 15-20.
2. SIDICO, *Arrear-wise Analysis of Loan portfolio*, 1994, pp. 8-10.
3. *Ibid.*, p. 11.
4. *Ibid.*
5. *Ibid.*, p. 14.
6. IDBI, *Performance Evaluation Study Report, 1992-93*, p. 13.
7. SIDICO, *Annual Report, 1994-95*, p. 5.
8. *All India Reporter*, Re. M/s. S. Kandasari Sugars,

   Narasimhunipet, Vs. Government of Andhara Pradesh and Others, 1976, p. 93, quoted by S. Sikidar, 'Development Banking', 1985, p. 118.

10

Industrial Scenario and Nature of Employment Generation

In view of arduous geographical location and topographical features, the Himalayan State of Sikkim suffers from constraints by way of lack of infrastructural facilities, particularly in respect of transport communication and socio-economic resources, limiting the scope for vigorous industrialisation in a big way, thereby resulting in the backwardness of the state.

Despite the bottlenecks in industrialisation, the state went for industries since the 'fifties. With the advent of planned economic development since 1954, a few medium scale industries were set up which in turn play a major role in the economy of the state. The state in the Process of ushering in a dawn of industrial development, established Sikkim Distilleries Limited, Government Fruit Preservation Factory, Sikkim Jewels Limited, Sikkim Time Corporation etc.

This chapter discusses the industrial picture of the state. A general industrial picture has been drawn. The assisted units have been examined with various parameters. The chapter also enumerated the employment generation in course of industrialisation.

Sikkim Distilleries Limited (SDL)

The SDL was established by Jimmy R. Contractor, a

seventh generation businessman of liquor, as a joint sector with the government of Sikkim. The Company was established by an invitation of the Chogyal of Sikkim in 1954. The State Government held 48.0 per cent equity in the SDL. It was registered with a Capital of Rs. 4.0 lakh, which rose to Rs. 460.0 lakh in 1993. Turnover escalated from Rs. 13.0 lakh in 1963 to Rs. 1150.0 lakh in 1993. The growth in turnover between the periods was more than 88 times. The SDL is a dividend-paying company since 1962-63. It also issued bonus shares on 13 occasions in the last twenty six years, so that 1 share held in 1965 has become 120 shares by 1992.[1]

The company employed 400 workers and 40 odd managerial and technical staff to run the distillery efficiently. It is the oldest and largest company in Sikkim. SDL produces different types of liquors—Whisky, Rum, Brandy, Gin etc. Besides, the company has a small but reputed Aromatics division. Among aromatics, important are after-shave lotion and perfume. Current liquor production capacity is over 2,000 cases per day and the distillery is gearing to increase production capacity to 3,000 cases per day. Maturation capacity (taken on the basis of a number of Vats vis-a-vis Sales) is by far the highest of any liquor manufacturing unit in this country. Storage capacity of rectified spirit is 6,50,000 litres. Installed capacity utilisation is 80-85 per cent.[2]

The major portion of the sales takes place in Sikkim followed by Kerala, Pondicherry, Western India and other parts of the country. Export from the SDL is occasionally made to England, Holland, Germany, Papua and New Guinea.

It being a joint sector enterprise, the working and policies are decided by a Board of Directors, comprising nominees representing the state government and the founder-entrepreneur's family, through a full time Managing Director.

Since its inception, by agreement the SDL is the sole producer of liquor in Sikkim. In early years, SDL possessed a renewable licence, and now a permanent licence is given to the Company to maintain the status quo of whole and sole producer of liquor in Sikkim. The Company has so far made no effort for specialised marketing agencies to market products. It has an available market which still demands more products.

Sikkim Time Corporation

Sikkim Time Corporation, was established in 1976, fully owned by the Government of Sikkim in collaboration with the Hindustan Machine Tools Limited (H.M.T.), Bangalore to assemble 2.5 lakh watches per year. During 1978-79, Corporation produced about 800 watches a day.[3]

During 1979-80, the Corporation had a paid-up capital of Rs. 38.0 lakh, which was raised to Rs. 233.0 lakh during 1990-91. The total capital investment also stood same as the paid up share capital. The turnover of Rs. 13.00 lakh during 1979-80 rose to Rs. 202.6 lakh during 1990-91. The amount of Profit earned was Rs. 2.4 lakh during 1979-80 which rose to Rs. 64.2 lakh during 1990-91. The Corporation contributed Rs. 11.7 lakh to the State Exchequer during 1990-91. In 1979-80, the Corporation employed 88 persons and in 1990-91 the number of employees rose to 202.[4]

Sikkim Tea Board

There is one tea garden in Sikkim—Temi Tea Estate near Singtam. To guide and regulate the tea garden, the Government of Sikkim established Sikkim Tea Board in the form of departmental public sector undertaking.

The number of employees in the garden stood at 400

during 1979-80, which registered a small increase to 415 employees during 1990-91. In 1979-80, the amount of capital investment was Rs. 117.8 lakh and in 1990-91 investment rose to Rs. 514.0 lakh. The amount of loss was Rs. 9.8 lakh during 1979-80. The loss was converted into a profit of Rs. 86.7 lakh during 1990-91. The contribution to the state exchequer rose from Rs. 5.4 lakh in 1979-80 to Rs. 140.0 lakh in 1990-91.[5]

Government Fruit Preservation Factory

The Government Fruit Preservation Factory was established in 1965 at Singtam. It was registered as a government Company. The factory uses agro-products like oranges, apples, ginger, tomatoes and similar other products locally grown in abundance and produces squashes and cordial juices, fruit in syrup, jams and jellies, marmalades and tomato products. The factory also manufactures orange oil and pectin out of the peel waste.

The Company registered a paid up Capital of Rs. 67.5 lakh, capital investment of Rs. 75.0 lakh and working capital of Rs. 39.1 lakh till March 1980. The turnover amounted to Rs. 45.5 lakh with a net profit of Rs. 0.6 lakh during the same period. The performance of the Company till March, 1987 revealed the investment of fixed capital of Rs. 34.9 lakh, capital investment of Rs. 93.2 lakh. The output was valued at Rs. 149.1 lakh. The net value addition was Rs. 67.8 lakh. The factory employed 122 persons of which 106 were workers.[6]

The factory had been leased out to a Private Company named M/s. Sikkim Food and General Industries Limited since 2 July, 1987.

Investment in Public Sector Enterprises

About 90.0 per cent of the State population is dependent

directly or indirectly on agriculture. Hence to achieve a rapid industrialisation and development of the financial sector, the State Government made an investment of Rs. 20.7 crore—Rs. 5.3 crore in 9 Government Companies, Rs. 15.2 crore in 6 Statutory Corporations and Rs. 0.2 crore in 5 Bank and Co-operative Societies.[7]

TABLE 10.1

INVESTMENT IN PUBLIC SECTOR UNDERTAKINGS

(Rs. in Crore)

Year	*Investment during the year*	*Total Investment*	*Dividend Received*	*Dividend as % to total Investment*
1979-80	3.1	3.1	0.4	13.0
1980-81	0.3	3.4	0.2	6.0
1981-82	1.5	4.9	0.1	2.0
1982-83	0.4	5.3	0.1	2.0
1983-84	0.3	5.6	—	—
1984-85	0.2	5.8	0.4	7.0
1985-86	0.4	6.2	0.4	6.4
1986-87	0.7	6.9	0.8	11.6
1987-88	1.6	8.5	0.7	8.0
1988-89	1.3	9.8	1.6	16.3
1989-90	1.1	10.9	0.7	6.4
1990-91	3.4	14.3	1.1	7.7
1991-92	2.0	16.3	1.0	6.0
1992-93	2.0	18.3	0.6	3.3
1993-94	2.4	20.7	0.2	—

Source: Study on Financial Position of the Government of Sikkim as on 31.3.94, GOS p. 20.

Table 10.1 exhibited yearwise breakup of the investments made and returns received by way of dividends therefrom.

The year 1990-91 experienced highest investment. The maximum amount of dividend was received during 1988-89. The average rate of dividend was about 5.8 per cent. The actual position, however, would be far worse if the return from the Sikkim Distilleries Limited which accounted for more than 90.0 per cent of the total return is considered separately.

An analysis of the performance of five public sector enterprises which account for 80.0 per cent of the total investment by the State Government, is depicted in Table 10.2.

TABLE 10.2

FINANCIAL POSITION OF MAJOR PSUs

(Rs. in Lakh)

	Public Sector Undertakings	*Year*	*Capital*	*Profit*	*Return on Capital Employed (in percent)*
1.	Sikkim Time Corporation	1992-93	586.0	32.0	3.0
		1991-92	458.0	59.0	7.0
2.	Sikkim Jewels Limited	1993-94	156.0	7.0	2.0
		1992-93	156.0	23.0	5.0
3.	State Trading Corporation	1990-91	35.0	16.0	12.0
		1989-90	30.0	1.0	1.0
4.	Sikkim Mining Corporation	1992-93	272.0	(19.0)	—
		1991-92	245.0	(0)	—
5.	SIDICO	1993-94	993.0	(197.0)	—
		1992-93	933.0	(71.0)	—

Note: Figures in parentheses denote net losses.
Source: Study on Financial Position, p.21.

Assisted Units: Equity Participation

The Corporation, till March, 1995, participated in the equity capital of 18 industries as evident in Table 10.3. However, after disinvestment in 3 industries during 1990-

91, the equity stock was reduced to 15 industries (Table 10.4).

TABLE 10.3

PARTICULARS OF EQUITY INVESTMENT HELD AS ON 31.03.1990

(Rs. in Lakh)

Sl. No.	*Name of Company*	*Total Paid-up Capi-*	*Year of Invest-ment*	*% owned by SIDICO*	*No. of share held*	*Amount of Invest-ment*	*Divend Recd.*	
							Year	*Amt.*
1.	West Bengal Consultancy Org. Ltd.	15.0	79-80 82-83	5%	50 25	0.5 0.3	—	—
2.	Sikkim Tobacco (P) Ltd.	10.0	80-81 81-82	49%	17000 32000	1.7 3.2	1983	11.8
3.	Sikkim Services Ltd.	3.0	82-83	49%	14700	1.5	1985	1.0
4.	Himalayan Distilleries Ltd.	25.0	83-84	25%	62500	6.3	—	—
5.	Yuksom Breweries Ltd.	180.0	83-84	16.7%	30000	30.0	—	—
6.	Sikkim Vanaspati Ltd.	175.0	85-86 86-87 87-88 88-89	51.5%	892500 40263	45.0 10.8 33.5 4.0	—	—
7.	Scan Industries Pvt. Ltd.	5.0	86-87	20.0%	1000	1.0	—	—
8.	Sikkim Jewels Ltd.	—	89-90 91-92	43 9%	25000 5432	25.0 43.5[1]	—	—
9.	Ancillary Units of Sikkim Jewels Ltd.	—	89-90 90-91	33.9%	32000 16750	32.0 16.8	—	—

Note: 1. Investment at a premium of Rs. 700 per share.
Source: Annual Reports, relevant issues, SIDICO.

Total participation in 18 industries was valued at Rs. 254.8 lakh. After disinvestment, the invested amount came down to Rs. 242.2 lakh. Out of this Sikkim Jewels Limited occupied the major share of Rs. 117.2 lakh i.e. 48.4 per cent of the total investment. Vanaspati industry shared Rs. 93.3 lakh, breweries Rs. 30.0 lakh.

TABLE 10.4

DISINVESTMENT BY SIDICO DURING 1990-91

(Rs. in Lakh)

Sl. No.	*Name of the Company*	*% owned by SIDICO*	*No. of Shares*	*Value at Cost*	*Value of Disinvestment*
1.	Sikkim Tobacco Pvt. Ltd.	49	49000	4.9	4.9
2.	Himalayan Distilleries Ltd.	25	62500	6.3	6.3
3.	Sikkim Services Ltd.	49	14700	1.5	6.0

Source: Annual Report, 1990-91, SIDICO, p. 8.

The East district gathered assistance of Rs. 118.9 lakh followed by the South District with Rs. 123.3 lakh. The West and North district is not having any industry with the equity holding of the Corporation. Among the recipient, Private Sector received the lion's share of Rs. 148.2 lakh i.e. 61.2 per cent of the investment.

The Corporation disinvested its holdings of 3 companies in the financial year ended in 1991. Among these Companies, Sikkim Tobacco Private Limited possessed an equity investment from the Corporation worth Rs. 4.9 lakh. But the Company paid dividend to the Corporation worth Rs. 11.8 lakh with 2 years of workings. Sikkim Services Limited paid a dividend of Rs. 1.0 lakh. By disinvesting its share, the Corporation gained Rs. 4.5 1akh. Another disinvested Company was Himalayan Distilleries Limited, where neither any dividend nor any profit on realisation was obtained by the Corporation.

We first review the performance of the equity participated units of the Corporation.

Sikkim Vanaspati Limited

The Sikkim Vanaspati Limited (SVL) was established in 1985 as a joint sector. This is the only company in which the Corporation has the highest equity investment i.e. 51.5 per cent. The Company was financed by the IDBI, IFCI and ICICI under the Project Financing Participation Certificate Scheme to the extent of Rs. 400.0 lakh.[8]

The company as on 31.3.92, as exhibited in Table 10.5, possessed share capital of Rs. 181.0 lakh ; loans Rs. 980.2 lakh ; Current assets of Rs. 43.8 lakh and Current liabilities worth Rs. 108.1 lakh. The net loss of the SVL amounted to Rs. 189.8 lakh which even exceeds the amount of capital of Rs. 181.0 lakh for the same period.

The SVL created a history of survival, since its inception. In the early 90s, the owner of the Company disposed of their holdings. By then, the Company stopped production. During 1992-93, the Corporation entered into partnership with the new owner and the government provided Rs. 200.0 lakh as soft loan, to revive the Company.[9] The company started production in early 1993 and again closed down within a few months. At present the Company has ceased to operate and production is at a standstill.

Sikkim Jewels Limited

Sikkim Jewels Limited (SJL), a joint sector concern, is one of the oldest industries Sikkim. It has been operating since 1962 i.e., from the time of Chogyal, the King of Sikkim. It is a sophisticated and precision oriented industry for the manufacture of Jewel bearings for electric metres, water meters and other measuring instruments like watches and clocks. It has a factory area of 9,500 square feet with well-trained personnel. Top technical staffs and engineers were trained in Switzerland.

TABLE 10.5

FINANCIAL POSITION OF SOME MAJOR ASSISTED INDUSTRIES ON 31.3.92

(Rs. in Lakh)

Sl. No.	*Companies*	*Share Capital*	*Loans*	*Current Assets*	*Current Liabilities*	*Net Profit*	*Turnover*	*Interest*
1.	Yoksom Breweries Ltd.	182.3	546.7	304.6	112.2	8.9	368.5	84.9
2.	Sikkim Jewels Ltd.	146.0	183.4	254.3	83.7	30.6	160.2	18.8
3.	Sikkim Vanaspati	181.0	980.2	43.8	108.1	-189.8	—	145.4
4.	Labott Pvt. Ltd.[1]	50.0	127.7	115.7	60.0	1.6	294.5	20.4
5.	Sikkim Minerals (P) Ltd.	12.0	32.6	7.1	6.5	4.2	41.6	3.9
6.	Metalex Inds. Pvt. Ltd.	7.7	46.0	8.3	2.9	-11.3	4.1	3.6
7.	Scan Inds. Pvt. Ltd.	5.0	190.0	—	—	-21.8	177.3	—

Note: 1. Figures are for the year ended 31.3.93. Source: Annual Reports of relevant companies.

Till March, 1992, the Share Capital was Rs. 146.0 lakh, loan amounted to Rs. 183.4 lakh, and working capital was Rs. 170.6 lakh, Table 10.5 recorded the financial position of the Company.

The debt equity ratio of SJL was satisfactory. The current ratio, however, is higher than the usual norm. The net profit to turnover is 19.0 per cent. Interest coverage ratio is 2.6:1.

To give fillip to the industry, SJL undertook a diversification programme with 10 ancillary units. The operation of those units, however, has not commenced.

Yoksom Breweries Limited

The Yoksom Breweries Limited (YBL) is the only joint sector profit-making beer company in the State. It is located at Melli, South district of Sikkim.

The Corporation invested Rs. 30.0 lakh and acquired 16.7 per cent holding in the Company. The Company with the most sophisticated plant earned a revenue of Rs. 730.0 lakh during 1992-93. As on 31.3.93, the Share Capital was Rs. 182.3 lakh, Fixed assets was Rs. 636.6 lakh and the amount of Secured loan was Rs. 513.3 lakh. Despite a net loss of Rs. 7.0 lakh in 1988-89, the Company earned a net profit of Rs. 67.3 lakh during 1992-93. The changes in Fixed assets were meagre and the share capital remained the same between 1988-93.[10]

As evident in Table 10.6, the debt-equity ratio is high. Its current ratio is slightly higher than the norm. Return on turnover is also marginal and interest coverage capacity of the YBL is low.

During 1993-94, the Corporation inducted the Managing Director of YBL, in its Board. This was an age long recommendation of the IDBI which has been fulfilled by this induction. The expertise of the MD of YBL would certainly be useful to the Corporation.

TABLE 10.6

RATIO ANALYSIS AS ON 31.3.92

Sl. No.	*Companies*	*Debt-Equity Ratio*	*Current Ratio*	*NP to Turn-over (%)*	*Interest Coverage Ratio*
1.	Yoksom Breweries Ltd.	3.0	2.7	2.4	1.1
2.	Sikkim Jewels Ltd.	1.3	3.0	19.1	2.6
3.	Sikkim Vanaspati Ltd.	5.4	0.4	—	—
4.	Labott Pvt. Ltd.	2.6	2.0	0.5	1.1
5.	Sikkim Minerals(P) Ltd.	2.7	1.0	10.1	2.1
6.	Metalex Indus. Pvt. Ltd.	6.0	2.9	—	—
7.	Scan Inds. Pvt. Ltd.	38.0	—	—	—

Source: Annual Reports of relevant Companies.

Scan Industries Private Limited

The Scan Industries (Private) Limited received equity base from the Corporation worth Rs. 1.0 lakh during 1986-87. The Corporation acquired 20.0 per cent equity in the Company (Table 10.3).

The company earned a sale proceed of Rs. 177.3 lakh during 1990-91. The Company has been a loss-making concern since 1988-89. During 1990-91, the Company suffered a net loss of Rs. 21.8 lakh (Table 10.5).

The company's fund is mainly supported by loan amount. During 1990-91, the loan was Rs. 190.1 lakh and fixed assets valued at Rs. 51.4 lakh. The debt-equity ratio was astronomical, i.e. 38:1 (Table 10.6).

Paucity of funds compelled the company to close down the operation. The Corporation, however, has not disinvested the shares. The proprietor has become an important leader in the newly formed Government in the State. Thus the hope for revival of the unit still persists.

West Bengal Consultancy Limited (WEBCON)

The Corporation made its first equity investment in the WEBCON in 1979-80 with an amount of Rs. 50,000. Reinvestment of Rs. 25,000 was made in 1982-83. The Corporation holds 5.0 per cent equity of the Company (Table 10.3).

Since inception, the WEBCON provided required consultancy to the Corporation. It has undertaken many studies on the Corporation, other state agencies and entrepreneurs. WEBCON has a branch named Sikkim Consultancy Limited (SICON) which works on Sikkim.

Ancillary Units of SJL

The Corporation invested a total of Rs. 48.8 lakh in the 10 ancillary units of the SJL, during 1989-91, (Table 10.3). However, the units have not started production so far.

The other three Companies where the Corporation had an equity stake before disinvestment were Sikkim Tobacco (Private) Limited, Himalayan Distilleries Limited and Sikkim Services Limited.

Sikkim Tobacco Private Limited

Sikkim Tobacco (Private) Limited has been operating since the early eighties. In its total paid up Capital of Rs. 10.0 lakh the Corporation's equity was Rs. 4.9 lakh i.e. 49.0 per cent, (Table 10.3). The Company manufactured Cigarettes and other tobacco related products.

It is interesting to note that within two years of investment the Corporation received a dividend of Rs. 11.8 lakh. This was more than double of the total investment of the Corporation in that Company.

The Company was one of the few off-spring companies which came into existence in Sikkim to evade tax especially, excise duty. Because, the excise duty came into force in Sikkim in 1983, this tobacco company, till 1983, earned several hundred crores of profit and evaded excise of Rs. 100.00 crore because then in other parts of India the excise on tobacco was to the extent of 300.0 per cent. Obviously, the Company wound up as soon as Central Excise Duty extended to the state in 1983.[11]

Sikkim Services Limited

The Sikkim Services Limited was also a profit-making company in early eighties. The Corporation held 49.0 per cent equity at a cost of Rs. 1.5 lakh. Till 1983, the Company had a paid up Capital of Rs. 3.0 lakh. During 1985, the Company gave dividend of Rs. 1.0 lakh to the Corporation (Table 10.3).

The Company was a victim of an age-old legal provision of the Chogyal Kingdom. As per the provision, any company on completion of 5 years of operation in Sikkim had to pay 3.0 per cent tax on turnover. In view of the heavy tax burden under that law, the management finally closed down the production in 1992-93.[12] By disinvesting the shares, the Corporation gained Rs. 4.5 lakh from the holding (Table 10.4).

The Corporation invested Rs. 6.3 lakh in the Himalayan Distilleries Ltd. and acquired 25.0 per cent equity capital in the Company. During 1990-91, the Corporation disinvested such shares at cost (Table 10.3 and Table 10.4).

Loan Assisted Units

Among the loan assisted industries, a few medium size industries submitted annual accounts to the Corporation. They are Sikkim Minerals Private Limited, Metalex Industries Private Limited and Labott Private Limited.

The Sikkim Minerals Private Limited is engaged in the

extraction of minerals like copper, iron ore etc. Till March, 1992, the Company had Share Capital of Rs. 12.0 lakh and loan of Rs. 32.6 lakh. The net profit during that period stood at Rs. 4.2 lakh (Table 10.5).

Table 10.6 represents ratio analysis in which debt equity was higher and current ratio was in unity. A reasonable return of 10.0 per cent on turnover gave birth to a moderate interest coverage ratio.

Labott Private Limited is producing bottles and bottle-caps. Most of its products are used in the State's beer and liquor factories. Till March 1993, the Company held Share Capital of Rs. 50.0 lakh and loans of Rs. 127.7 lakh. The loan outstanding to SIDICO was Rs. 95.7 lakh.[13] The Company earned a net profit of Rs. 1.6 lakh during that period (Table 10.5).

The ratios, (Table 10.6), are ideal in case of debt-equity and current ratio. The Profit margin was, however, very low i.e. 0.5 with lower interest-coverage ratio.

The Metalex Industries Private Limited was registered with a paid up Capital of Rs. 7.7 lakh, fixed assets of Rs. 19.0 lakh and loans amounting to Rs. 46.0 lakh during 1991-92. SIDICO's contribution to the total loan accounted for Rs. 25.8 lakh for the period.[14] The Company slumped into losses since 1989-90. Till March, 1992, the net loss was depleted to Rs. 11.3 lakh. Ratio analysis indicates high debt-equity and current ratio of the company, (Table 10.5 and Table 10.6).

Loan Assistance

The Corporation as the Primary term-lending institution, sanctioned term loanS amounting to Rs. 2,430.6 lakh and disbursed upto Rs. 2,159.3 lakh till March, 1995. In the last three years fund-constraint declined the quantum of sanction to a record low. Table 10.7 depicts the amounts of assistance over the years.

TABLE 10.7

TERM LOAN SANCTION AND DISBURSEMENT BY THE SIDICO

(Rs. in Lakh)

Year ending 31 March	*Sanction*	*Disbursement*	*Per cent Disbursement to Sanction*
1978	5.2	0.6	11.5
1979	18.1	3.6	19.9
1980	12.0	17.4	145.0
1981	31.3	26.8	85.6
1982	35.3	22.8	64.6
1983	34.5	40.2	116.5
1984	75.9	40.3	53.1
1985	142.0	117.4	82.7
1986	202.7	124.3	61.3
1987	305.3	161.2	52.8
1988	237.2	341.5	144.0
1989	345.2	207.5	60.1
1990	308.2	257.9	83.7
1991	196.4	278.6	141.8
1992	365.0	254.4	69.7
1993	20.8	121.6	584.6
1994	51.7	48.1	93.0
1995	43.6	94.6	217.0
Total	2430.6	2159.3	
Compound Growth Rate	12.6	32.4	

Source: Annual Reports, 1994-95, SIDICO, p.22.

The rate of disbursement to the amount sanctioned was moderate. In the mid-eighties, the share of disbursement was on an average 60.0 per cent to that of sanction. In later years, i.e. 1991-95, the rate of disbursement to sanction improved to an average of 221.2 per cent. This was largely due to disbursal of old sanctioned amounts in later years. In 1993, the percentage of disbursement mounted to a record high of 584.6 per cent. The compound growth rate was not high. This was due to low activity in the last year i.e., in 1995.

The Corporation provided loan assistance on various accounts. The term loan sanction and disbursement till 31.3.94 on various headings have been depicted in Table 10.8 to Table 10.14.

TABLE 10.8

TERM LOAN: SCHEME WISE (1993-94)

(Rs. in Lakh)

Sl. No.	*Scheme*	*No. of Units*	*Sanction*	*Disbursement*
1.	Normal Term Loan	1263	2214.6	1892.2
		(99.1)	(92.8)	(91.7)
2.	Modernisation Loan	6	161.5	161.6
		(0.5)	(6.7)	(7.8)
3.	Rehabilitation Loan	1	4.6	4.6
		(0.1)	(0.2)	(0.2)
4.	Others (SEMFEX)	4	6.3	6.3
		(0.3)	(0.3)	(0.3)
		1274 (100.0)	2387.0 (100.0)	2064.7 (100.0)

Note: Figures in Parentheses denote percentages.

Source: *Annual Report*, 1990-94, SIDICO and Official Records.

Schemewise, till March, 1994, the Corporation as mainly a term-lending financial institution, disbursed 92.8 per cent of the total sanction as Normal term loan. However, unitwise more than 99.0 per cent of the total units received normal term loan. The loan for modernisation occupied only 6.7 per cent of the sanction and 7.8 per cent of the disbursement. Rehabilitation and SEMFEX Schemes were allotted a very meagre percentage of 0.2 and 0.3 respectively (Table 10.8).

Sizewise, until March, 1994, although 1232 units out of a total 1274 units i.e. 96.7 per cent received loan upto Rs. 10.0 lakh amountwise these units accounted for Rs. 1,118.8 lakh i.e. 47.0 per cent of the total sanction. This was followed by 21.4 per cent sanction to the units upto a loan of Rs. 30.0 lakh. A total of 7 units obtained 15.2 per cent of the loan sanctioned within the limit of Rs. 40.0 lakh to Rs. 60.0 lakh. Only 3 units were provided with 10.4 per cent of the total term loan sanction exceeding Rs. 60.0 lakh per unit (Table 10.9).

TABLE 10.9

TERM LOAN: SIZE WISE (1993-94)

(Rs. in Lakh)

Size	*No. of Units*	*Amount*
Upto Rs. 10.0 Lakh	1232 (96.7)	1118.8 (47.0)
Rs.10.0 - Rs. 30.0 Lakh	28 (2.2)	511.6 (21.4)
Rs.30.0 - Rs. 40.0 Lakh	4 (0.3)	144.0 (6.0)
Rs.40.0 - Rs. 60.0 Lakh	7 (0.5)	364.6 (15.2)
Over Rs. 60.0 Lakh	3 (0.3)	248.0 (10.4)
Total	1274 (100.0)	2387.0 (100.0)

Note: Figures in Parentheses denote percentages.
Source: *Annual Report*, 1993-94, SIDICO and Official Records.

Purposewise, till March, 1994, the Corporation gave priority to new projects. Unitwise, about 1206 units i.e. 95.0 per cent of the total units obtained term-loan of Rs. 2,128.0 lakh i.e. 89.0 per cent of the total sanction for setting up new projects. The sanction and disbursement as percentage to total sanction and disbursement figured almost the same i.e. about 89.0 per cent for different purposes. The loan assistance for diversification was 6.3 per cent to the total and overrun and rehabilitation occupied very nominal percentages to the total (Table 10.10).

TABLE 10.10

TERM LOAN: PURPOSE-WISE (1993-94)

(Rs. in Lakh)

	Purpose	*No.*	*Sanction*	*Disbursement*
1.	New Projects	1206 (94.7)	2124.4 (89.0)	1819.7 (88.2)
2.	Expansions	41 (3.2)	64.8 (2.7)	64.8 (3.2)
3.	Diversification	6 (0.5)	150.0 (6.3)	137.2 (6.6)
4.	Rehabilitation	1 (0.1)	4.6 (0.2)	4.6 (0.2)
5.	Overrun Financing	20 (1.5)	43.2 (1.8)	38.3 (1.8)
		1274 (100.0)	2387.4 (100.0)	2064.7 (100.0)

Note: Figures in Parentheses denote percentages.

Source: *Annual Report*, 1990-94, SIDICO, and Official Records.

Sectorwise, till March, 1994, sole-proprietorship and partnership business accounted for more than 96.0 per cent units of the total assisted units. But, private limited companies obtained maximum sanction i.e. 47.3 per cent of the total. Sole Proprietorship and Partnership accounted for 44.7 per cent of the total sanction. However, this sector accounted for 58.1 per cent of the total disbursement (Table 10.11).

TABLE 10.11

TERM LOAN: SECTOR-WISE (1993-94)

(Rs. in Lakh)

	Sector	*No. of Units*	*Sanction*	*Disbursement*
1.	Public Sector	4 (0.3)	193.2 (8.0)	164.2 (7.9)
2.	Private Limited Cos.	46 (3.6)	1130.4 (47.3)	702.3 (34.0)
3.	Others (Sole-·Proprietorship, Partnership etc.)	1224 (96.1)	1063.4 (44.7)	1198.2 (58.1)
		1274 (100.0)	2387.0 (100.0)	2064.7 (100.0)

Note: Figures in Parentheses denote percentages.

Source: Annual Report, 1993-94, SIDICO, pp. 30-40.

Districtwise, till March, 1994, most of the term loans have provided in east district. East district accounted for 63.3 per cent of the total units amounting to 81.3 per cent of the total sanction and disbursement. North district holds second position unitwise, followed by south and west districts. Similarly, amountwise South district occupied 10.4 per cent, West 5.5 per cent and north 2.8 per cent of the assistance (Table 10.12).

Categorywise, till March, 1994, SSIs account for major term loan assistance in terms of both sanctions and disbursement. Unitwise, SSIs accounted for 66.7 per cent of the total units. Amountwise, SSI possessed 65.6 per cent of the total sanction and almost the same i.e. 69.8 per cent of the total disbursement. Unitwise, Small Vehicle Operators stood second with 18.3 per cent of the total. Amountwise, hotel industry received 25.1 per cent of the total sanction and SVOs only 9.3 per cent of the total (Table 10.13).

TABLE 10.12

TERM LOAN: DISTRICT-WISE (1993-94)

(Rs. in Lakh)

Districts	*No. of Units*	*Sanction*	*Disbursement*
1. East	806 (63.3)	1940.4 (81.3)	1677.5 (81.3)
2. West	112 (8.8)	131.0 (5.5)	112.6 (5.5)
3. North	182 (14.3)	67.9 (2.8)	56.6 (2.7)
4. South	174 (13.6)	247.7 (10.4)	217.8 (10.5)
	1274 (100.0)	2387.0 (100.0)	2064.7 (100.0)

Note: Figures in Parentheses denote percentages.
Source: *Annual Report*, 1993-94, SIDICO, pp. 30-37.

TABLE 10.13

TERM LOAN: CATEGORY-WISE (1993-94)

(Rs. in Lakh)

Category	*No. of Units*	*Sanction*	*Disbursement*
1. SSIs, Vill. & Cottage Inds.	850 (66.7)	1564.0 (65.6)	1440.0 (69.8)
2. Hotels	191 (15.0)	600.0 (25.1)	410.8 (19.8)
3. SVOs	233 (18.3)	223.0 (9.3)	214.0 (10.4)
	1274 (100.0)	2387.0 (100.0)	2064.7 (100.0)

Note: Figures in Parentheses denote percentages.
Source: *Annual Report*, 1993-94, SIDICO, pp. 30-36.

Industrywise, upto March, 1994, as an individual industry, hotel accounted for the highest sanction i.e. 25.1 per cent of the total. Food manufacturing industry and Road Transport or SVOs or Taxi Loans represent 9.4 per cent and 9.3 per cent respectively of the total sanction. Other service industries and other industries consisting of Jewels, Motor repairing, Tailoring, Laundries, Rice Mills etc., however, groupwise account for 38.7 per cent of the total sanction. Disbursement of term loan also follows the same trend as observed in sanctioned head. Unitwise, however, the textile sector, mostly composed of Carpet Weaving, Woollen Products etc., occupies 23.4 per cent of the total unit. This is followed by SVOs and hotels with 18.3 per cent and 15.0 per cent respectively. Other industries jointly account for 30.1 per cent of the total units (Table 10.14).

Review

To evaluate the Corporation's term loan assistance in various ways, it can be said that despite inherent hindrances to promoting industries in the State, a fairly large amount was sanctioned and disbursed. The disbursal was 88.9 per cent to the sanction in total. However, in districtwise analysis, the shares of sanction and disbursement were identical to the total sanction and disbursement.

An uneven concentration of loan assistance has been observed in the east district. With less per cent of units the district got loans at a much higher percentage and in other districts just the opposite trend happened. Thus to avoid imbalances, all the districts should be given equal priority as far as loan sanction and disbursement is concerned. The type of industries may be different, but efforts should be made to give financial assistance as evenly as practicable.

The Corporation should increase allocation on

rehabilitation and SEMFEX Scheme. This is necessary to set right huge arrear-amounts. The Corporation should encourage the setting up of medium and large scale industries, as viable, to enrich the state with better technology and entrepreneurship. The sizewise sanction should be shifted from low range to medium and upper range.

TABLE 10.14

TERM LOAN: INDUSTRY-WISE (1993-94)

(Rs. in Lakh)

Industry		*No. of Units*	*Sanction*	*Disbursement*
1.	Food Manufacturing	84 (6.6)	224.6 (9.4)	221.6 (10.7)
2.	Textiles (Carpets)	298 (23.4)	82.9 (3.5)	75.0 (3.6)
3.	Printing & Paper Product	30	37.4	26.7
4.	Rubber Products	4	31.4	27.5
5.	Chemical Product	20	102.7 (4.3)	87.1 (4.2)
6.	Metal Product	17	110.2 (4.6)	116.5 (5.6)
7.	Electrical Product	13	54.0	47.8
8.	Hotels	191 (15.0)	600.8 (25.1)	410.8 (19.9)
9.	Road Transport (SVOs)	233 (18.3)	223.0 (9.3)	214.0 (10.3)
10.	Others (Services and Inds.)	384 (30.1)	920.0 (38.7)	837.7 (40.6)
		1274 (100.0)	2387.0 (100.0)	2064.7 (100.0)

Note: Figures in Parentheses denote percentages.

Source: *Annual Report*, 1993-94, SIDICO, pp.30-36.

Besides term loan facility, the Corporation provided a stop-gap loan equivalent to the Central investment subsidy of each unit. This loan was provided to the assisted units to make available funds for their uninterrupted activity. As disbursal of Central investment subsidy was generally delayed, to make a bridge in requirement and time taken, such loan was provided as a part of total sanction.

The Corporation started bridge loan provision since 1981-82. Since the discontinuance of Central investment subsidy, bridge loan provision has been affected. Total bridge loan sanctioned till 1994 is Rs. 317.6 lakh and disbursement is Rs. 181.7 lakh i.e. 57.2 per cent.[15] Bridge loan sanction had been stopped since 1989-90 as Central Investment subsidy also discontinued since that time.

The Corporation also provided soft loan on minimum rates of interest. The maximum amount provided as soft loan was during 1992-93, when it provided Rs. 200.0 lakh to the Sikkim Vanaspati Limited.

Amidst the assisted units, both in terms of equity and loan capital, the Yoksom Breweries Limited occupies the major share. However, during 1993-94, Yoksom Breweries, Sikkim Jewels, Vanaspati Limited and Labott Limited were the only functioning units.

Sikkim Jewels Limited is the maximum profit-earning company assisted by the SIDICO. Yoksom Breweries generated the highest turnover followed by Labott Private Limited.

Debt-equity ratio of the Sikkim Jewels appears unique. However, it can be extended to 2:1, the standard norm. The Labott industry and Yoksom Breweries possesses a higher debt-equity ratio.

The current ratio of Labott is ideal and for Yoksom and Vanaspati a bit high. Sikkim Jewels earned a lucrative return on turnover i.e. 19.1 per cent. Its interest-coverage ratio too is satisfactory.

Thus, in terms of ratio analysis, Sikkim Jewels Limited outnumbered other assisted industries by profitability and better financial management in Sikkim.

Credit Facilities to Small Borrowers

The meaning of tiny, cottage, and small scale industries has been well-defined by different committees under the Govt. of India.[16] All these sectors enabled small borrowers to avail of loans on easier terms.

The Corporation formulated certain liberal credit policies to suit the requirement of small borrowers. The policy of finance of the Corporation has been to nourish and flourish the growth of promising small concerns. In order to enable the Corporation to play a more effective role in the development of small scale industries in the backward region it has had to consider a number of relaxations to attract industries in the State. As per the consensus of financial institutions, the IDBI evolved some norms. As a result of relaxations, it can be noticed that, 1) the earlier limit of loans of Rs. 20,000 was lowered to Rs. 10,000 for small scale units in backward regions. This enabled SIDICO to provide loan with lesser amount i.e. above Rs. 10,000 which increased the number of small borrowers.

2) the norm relating to debt-equity ratio was relaxed to 75:25 with further relaxations for special categories of entrepreneurs like technicians etc.;

3) the initial moratorium period of three to four years to be allowed to backward areas;

4) the security margin i.e., promoters contribution was reduced from 50.0 per cent to 25.0 per cent of the value; and

5) the rate of interest was fixed by the IDBI which certainly costs the borrower less compared to the market rate.

These relaxations were further reduced in one case in Sikkim. The promoters' contribution was reduced to 12.5 per cent. Besides, 25.0 per cent subject to maximum Rs. 25.0 lakh as central investment subsidy and 90.0 per cent transportation cost from the nearest Railway or Air link was allowed as central transport subsidy. The important point to note here is that the scheme covered a large number of small entrepreneurs in tiny and village industries but the amount involved was comparatively small.

The loan assistance was provided to comparatively small industries while medium scale industries were assisted with equity investment. The logic behind such division was to be a party and dividend-getter from the big concern and to utilise own resources and earnings from other investments to promote and develop tiny, village and small scale industries.

In the loan-portfolio of the Corporation, cottage industry occupied a significant position. However, in plan documents cottage industry is included in Khadi and Village industries. This sector has been granted loan mainly under composite loan scheme. This loan was provided upto Rs. 25,000 with the lowest rate of interest to the artisans, village and cottage industries. Till 31 March, 1995 the maximum number of beneficiaries were in composite loan. Small scale industries on the other hand occupied maximum amount of assistance with lesser number of beneficiaries. Table 10.15 exhibited detailed allocation of assistance to Khadi and Village level industries under composite loan, SSIs and others.

TABLE 10.15

PLAN ACHIEVEMENT FOR KVIs AND SSIs IN SIKKIM

(Rs. in Lakh)

Item	*1985-86*		*1986-87*		*1987-88*	
	Prodn.	*Emp. (in Nos)*	*Prodn.*	*Emp. (in Nos)*	*Prodn.*	*Emp. (in Nos)*
1. Khadi						
Cotton	3.1	60	4.7	80	4.5	90
Woolen	1.3	30	1.2	15	2.0	20
	4.4	*90*	*5.9*	*95*	*6.5*	*110*
2. Village Industries						
Handmade Paper	0.3	15	—	—	1.0	19
Fibre	—	1	—	—	0.6	4
Leather	—	—	0.6	8	0.7	12
Cane & Bamboo	5.0	110	3.5	200	10.0	315
Beekeeping	1.5	95	2.0	100	2.5	110
Processing of Cereals & Pulses	2.1	100	3.0	140	3.2	125
Carpentry & Blacksmithy	2.1	109	3.3	105	7.0	147
Fruit Preservation	1.0	3	1.6	7	2.6	5
Village Oil	—	—	—	—	1.0	2
Lime Industry	—	—	1.0	18	1.5	36
	12.0	433	15.0	578	30.1	775
3. Small Scale Industries	23.0	575	35.0	1000	40.0	800

Note: Emp. = Employment.

Source: Draft Annual Plan, 1988-89, Department of Industries, GOS, pp. 15-17.

The growth of Khadi and Village industries (KVI) and

SSIs in the state was remarkable. The growth rate of KVI production was 27.4 per cent during 1986-87 which shot up to 75.0 per cent during 1987-88 compared to the previous year. However, production of village industries grew heavily, registering 100.0 per cent growth during 1987-88, compared to the previous year.

During 1985-88, KVI registered an employment of 2081 persons in which village industries provided more than 85.0 per cent of employment.

The SSIs raised the production at a slower rate. The production was Rs. 23.0 lakh in 1985-86; Rs. 35.0 lakh in 1986-87 and Rs. 40.0 lakh in 1987-88. During 1985-88, the employment in SSIs was 2,375 persons.

The performance of Khadi, Village and Small Scale Industries is greatly influenced by the SIDICO because more than 90.0 per cent of the State's industrial activities are financed by the SIDICO. The Corporation has also promoted industrial estates. It has also geared entrepreneurship by various entrepreneurship development programmes (EDP) in collaboration with the Directorate of Industries.

A number of variable effects were observed in the course of development for KVIs and SSIs:

1. Promotion and development of village and SSIs were materialised by the loan of the Corporation.
2. Quantum of loan and size of industries were directly related.
3. The subsidy assistance by the Corporation enlarged the capacity of loanees.
4. Poor recovery performance synchronised the fund for the entrepreneur.

5. The Corporation made assisted units accountable through follow-up.
6. By providing loans to composite and SSI sector, it created ancillary activities and catered for hotels and vehicles to promote tourist industries.

The portfolio balance of the Corporation is largely tilted to SSIs followed by hotel, SVO and tiny, cottage and village industries in the form of composite loan. The cottage and village industries to be allotted a higher share in the loan portfolio. The dispersal of village industries can be more beneficial than to provide loans for large scale industries. In the difficult terrain of Sikkim household industries and small scale industries with required expertise can tap natural resources to the fullest extent.

The experience of more than two decades of merger shows an upsurge of small and tiny industries in Sikkim. As a place of tourist interest, the state was bound to be tilted to the development of transport and hotels. These factors have circumscribed the activity of the Corporation within SSIs, hotels and Small Vehicle Operators (SVO). The Corporation, however, provided loan to medium scale which with the increase of ceiling for Small-Scale Units lost their nomenclature and became SSIs. Thus, loan assistance to two medium scale industries worth Rs. 297.0 lakh was merged in the nomenclature of SSIs with the increase in its ceiling in 1990.

Till March, 1994, the Corporation provided loans including term loan, bridge loan and other soft loans to 1274 units worth Rs. 2,904.6 lakh. Table 10.16 exhibited the loan assistance to SSIs, hotels, SVOs and the composite sector.

Amountwise, SSIs were the largest recipients of loans followed by hotels, SVOs and composite loan. Out of a total of Rs. 2,904.6 lakh, SSIs received Rs. 1,673.2 lakh, hotels Rs. 646.4 lakh, SVOs Rs. 223.5 lakh and composite in the form of village and cottage industries of Rs. 161.4 lakh. During 1993, soft loan of Rs. 200.0 lakh was provided by the Corporation to revive the Sikkim Vanaspati Limited. In early years too, a few soft loans and short term loans were provided which inturn consolidated with the term loan.

TABLE 10.16

TOTAL LOAN SANCTION BY THE SIDICO TILL 31 MARCH, 1994

(Rs. in Lakh)

Year	*Composite*		*S.S.I.*		*Hotel*		*S.V.O*		*Others*		*Total*	
Ending 31 March	*No.*	*Amnt.*	*No.*	*Amnt.*	*No.*	*Amnt.*	*No.*	*Amnt.*	*No.*	*Amnt.*	*No.*	*Amnt.*
1978	4	0.9	4	4.3	—	—	—	—	—	—	8	5.2
1979	—	—	4	6.1	1	12.0	—	—	—	—	5	18.1
1980	2	0.3	8	8.7	2	3.0	—	—	—	—	12	12.0
1981	9	1.8	8	17.6	5	16.9	—	—	—	—	22	36.3
1982	8	1.4	13	22.6	8	16.6	—	—	—	—	29	40.6
1983	7	1.4	12	40.3	—	—	—	—	—	—	19	41.7
1984	23	4.9	22	54.8	16	36.4	—	—	—	—	61	96.0
1985	77	17.1	19	104.8	16	26.1	36	26.6	—	—	148	174.5
1986	58	8.9	26	183.9	18	32.2	37	27.0	—	—	139	252.0
1987	96	17.5	17	290.4	19	67.2	18	15.4	—	—	150	390.6
1988	83	10.5	24	261.1	11	24.8	21	15.3	—	—	139	311.6
1989	35	8.7	25	325.9	12	20.5	11	7.8	—	—	83	363.0
1990	43	16.7	11	267.9	5	2.5	38	37.2	—	—	97	324.4
1991	30	24.1	9	62.3	22	84.4	21	25.8	—	—	82	196.7
1992	145	40.5	3	22.5	37	253.3	38	53.0	—	—	223	369.3
1993	12	4.7	—	—	6	4.5	12	11.6	—	200.0	30	220.8
1994	6	2.0	—	—	18	46.0	3	3.7	—	—	27	51.7
Total	638	161.4	205	1673.2	196	646.4	235	223.5	—	200.0	1274	2904.6

Source: *Annual Report, 1993-94,* SIDICO, p. 31.

Unitwise, however, composite loan account is the highest at 638 units out of 1,275 units i.e. 50.0 per cent. This, coupled with SSIs, occupies the major share both unitwise and amountwise

TABLE 10.17

INCREASE AND DECREASE IN NUMBER AND AMOUNT OF SANCTION TO SSIs & OTHERS

(Rs. in Lakh)

Year Ending 31 March	*Sanction to SSI (Cumulative)*		*% increase or decrease in No.*	*% increase or decrease in amnt.*	*Sanction to SSI & Others (Cumulative)*		*% share of SSIs to total number*	*% share of sanctioned amount of SSIs to the Total*
	No.	*Amnt.*			*No.*	*Amnt.*		
1978	4	4.3	—	—	8	5.2	50.0	82.7
1979	8	10.4	100.0	141.9	13	23.3	61.5	44.6
1980	16	19.1	100.0	83.6	25	35.3	64.0	54.1
1981	24	36.7	50.0	92.1	47	71.6	51.1	51.2
1982	37	59.3	54.2	61.6	76	112.2	48.7	52.8
1983	49	99.6	32.4	67.9	95	153.9	51.6	64.7
1984	71	154.4	44.9	55.0	156	250.0	45.5	61.8
1985	90	259.2	26.8	67.9	304	424.4	29.6	61.1
1986	116	443.1	28.9	70.9	443	676.4	26.2	65.5
1987	133	733.5	14.6	65.5	593	1067.7	22.4	68.7
1988	157	994.5	18.0	35.6	732	1378.6	21.4	72.1
1989	182	1320.5	15.9	32.8	815	1741.6	22.3	75.8
1990	193	1588.4	6.0	20.3	912	2066.0	21.2	76.9
1991	202	1650.7	4.7	3.9	994	2262.7	20.3	72.9
1992	205	1673.2	1.5	1.4	1217	2632.0	16.8	63.6
1993	—	—	—	—	1247	2853.0	—	—
1994	—	—	—	—	1274	2904.6	—	—

Source: *Annual Reports*, relevant issues, SIDICO.

Analysis, as evident in Table 10.17, has been carried out on total assistance sanctioned to small scale units since inception upto the end of different years and percentage increase or decrease thereon and also the share of SSIs compared to all the sectors i.e. SSIs and others.

It is transparent from the table that, the loan assistance both unitwise and amountwise fell down successively over the years. The trend persists in the share of SSIs to total number and amounts, too. The situation worsened in 1993 and 1994, when no sanction could be made to SSIs. This reveals that the dearth of funds has impeded the Corporation in new sanctions.

The number of loan proposals sanctioned is to be substantially increased so that a large number of small borrowers can avail the facilities offered by the Corporation. It is wise that the risk of financing should be diversified over a large group of borrowers.

In case of loan to SSIs, maintenance cost and cost for administering the loan is higher in comparison to that of other than SSIs. Risk involvement is higher in other than SSIs involving huge amounts of loan, but it is lower in case of SSIs. Sanctioning of small and smaller loans to village and cottage industries is for meeting Corporation's social obligations whereas sanctioning loan to comparatively big units in small scale and medium scale sectors is meant to prove Corporation's viability. As regards SSIs and tiny and village industries, risk involvement is lesser in that default by one units will have little effect on total default figure since the amount involved is less. For example, huge investment in SVL alone with Rs. 93.3 lakh disdained the optimism of large scale investment.

A study in 1990 revealed only 94 operating industrial units in the state. In Table 10.18, maximum 22 Units were

TABLE 10.18

POSITION OF SSIs AND MSIs IN SIKKIM

(Rs. in Lakh)

Industies	*No. of units*	*Fixed Capital*	*Working Capital*	*Gross Output*	*Net Value Addition*	*Employment*	*Emoluments*
1. Flour Mills	22	106.6	28.5	128.7	21.0	108	13.0
2. Printing	11	49.1	—	18.0	7.2	99	7.5
3. Electrical Product	8	69.1	37.2	14.1	0.1	93	4.1
4. Confectionery	7	41.3	2.4	39.6	4.2	35	2.1
5. Wooden Furniture & Fixtures	5	1.9	0.6	3.7	1.8	24	1.3
6. Textiles	4	2.2	0.1	2.7	—	22	1.0
7. Rice Mill	4	3.7	0.02	0.5	0.1	9	0.2
8. Cosmetics & Cleansers	4	3.0	1.1	8.6	0.7	19	0.5
9. Structural Metal & Steel Product	4	47.4	40.8	58.7	35.8	144	8.6
10. Soaps & Detergents	3	2.5	0.3	5.8	3.5	16	0.9
11. Carpet, Rugs Weaving	2	6.9	2.6	7.8	5.5	84	1.6
12. Jewellery	2	0.2	2.4	7.0	3.2	13	0.8
13. Food Processing	2	1.4	—	1.6	0.3	8	0.3
14. Malt Liquor & Beer	2	769.6	334.0	677.1	225.9	579	45.0
15. Allopathic & Ayurvedic Medicine	2	31.3	83.2	431.0	185.7	96	7.7
16. Leather	2	5.0	—	2.6	0.2	22	1.0
17. Tea Processing	1	8.5	0.7	44.7	28.6	39	2.3
18. Others	9	141.0	114.5	217.2	91.7	266	23.2
Total	94	1290.7	648.4	1669.4	615.5	1676	121.2

Note: MSI = Medium Scale Industries.
Source: *Industrial Economy of Sikkim*, 1990, B.E. & S., GOS, pp. 25-35.

found engaged in the production of flour. Printing and Press appeared second largest units followed by Electrical product manufacturing units, Confectioneries and wooden furniture and fixtures etc.

Two medium scale companies engaged in the production of malt liquor and beer possess maximum fixed and working capital, output, net value addition, employment and provide highest emoluments.

SSIs and MSIs hold fixed capital of Rs. 1,290.7 lakh, working capital being Rs. 648.4 lakh. Total output stood at Rs. 1,669.4 lakh and net value added was Rs. 615.5 lakh. Total employment generation was 1,676 persons with an accumulated emolument of Rs. 121.2 lakh.

Capital Output and Other Ratios

The tool of ratio analysis has been followed to evaluate the intrinsic condition of these 94 industrial units.

For all industries, capital-output ratio is 0.8:1.0 as shown in Table 10.19. The highest ratio of 7.4 was in rice mill units. The lowest of 0.03 capital-output ratio was observed in jewellery units.

The contribution of capital to net value, net value to output and emolument to net value appeared as 2.1, 0.4 and 0.2 respectively. The output per factory and employee is satisfactory. Net value addition per factory is also high. The emoluments of the employees are Rs. 7,219.6. Employees per factory was 18 and value addition per employee was 0.4 lakh. All these ratios are high due to presence of MSIs in the calculation, because two MSIs account for 60.0 per cent of the fixed capital, 50.0 per cent of the working capital and 40.0 per cent of the gross output.

The capital-output ratio of SSIs (excluding MSIs) would

be 0.5:1. Capital to net value, net value to output and output per factory would be 1.3, 0.4 and 10.8 respectively.

By Questionnaire, besides collecting monetary information, an effort had been made to bring out the problems of the entrepreneurs in various fields. The problem areas were identified as Financial, Raw Material, Production and Marketing Arenas. Moreover, reasons for sickness and measures to be taken to improve the workings of the Corporation and the Government were also asked to the respondents. Performance of some SIDICO assisted industries and proforma of Questionnaire are included in Appendix II and III.

Some of the problems mentioned by the respondents on various fields were as follows:

	Questions to SSIs	*Yes(%)*	*No(%)*
1.	Is SIDICO's loaning procedure satisfactory?	80.0	20.0
2.	Any difficulty in the procurement of raw materials?	80.0	20.0
3.	Any guidance provided by the SIDICO?	—	100.0
4.	Any complaint against the SIDICO?	40.0	60.0
5.	Any Marketing Problem?	100.0	—
6.	Is your unit sick?	30.0	70.0

Observations

1. SIDICO is oblivious to the task of providing necessary guidance to the assisted units.

2. All units envisage marketing problems.

3. Impediment to procuring raw-materials.

4. Loaning Procedure was satisfactory.

TABLE 10.19

RATIO ANALYSIS OF SSIs AND MSIs PERFORMANCE

(Rs. in Lakh)

	Industries	*Capital Output ratio*	*Capital to Net val. Add.*	*Net val. to output*	*Emoluments to net val.*	*Output per factory*	*Output per employee*	*Net val. per factory*	*Emolument per employee (in Rs.)*	*Employees per factory*	*Net val. per employee*
1.	Flour Mill	0.8	5.1	0.2	0.6	5.9	1.2	0.9	0.1	5	0.2
2.	Printing	2.7	6.8	0.4	1.0	1.6	0.2	0.6	0.1	9	0.1
3.	Electrical Product	4.9	691.0	N	41.0	1.8	0.1	N	N	12	N
4.	Confectionery	1.0	9.8	0.1	0.5	5.6	1.1	0.6	0.1	5	0.1
5.	Wooden Furniture & Fixture	0.5	1.1	0.5	0.7	0.7	0.1	0.4	N	5	0.1
6.	Textiles	0.8	—	—	—	0.7	0.1	—	N	5	—
7.	Rice Mill	7.4	37.0	0.2	2.0	0.1	0.1	N	N	2	N
8.	Cosmetics & Cleansers	0.3	4.3	0.1	0.7	2.2	0.4	0.2	N	5	0.04
9.	Structural Metal & Steel Prod.	0.8	1.3	0.6	0.2	14.7	0.4	9.0	0.06	36	0.2
10.	Soaps & Detergents	0.4	0.7	0.6	0.3	1.9	0.4	1.2	0.06	5	0.2
11.	Carpet, Rugs Weaving	0.9	1.3	0.7	0.3	3.9	0.1	2.7	0.02	42	0.1

12. Jewellery	0.03	0.1	0.5	0.3	3.5	0.5	1.6	0.1	6	0.2
13. Food Processing	0.9	4.7	0.2	1.0	0.8	0.2	0.2	0.04	4	0.03
14. Malt Liquor & Beer	1.1	3.4	0.3	0.2	338.6	1.2	112.9	0.1	290	0.4
15. Allopathic & Ayurvedic Medicine	0.1	0.2	0.4	0.04	215.5	4.5	92.8	0.1	48	1.9
16. Leather	1.9	25.0	0.1	5.0	1.3	0.1	0.1	0.05	11	N
17. Tea Processing	0.2	0.3	0.6	0.1	44.7	1.1	28.6	0.06	39	0.7
18. Others	0.6	1.5	0.4	0.3	24.1	0.8	10.2	0.1	30	0.3
TOTAL	0.8	2.1	0.4	0.2	17.8	1.0	6.5	0.07	18	0.4

Note: N = Negligible.

Source: Computed from The Industrial Economy of Sikkim, 1990, GOS.

5. Only one-third of the units is sick. It is worth mentioning that entrepreneurs were confident, optimistic and reluctant to declare the unit sick.

The location of the state entails procurement of raw-materials and marketing as the two most important bottlenecks in setting up a congenial industrial base in Sikkim. The problems of guidance, supply of scarce raw-materials, transportation cost and documentation complications can be addressed immediately, on the following lines:

1. The Corporation requires to simplify documentation in loaning procedures.
2. It must render necessary post-sanction guidance to the entrepreneurs. Advisory Board can be constituted with specialised personnel for guidance and surveillance.
3. Scarce raw-materials must be supplied by the Corporation.
4. Transportation subsidy must be sustained.
5. Price preference and local purchase, especially of the state's products should be made obligatory.

Hoteliers in Sikkim are optimistic about the bright future of their business. Responses to the Questionnaire revealed problem areas to be resolved for the rapid development of hotels as an important infrastructure for tourism industry. Performance of a few major SIDICO assisted hotels and proforma of Questionnaire have been shown in Appendix IV and V.

According to the responses of the hoteliers the following are the obstacles.

Observation

1. Moratorium period is short;

2. Higher rate of interest;
3. Infrastructural facilities are inadequate; and
4. New tourist places in the state to be developed.

In reconciling observations with ground realities, it is clear that the tourist influx in the State had caused a boom in hotel business. Regarding problem areas, moratorium is granted for more than 5 years by the Corporation. However, due to seasonal business, hoteliers often found difficulties in the repayment of loan and interest. The rate of interest, however, was not relaxed for the State. Political imbroglio in the adjacent state, adverse climatic conditions had often caused sorrow to the entrepreneurs. Especially, during the peak season any such uncertainties depressed the earnings of hotel business.

Infrastructural facilities in the State need to be improved. With this, new places and means of tourist interest should be developed to cater for and attract more tourists. Many parts of the state are yet to be connected by road to mobilise more tourists.

Since early nineties, the state started experiencing heavy tourist inflow necessitating the establishment of hotels, lodges etc. in sizeable numbers. Sikkim being a hilly area, construction was not easy as in the plains. Thus to provide lodging, residential houses were converted to hotels and lodges. Tenants of those residential buildings had to be shifted to far-flung areas. The rate of house rent increased heavily. The Capital Gangtok was extended on all sides. Other districts of Sikkim started beautifying and glorifying their places to attract tourists. A sizeable number of foreign tourists also visited with foreign exchange contributions to the exchequer. A large number of employment was also generated in transport oriented business. The Corporation advanced loans to the Small Vehicle Operators to purchase vehicles for employment. The economy of Sikkim increasingly tilted in favour of tourism.

In conclusion, the Corporation should not act only as a passive provider of loans. It should enhance activities mainly to follow up the assistance required by the assisted units for their sustenance and growth. It should adjust to the changing situation of various industries from time to time. The Corporation should find out avenues of resource generation. It should be well-informed about the workings of similar SIDCs in other parts of the country. The research and development activities must be augmented immediately. To lay a sound financial base, the Corporation should also invest outside the state. This would enable the Corporation to meet the growing financial demands of the State.

REFERENCES AND NOTES

1. Sikkim Distilleries Ltd., *Booklet on Sikkim Distillery Limited*, 1994, p.3.
2. *Ibid*, p.4.
3. Government of Sikkim; *Industrial Development in Sikkim*, 1979, p.8.
4. GOS, *A Statistical Profile (1979-80 & 1991-92)*, p.53.
5. *Ibid*, p.54.
6. GOS, *A statistical profile*, op.cit., p.54 and 'Industrial Economy of Sikkim,' GOS, 1990, p.25.
7. GOS, *Report on the study on Financial position of the Government of Sikkim*, 1994, p.20.
8. SIDICO, *Annual Report*, 1985-86, p.10.
9. SIDICO, *Annual Report*, 1992-93, p.5.
10. Yoksom Breweries Limited, *Annual Report,1992-93*, p.6.
11. Revealed in an interview with the DGM-I of the SIDICO.
12. *Ibid*.
13. Labott Private Limited, *Annual Report, 1992-93*, p.3.
14. Metalex Industries Private Limited, *Annual Report*, 1991-92, p.6.

15. SIDICO, *Annual Report*, 1993-94, p.30.

16. The definitions of tiny, cottage, village and small scale industries clarify the conceptual differences among them. Bhatt Committee report in 1950, created a subcategory of small unit and designated it as a 'Tiny Unit'. The tiny unit was defined as: "meaning a unit in which total capital investment does not exceed Rs. 1.0 lakh and investment per worker does not exceed Rs. 4,000.0 and turnover of which does not exceed Rs. 5.0 lakh per annum." The tiny unit is significant in SIDICO as most of the small units in Sikkim are tiny units.

    Cottage industries play a prominent role in our national economy. But there is no clear cut definition of cottage industries. Different definitions were put forward for different purposes. Sometimes they were lumped with small scale industries, which creates much confusion.

    At one time, the Government of India grouped these industries into two categories — those using power with fewer than 50 workers and those not using power with fewer than 50 workers and those not using power with fewer than 100 persons with the maximum investment of Rs. 5.0 lakh. The criterion for ownership was sole proprietorship or partnership. The major industries were classified under two heads: the traditional small industries, like khadi and handloom, village industries, handicrafts, sericulture, coir etc. and the other modern small scale industries, ancillary industries etc. (Jaiswal, N.P., Image of Village Industry, Commerce Journal, 13.3.82).

    The working group on Khadi and Village industries said that, "the definition given in the Khadi and Village industries commission act need not be changed, since a suitable definition by connotation is almost impossible". (Khare Committee on the Problems of Cottage, Village and SSIs, 1955).

    Cottage industries are thus called village industries, rural industries, agro industries and unorganised industries. The broad classification and criteria for identification as given by the industrial policies are vague and often confusing with small scale industries.

    A cottage industry is thus one which is carried on wholly or primarily with the help of members of the family, either as a whole or part-time occupation. An SSI on the other hand, is one which is operated mainly with hired labour usually 10 to 50 hands (Report of the Fiscal Commission, Government of India, 1950, pp. 99-100).

The only meaningful and clear-cut definition of cottage industries is given by census guidelines, 1981, in which cottage industries are termed household industries (H.H.I.). According to guidelines, the main characteristics of the household industries are the following:

1. One or more members of the household must participate in work. Participation by hired labour must be minimum;

2. The activity should relate to some production, processing, servicing, repairing or making and selling of goods;

3. The goods produced should not be for consumption by the household itself but should be wholly or partly for sale;

4. In urban areas the industry must be carried on in the precincts of the house in which the household lives. In rural areas the industry may be anywhere within the limits of the village;

5. The activity should not be on the scale of a registered factory; and

6. Professions such as pleader, barber, doctor, dhobi etc. will not be household industries;

In view of above characteristics a few industries that may be termed cottage industry are as follows:

1. Khadi;

2. Handloom (spinning and weaving);

3. Sericulture;

4. Coir;

5. Handicrafts like Pottery, Blacksmithy, Cane and Bamboo Products, Jewellery except that traded in shop.

6. Village industries like confectionery, food stuff processing, ghani oil preparation etc.

Small Scale Industry (SSI) is a concept which gained momentum in mid-seventies. This sector is defined by the ceiling of investment. In 1975, the units with Rs. 10.0 lakh fixed capital investment were termed SSIs and units with Rs. 15.0 lakh investment were termed ancillary units of SSIs. With the promulgation of Industrial Policy Resolution, 1980, the limit was raised to Rs. 15.0 lakh for SSIs and Rs. 20.0 lakh for ancillary units. In March 1985, the limit was raised to Rs. 35.0 lakh, for SSIs and Rs. 45.0 lakh for ancillaries. On May, 1990, with the announcement of New Industrial Policy, the investment ceiling in Plant and Machinery for SSIs were raised to Rs. 60.0 lakh and for ancillary units to Rs. 75.0 lakh. In 1993 again, the limit is raised to Rs. 1.0 Crore. This hectic change signifies the growing attention to the rising trend of SSIs in the country.

Medium Scale Industry (MSI) is an industry with more than Rs. 1.0 crore of investment.

11

Financial Analysis

Income Analysis

An introspection in the financial management of the Corporation reveals unsound fund management leading to immobilisation and dearth of resources. Lack of financial discipline both in lending and recovery has caused serious threat in enhancing loan to the entrepreneurs in recent years.

This chapter assessed the income and expenditure components of the Corporation. The asset structure and ratios have been analysed to evaluate the financial position of the Corporation.

The profitability of the Corporation can be ascertained primarily by making a comparative review of the interest income earned, interest paid on borrowings and from other incomes and expenditures.

The total income of the Corporation comprised of interest on loan, income from trading activity of procurement and distribution of raw materials, interest on fixed deposits, dividends, subsidy on woollen yarn etc. Table 11.1 enlisted major items of income and expenditure of the Corporation, since inception.

TABLE 11.1

BREAK UP OF MAJOR ITEMS OF INCOME AND EXPENDITURE OF SIDICO

(Rs. in Lakh)

Year	*Interest on Loans to Industries*	*Miscellaneous Income*	*Total Income*	*Administrarive & Other Cost*	*Int. Paid on Borrowings*	*Total Expenditure*	*Net Profit*	*% of Expenditure to Income*
1977-78	0.3	0.5	0.8	0.5	—	0.5	0.3	62.5
1978-79	1.0	1.3	2.3	1.4	—	1.4	0.9	60.9
1979-80	2.8	3.3	6.1	3.6	0.5	4.1	2.0	67.2
1980-81	5.0	3.6	8.6	4.6	1.6	6.2	2.4	72.1
1981-82	7.2	14.0	21.2	16.0	2.3	18.3	2.9	86.3
1982-83	10.9	65.9	76.8	59.0	3.8	62.8	14.0	81.8
1983-84	15.8	15.8	31.6	21.7	6.5	28.2	3.4	89.2
1984-85	22.4	14.0	36.4	23.5	9.4	32.9	3.5	90.4
1985-86	36.8	2.5	39.3	20.5	14.9	35.4	3.9	90.1
1986-87	58.1	0.8	58.9	24.4	29.8	54.2	4.7	92.0
1987-88	83.2	0.6	83.8	36.4	41.7	78.1	5.7	93.2
1988-89	112.7	0.7	113.4	45.4	60.1	105.5	7.9	93.0
1989-90	61.9	1.4	63.3	24.0	41.8	65.8	(-) 2.5	103.9
1990-91	30.3	3.1	33.4	25.1	72.5	97.6	(-)64.2	292.2
1991-92	65.7	2.4	68.1	29.2	83.8	113.0	(-)44.9	165.9
1992-93	54.1	1.5	55.6	31.5	95.4	126.9	(-)71.3	228.2
1993-94	72.5	1.5	74.0	170.8[1]	100.4	271.2	(-)197.2	366.5
1994-95	58.7	0.5	59.2	537.9[2]	99.5	637.4	(-)578.2	1076.7

Note:1. includes Provision for Doubtful assets of Rs. 140.8 lakh.

2. includes Provision for Doubtful assets of Rs. 408.8 lakh and Provision for diminution of Rs. 93.3 lakh.

Source: *Annual Reports*, 1977-95, SIDICO.

The share of interest income and other miscellaneous income in total income disclosed different trend over the years. Till 31 March, 1989, miscellaneous income occupied major portion in the total income. Since 1985-86 onwards the interest income outnumbered other incomes and accounted for more than 90.0 per cent share in the total income. The Corporation's miscellaneous income came down heavily in 1995. For the period, against the interest income of Rs. 58.7 lakh, the miscellaneous income was only Rs. 0.5 lakh. This, obviously substantiate the inability of the Corporation in generating income from other activities. Thus the Corporation's sole dependence on interest income affected resource mobilisation adversely in the sluggish industrial growth of the state.

On the expenditure part of the Corporation, the interest paid on borrowings constitute lion's share in the total expenditure. But very recently during 1993-95, the administrative expenditure outcasted interest payment. This was, however, due to huge provision for doubtful debts of Rs. 100.4 lakh and Rs. 408.8 lakh respectively, included in the administrative expenditure of 1993-94 and 1994-95.

It is evident from Table-11.1 that before 1986, the administrative cost component was more than 90.0 per cent in total expenditure. Administrative cost includes cost of sales, establishment costs including salaries, Corporate costs, provision for bad and doubtful debts and provision for depreciation. Almost entire interest payment went to the IDBI. It had increased gradually with the quantum of refinance.

There was substantial increase in the cost of sales during 1982-83. This made a spurt in administrative costs. Besides, increase in the provision for bad and doubtful debts and expansion in the Organisational structure necessitated all round increase in expenditure.

The overall review of the income and expenditure position has disclosed that on an average 60.0 per cent of the income was spent by the Corporation. The expenditure as a percentage of income gradually increased. Since 1989-90, with the introduction of cash system of accounting, expenditure exceeds income by 292.0 per cent. Income-Expenditure Graph 11.2, shows the movement of income and expenditure since its inception.

TABLE 11.2

INCOME AND EXPENDITURE

Table-XI.2

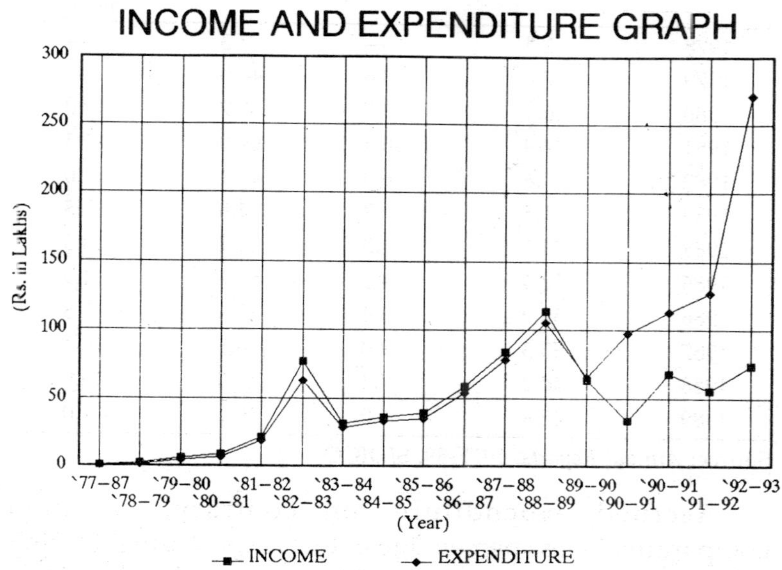

The interest income and interest payment constitutes a sizeable amount of accrued income and expenditure.

However, since 1989-90, with the advent of Cash System, accrued interest income was discarded by actual income only.

As is evident in Table-11.3, accrued income as percentage of total income increased gradually. Accrued income, on an average between 1977-89, accounted for 30.0 to 40.0 per cent of the total per cent income.

TABLE 11.3

ACCRUED INCOME AND EXPENDITURE

Year ended 31 March	*Accrued Inc. as % to total inc.*	*Accrued Exp. as % to total exp.*	*Accrued inc. as % to Intt. inc.*	*Accrued Exp as % to Intt. Payment*
1978	1.3	—	3.3	—
1979	17.4	3.6	40.0	—
1980	16.4	3.7	35.7	10.0
1981	34.9	48.4	60.0	12.5
1982	14.6	16.9	43.1	13.0
1983	1.8	2.2	12.8	15.8
1984	24.1	4.3	48.1	18.5
1985	32.4	4.3	52.7	14.9
1986	38.9	5.4	41.6	12.8
1987	55.3	9.0	56.1	16.4
1988	40.2	7.4	40.5	13.9
1989	45.9	4.0	46.1	7.0

Source: *Annual Reports*, 1977-89, SIDICO.

Accrued expenditure, on contrary, occupied comparatively less percentage in total expenditure. During 1978-89, average accrued expenditure to total expenditure accounted for only 10.0 per cent. During 1979-89, accrued expenditure as percentage to interest payment was an average of 13.5 per cent.

Had the Corporation adopted cash basis of accounting

since inception, the net profit position would have shown different picture as per Table-11.4. Although, mercantile system of accounting resulted net profit till 1989, the cash basis would have resulted net loss during 1980-82 to 1983-84 onwards uninterruptedly. Thus the mercantile system provided at least some degree of window dressing in profit figure of the Corporation till the adoption of cash basis.

TABLE 11.4

TREND IN NET PROFIT ON CASH BASIS TILL 31.3.89

(Rs. in Lakh)

Year ended 31 March	*Net Profit on Accrual basis*	*Accrued Income*	*NP on Cash basis*
1978	0.3	0.01	0.29
1979	0.9	0.4	0.5
1980	2.0	1.0	1.0
1981	2.4	3.0	(0.6)
1982	2.9	3.1	(0.2)
1983	14.0	1.4	12.6
1984	3.4	7.6	(4.2)
1985	3.5	11.8	(8.3)
1986	3.9	15.3	(11.4)
1987	4.7	32.6	(27.9)
1988	5.7	33.7	(28.0)
1989	7.9	52.0	(44.1)

Note: Figures in Parentheses denote net losses.
Source: Annual Reports, 1977-89, SIDICO.

In the initial period of its operation, the Corporation earned major portion of its income by way of interest on short-term deposit with commercial banks. The short term deposit made with the commercial banks based on sound financial planning. The Corporation being a development institution must aim at increase in profitability by long term investment rather than earning from short-term investment in commercial banks. The administrative cost need be financed from the share capital and not from the borrowed capital because borrowed capital is costlier than share capital. On the contrary, if borrowed capital is kept in commercial banks without investing the same in business units there would obviously be loss to the Corporation since blockage of such resources in banks would yield lesser interest rate than against loan to business units. Efficient management of resources would increase the profitability of the Corporation.

The adoption of cash system of accounting has declined the amount of interest on loans from industrial concerns. The Corporation has been following the cash system on interest income on loans and accrual basis on interest on borrowings and other expenditures.[1] The change in the basis of accounting, perhaps, indicates that the Corporation could not exercise proper control over the realisation of interest from the assisted units as per terms of loan agreement. This new procedure may result in encouraging slackness in actual realisation of accrued income during the year.

Another important point to be considered is of the provision of Income tax. The Central Income tax has not been imposed on Sikkim. Hence, the Corporation is not making any deduction of tax. The Income tax relaxation has given the Corporation ample scope for savings. Despite the exemption of tax, the Corporation is overburdened with ever-increasing net loss over the years.

To succumb hard reality of profit-earning, the Corporation must be bestowed with machinery for arrear collection. In recent times, however, the Corporation through the Sikkim Public Demand Recovery Act, 1988, attached the property of defaulters to realise the loan of the

Corporation. This effort, however, envisages oppositions from various pressure groups.

Asset Position

The growth in asset is depicted in Table-11.5. The current asset of the Corporation occupies major share in the total assets.

TABLE 11.5

GROWTH IN ASSETS AND LIABILITIES

(Rs. in Lakh)

Year	*Current Assets*		*Current Liabilities*		*Growth in Total Assets*	
	Amount	*Annual Growth (in %)*	*Amount*	*Annual Growth (in %)*	*Amount*	*Annual Growth (in %)*
1977-78	13.8	—	0.5	—	14.6	—
1978 -79	37.8	173.9	18.7	3640.0	42.4	190.4
1979-80	40.6	7.4	9.8	47.6d	64.5	52.1
1980-81	33.3	18.0d	10.2	4.0	96.5	49.6
1981-82	22.4	32.7d	14.5	42.1	116.9	21.1
1982-83	52.7	135.3	15.5	7.0	173.6	48.5
1983-84	60.9	15.6	11.4	26.4d	273.7	57.7
1984-85	38.8	36.3d	10.4	8.8d	363.3	32.7
1985-86	48.7	26.6	24.7	137.5	533.9	46.9
1986-87	31.4	35.5d	24.2	2.0d	706.4	32.3
1987-88	158.7	405.4	99.6	311.6	1117.9	58.2
1988-89	41.3	74.0d	43.6	56.2d	1285.0	14.9
1989-90	111.3	169.5	7.6	82.6d	1563.4	21.7
1990-91	68.6	38.4d	6.7	11.8d	1727.4	10.5
1991-92	31.0	54.8s	17.6	162.7	1923.3	11.3
1992-93	38.5	24.2	107.7	511.9	2192.3	14.0
1993-94	64.1	66.5	48.4	55.0d	2078.0	5.2d
1994-95	21.1	67.1d	48.3	—	1591.8	23.4d

Note: d = decrease.

Source: Computed from the Annual Reports, 1977-95, SIDICO.

The current asset varies mostly with the changes in the Cash and Bank balances of the Corporation. The increase in the amount of current assets during 1987-88 to 1989-90 was due to realisation from sale of assets and central subsidies respectively.

The current liabilities were mainly fluctuated by the provisions and subsidies owed to the assisted units. The increase in liabilities during 1987-88 to 1992-93 were the resultant of the arrear of central subsidies and interest on loan to IDBI and SIDBI, respectively.

The growth in current assets was not always positive. The decrease in growth rate compared to previous year was mainly for changes in Cash and Bank balances and subsidies. The growth in total assets was, however, moderate. In last two years i.e., 1993-95, total assets witnessed a negative growth owing to reduction in advances and diminution in the investment.

In consonance with the policy matter of the Government of India, the IDBI conducted a study on the asset structure of the SIDICO assisted units.[2] This was done to know the true and fair view of financial position of the assisted units as they are the root on which the performance of the Corporation is circumscribed.

In general, the Corporation follow bi-annual instalment payment system. In calculating the asset position, the Corporation has considered the periodicity of instalment payment as the standard of assets. Thus, lesser outstanding treated as better asset and vice versa. This way assets have been classified in three groups:

1. **Standard Assets (0 to 1 year)** — The units defaulted for 0, 1 and 2 instalment of principal repayment are included in standard assets i.e., the amount of principal outstanding is treated as the amount of asset.

2. **Sub-standard Assets (1 year to 2 years)** — The Units having been defaulted for 3 or 4 instalment repayment considered as sub-standard assets.

3. **Doubtful and Loss Assets (above 2 years)** — The units defaulted for 5 or 6 instalment repayment are categorised in doubtful assets. The defaulters for more than 6 instalments are dumped in loss assets.

Asset classification, as is evident in Table-11.6 exhibited the supremacy of doubtful assets in the total. Total principal outstanding amounted to Rs. 1,668.1 lakh for 840 units. Out of this, doubtful assets accounted for Rs. 1,016.4 lakh i.e. 60.9 per cent of the total outstanding. Standard assets occupied 13.2 per cent, sub-standard 13.9 per cent and loss assets were 12.0 per cent to the total principal outstanding.

Unitwise, doubtful and loss assets were accounted for 534 units i.e. 63.6 per cent of the total units under classification. Standard assets were found for 242 units followed by sub-standard's 64 units.

In total Principal outstanding, SSIs account for 1171.2 lakh i.e., 70.2 per cent. Hotels and S.V.O.s possessed Rs. 327.2 lakh and Rs. 87.5 lakh i.e. 19.6 per cent and 5.2 per cent respectively. In case of composite loan out of total Principal outstanding of Rs. 82.2 lakh no loss assets were recorded. Again, 19 units of SSIs and hotels with a total principal outstanding of Rs. 248.2 lakh and total principal and interest in arrear of Rs. 160.2 lakhs were projects under implementation but in default. 552 units with principal outstanding of Rs. 824.8 lakh and arrears of Rs. 980.2 lakh were recalled and suit filed projects. A total of 271 units having principal outstanding of Rs. 596.3 1akh and arrears of Rs. 405.1 lakh were considered as safe projects in terms of risk and profitability.[3]

TABLE-11.6

ASSET CLASSIFICATION OF SIDICO ASSISTED UNITS AS ON 31.3.94

(Rs. in Lakh)

Categories of Investment	*Standard*		*Sub-Standard*		*Doubtful and Loss Assets*				*Total Principal Outstanding*
	No. of units	*Total Principal Outstanding*	*No.*	*Total Principal Outstanding*	*No.*	*Total Doubtful Outstanding*	*Total Loss Outstanding*	*Total Principal Outstanding*	
A. S.S.I.	8	27.4	9	169.9	72	817.5	156.0	973.5	1171.2
B. Composite	154	16.4	13	2.0	341	63.7	—	63.7	82.2
C. Taxi (S.V.O.)	33	20.2	31	25.3	52	33.0	9.0	42.0	87.5
D. Hotel	47	155.4	11	34.7	69	102.2	35.0	137.2	327.2
Total	242	219.8	64	231.9	534	1016.4	200.0	1216.4	1668.1

Source: Compiled from the "Study Report on Assets Classification.... "Executive Summary, No.1, 1994, WEBCON.

Till the end of March, 1995, the Corporation calculated specific cases for sub-standard, doubtful and loss assets for Rs. 1225.3 lakh of which Rs. 612.6 lakh i.e. 50.0 per cent were earmarked as provision for these assets.[4]

The rate of interest earned on average term loan was higher till 1988-89, as exhibited in Table-11.7. In latter years, the Corporation lagged behind in interest earnings from loan amount. The adoption of cash basis system or realisation concept of interest income is responsible for lessening the rate since 1989-90.

TABLE 11.7

TREND IN INTEREST COST, INCOME AND COST COVERAGE

Year	*Interest on Av. TL* (IN PERCENT)	*Cost of Av. Borrowings* (IN PERCENT)	*Interest Coverage Ratio*
1979-80	21.5	3.9	5.0
1980-81	14.3	7.2	2.5
1981-82	13.5	6.8	2.3
1982-83	12.6	6.9	4.9
1983-84	13.2	8.0	1.5
1984-85	11.3	8.1	1.4
1985-86	11.5	7.6	1.3
1986-87	12.7	10.0	1.2
1987-88	12.1	8.4	1.1
1988-89	12.0	9.0	1.1
1989-90	5.6	5.5	0.9
1990-91	2.3	8.3	0.1
1991-92	4.4	8.7	0.5
1992-93	3.1	9.4	0.3
1993-94	3.8	9.6	0.3
1994-95	3.1	9.1	0.4

Note: Term Loan (TL) excludes Provision and Accrued Interest on Loan.

Source: *Annual Reports*, 1979-95, SIDICO.

The cost of borrowings, calculated as the percentage of interest payment to the average long-term debt, increased gradually over the years. The rate of borrowings appeared higher than the rate of earnings. In case of interest payment the Corporation follow accrual basis, hence more disbursement is made on account of interest payment. This practice induce the convention of conservatism to maintain adequate capacity to meet obligations. However, apparently the gap between the cost and revenue for interest widened in recent years. This uneven trend in the earning and borrowing rate requires to be converged.

The interest-coverage ratio shows the capacity of the profit before interest & tax (PBIT) in covering the interest charge of the Corporation. The ratio in the initial stage was higher. Since 1989-90, the ratio decreased sharply and during 1993-95 only 30.0 to 40.0 per cent of the interest charge could be provided out of the PBIT.

Solvency Ratios

The Debt-Equity ratio indicates the proportion of the Corporation's owned and borrowed funds. It reflects the capital gearing ability, as is evident in Table-11.8.

The IDBI has been following the norm of 3:1 for the projects financed by it. The variation in this ratio over the assisted units among different SFCs of the country is so high and flexible that it reduces the ratios apparently to a hypothetical affair. The widely accepted norm of this ratio is 2:1. The Corporation accounted lower ratio resulting less loan assistance generation capacity and less fund for assistance. The excess dependence on equity capital relegating outsiders' fund causes inefficiency in its administration which inturn affected the repayment position of the Corporation. The poor repayment of the borrowings reduced refinance from the IDBI and SIDBI lowering the loan fund and the debt-equity ratio.

TABLE 11.8

SOLVENCY RATIOS

Year	*D-E Ratio*	*DSCR*	*Cost of Capital*	*Current Ratio*	*Proprietary Ratio*
1978-79	0.3	3.3	—	0.04	0.4
1979-80	0.4	2.6	—	0.2	0.6
1980-81	0.7	2.0	1.3	0.1	0.5
1981-82	0.6	1.3	2.6	0.6	0.5
1982-83	0.9	1.9	2.9	0.9	0.5
1983-84	0.5	1.5	3.0	3.2	0.6
1984-85	0.6	1.3	3.0	1.9	0.6
1985-86	0.8	1.0	3.3	0.6	0.5
1986-87	1.0	1.4	4.8	0.7	0.5
1987-88	1.3	1.4	4.6	0.2	0.4
1988-89	1.2	1.0	5.0	0.3	0.4
1989-90	1.1	1.1	3.0	7.7	0.5
1990-91	1.1	0.3	4.5	2.8	0.5
1991-92	1.2	0.4	4.6	1.1	0.5
1992-93	1.0	0.4	4.9	0.2	0.4
1993-94	1.0	0.9	5.0	0.4	0.5
1994-95	1.0	0.6	4.6	0.01	0.7

Source: *Annual Reports*, 1977-95, SIDICO.

The Debt Service Coverage Ratio (DSCR)[5] of the Corporation is not satisfactory. Till 31.3.81, the ratio was ideal, but in later years it decreased gradually.

The ideal DSCR for the State Financial Corporation and for the IDBI should be 1:1 and 2:1, respectively.[6] In SIDICO, the ratio is less than one, as evident in Table-11.8. Such lower ratio signify poor cash management. The Corporation at present is paying the obligations not only from earnings but from the accretion of share capital and reserve. Such diversion of fund to meet debt-service requirements inculcating inefficiency in recovery from the assisted units. During 1993-95, debt-service amount mainly consists of interest payment. Repayment of Principal to IDBI during 1993-94 to 1994-95 was Rs. 2.1 lakh and Rs. 23.2 lakh respectively, whereas interest charge for these two financial years amounted to Rs. 100.4 lakh and Rs. 99.5 lakh. The priority is on the repayment of interest arrears than to the repayment of principal.

The cost of capital was low in the early years. The rate has moderately increased over the years. The rate of increase in interest payment was more than the rate of increase in average capital employed, showing the rise in cost of capital. This reflects the Corporation's better obligation repayment capacity in the event of poor recovery.

The current ratio represents the liquidity position of the Corporation.[7] The ratio in general was less than the usual norm of 2:1, as evident in Table-11.8. The ratio was very high at 7.7:1 during 1989-90. This was due to the reduction in current liability on account of accrued interest resulted from the adoption of cash basis of accounting.

The Corporation spent, on an average, 50.0 per cent of its owned fund in total assets. This proprietary ratio shows average capability of the Corporation to finance its assets. The ratio has improved to 0.7:1 during 1994-95. The Corporation should maintain the ratio between 60.0 per cent and 75.0 per cent.

Profitability Ratios

The profitability of the corporation is dwindling over the years. This is causing low returns, as evident in Table-11.9.

The net profit to total assets reveals the asset utilisation capacity for profit-generation. The return was comparatively high in 1982-83, owing to increased income from the sale of scarce raw materials like paraffin wax, cement, carpet, woollen yarn etc. to the industrial units. In later years, the return decreased gradually reflecting underutilisation and blockage of assets leading inefficient asset management.

TABLE 11.9

PROFITABILITY RATIOS

(In Percent)

Year	*Net Profit to Total Assets*	*Net Profit to Working Fund*	*Return on Average Equity*	*Return on Average Capital Employed*
1978-79	2.1	2.2	7.9	6.3
1979-80	3.1	2.9	8.8	6.4
1980-81	2.5	3.4	3.3	3.8
1981-82	2.5	5.2	6.2	3.3
1982-83	8.1	13.9	23.2	12.4
1983-84	1.2	2.1	3.0	1.6
1984-85	1.0	1.9	2.1	1.1
1985-86	0.7	1.5	1.7	0.9
1986-87	0.7	1.5	1.6	0.7
1987-88	0.5	0.9	1.5	0.6
1988-89	0.6	1.9	1.6	0.6
1989-90	Neg.	Neg.	Neg.	Neg.

Note: 1. Neg. = Negative.

2. Working Fund is the 'Source of Fund'.

Source: Annual Reports, 1978-90, SIDICO and Appendix No.I.

The working fund of the Corporation has been computed on the basis of Sources of fund, as exhibited in Appendix No. I. The return on fund grew with a low return of 2.2 per cent during 1978-79 and reached its pinnacle with 13.9 per cent during 1982-83. Thereof, the return took steep recession and slumped down even 0.9 per cent during 1987-88.

It is to be noted that, contrary to the regular expansion in the working fund, net profit grew meagrely. It is also pertinent to note that with the increase in working fund, the percentage return on it reveals a gradual decline precisely, since 1983. This implies the infusion of additional capital by the IDBI since 1983 could not result in additional return. It signifies that the additional fund employed could not be utilised fruitfully to yield sufficient return on it. This is also because the fund utilised by way of loan to the business concerns could not be realised as scheduled and it caused blockage of funds in the hand of loanees. The control and management of loan assistance by the assisted units in turn makes or unmakes the profitability of the Corporation.

The return on average equity till 1983 was higher compared to the return of later years. During 1982-83, the return was maximum at 23.2 per cent. The return reduced since 1983 and registered a meagre 1.6 per cent. In regard to the utilisation of equity capital, the Corporation was vulnerable. Annual contribution in the equity capital by the state government, IDBI and SIDBI could not overhaul better equity management to accentuate owned fund.

The return on capital employed is an important ratio to evaluate overall performance of the Corporation. This is similar to the return on investment (ROI). The return on average capital employed of the Corporation is in sharp erosion. During 1978-82 the average return was about 5.0 per cent, in the last four years the average return was only 0.7 per cent.

The gap between the return generation on average capital employed and the cost of average capital employed lopsided the financial prudence of the Corporation. As is evident from Table-11.8 and Table-11.9, the Corporation till 1983 was earning at a higher rate than the rate of payment on capital employed. Since then, despite the rise in the cost of average capital, there was a constant fall in the return on investment. The growth of the Corporation is affected for uneven rate of cost and return on overall investment. The Corporation for meeting obligations effectively, divert funds sacrificing the interest of the prospective loanees.

The ratio analysis of the Corporation reveals a dismal picture. All the ratios relating to Revenue and Balance Sheet are below the expected norm. The trend has been deteriorated further in recent years. The recurring net losses since 1989-90, because of the switch-over to cash system of accounting made the analysis meaningless and impractical, thereafter.

As a remedial measure, the Corporation should revamp its earning capacity to assist nascent industries in the state. The income components viz, recovery needs utmost priority, because poor recovery is the root-cause of all the financial hurdles. On the contrary, austerity measures must be taken to lessen administrative expenditures.

Accounting Method

The Corporation has introduced cash system of Accounting with effect from 1 April, 1989. Under Mercantile or Accrual basis of accounting, huge amount of unrealised interest income was added to interest received component. As is evident in Table 11.4, the Corporation out of its operation, virtually incurs a loss when Profit and Loss account is prepared on cash basis of accounting.

Though in case of income, cash basis of accounting is followed, for expenditure the Corporation still follow Mercantile System of Accounting to deflate profit position following conservative convention of accounting.

Since the adoption of Cash System, subsidies from the Central and State Governments and distribution of the same to assisted units are recorded on cash basis. Similarly, non-financing activities are also accounted on cash basis. All investments made by the Corporation have been taken at cost for not being quoted. No fixed assets have been revalued, so far.

The Corporation follows diminishing balance method for depreciation. The rate of depreciation as on 31.3.93 was for Buildings @ 5.0 per cent, Furniture and fittings @ 10.0 per cent, Office equipments @ 15.0 per cent and vehicles @ 20.0 per cent per annum.[8]

The Corporation maintains Bank Reconciliation Statement since 1989. The provision for bad and doubtful debts was not ascertained on realistic basis especially against the sticky loans.

The Corporation has installed a Computer at its head office at Gangtok. It is expected that in a progressive manner the entire Corporate accounts be computerised so that the Profit and Loss Account and Balance Sheet can be prepared in time and accurately with the help of the Computer.

There is a persistent effort in all the Auditors Report regarding the Reconciliation of Loan Control Ledger with the General Ledger of the Corporation. The Corporation should issue balance Confirmation letters to all the debtors and borrowers and obtain their confirmation.

Owing to the absence of Income Tax in the State, accounting procedures have been simplified from the complicacies of tax calculation etc.

Audit

The accounts of the Corporation are audited by internal auditor, statutory auditor and auditors of the office of the

Accountant General (AG) of Sikkim. In most of the years, both internal and statutory audit were conducted by the same audit firm.

The audit reports, by the outside firm of chartered accountants, contained many findings and suggestions to the Corporation. In the follow up of such instructions, the Corporation took necessary steps as and when required. Besides the audit report, the Corporation also received suggestions from the IDBI in course of the preparation of Performance Evaluation Study Report (PES) every year. The Corporation took up the recommendations seriously and implemented them from time to time to strengthen the functions of the Corporation.

The Corporation has appointed six auditor i.e. audit firm, till March 31, 1995. Following are the names and tenure of those auditors.

1. Agarwal Mundra & Company, Calcutta, 1977-82;
2. P.K. Bansal Associates, Gangtok, 1982-84;
3. K. Ray & Company, Gangtok, 1984-89;
4. Advani & Associates, Gangtok, 1989-92;
5. Ashok Pradhan & Associates, Calcutta, 1992-94;
6. Price Water House, Calcutta. 1994 onwards.

It is apparent that the first and third auditor were continued for 5 years. In view of rapid change in auditors, consistency of accounting procedure was affected. It is wise to appoint an auditor for at least 5 years for better management of accounts.

The present system of audit, however, suffers from certain limitations such as:

a) Coverage and Scope of audit is very limited;

b) the audit is more of a routine nature and there is hardly any trace of operational audit;

However, it is felt that SIDICO do not require any full-fledged Internal Audit Department of its own at present. The Corporation may continue with the existing system of getting things done by outside audit firms. Only the coverage and scope of the audit can be widened substantially so as to embrace all the operations of the Corporation. To this end some sort of agreement with the outside audit firm may have to be made so that the outside firm can develop a fairly good idea about the entire operation of the Corporation. Besides overall operational audit, the Internal Audit team will have to cover the following areas by

i) examining the time taken in processing different cases;
ii) checking the Appraisal notes;
iii) checking the disbursement, including mode of release of payments;
iv) checking the documentation work relating to sanctions and disbursements;
v) examining all cases of defaults and suggesting corrective measures; and
vi) checking whether all policies, guidelines and norms issued by the management from time to time are being adhered to.

It is expected that the Corporation could find out an efficient and competent audit firm as retainer who will be able to present factual views of the problems identified in a controlled and objective manner.

Instead of measuring the performance of the Corporation on the basis of financial results only, it is relevant to judge its socio-economic effects to the state as a whole. The

Corporation, in line with the Directive Principles of State Policy attuned to judicious distribution of wealth. However, distributive justice was the core of establishing state level financial and industrial corporations in our country.

The Corporation has generated sizeable employment with various activities in the last two decades. It was the main source to the small borrowers for tiny, cottage and village industries, SSIs, hotels and transport operators. In enhancing loan to these sectors, the Corporation provided enormous employment directly in these industries and indirectly to allied sectors. In the process, tourism has been augmented to create multifaced avenues for employment.

The Corporation dispersed wealth to reduce the regional imbalances. In composite loan, mostly weavers were benefited and in SSIs loan agro-based industries viz, flour, rice, malt beer, spices, bamboo, timber and tea set a firm root in the economy of the State. Moreover, various medicinal plants, orchids are also marketed with great potential. The local products are being used for making goods of tourist-interest. All these paved the agro-based development in the state.

The Corporation must be assessed from the viewpoint of its role in the upliftment of the socio-economic status of the state. It worked with the social objective rather than the economic objective of the business.

REFERENCES

1. SIDICO, *Annual Report*, 1992-93, p.3.
2. WEBCON, *Study Report on Asset Classification*, Financial and Organisational Restructuring, No.1, 1994, p.14.
3. *Ibid.*
4. SIDICO, *Annual Report*, 1994-95, p.6.

5. DSCR has been calculated as a proportion of (Recovery and Interest income minus Administrative Expenses) to (Repayment of Principal and Interest Charges).
6. Sikidar, Sujit, *'Development Banking'*, S. Chand & Company Limited, New Delhi, 1985, pp. 106-107.
7. It being a financial Corporation, in calculating current ratio cash in hand and at bank has been excluded since these liquid balances are subject to certain obligations which may be required to be met soon. Moreover, such cash in hand and at bank is obtained to some extent by way of refinance, deposits, loan, subsidy etc. from different sources.
8. SIDICO, *Annual Report*, 1992-93, Schedule-4, p.14.

12

Summary and Conclusion

The environmental factors in Sikkim are not congenial to the establishment of large-scale industries as possible in other parts of the country. The heavy rainfall and soil structure need extensive 'afforestation' in the region. This, together with measures for social forestry can pave the way for forest based small scale industrial units.

The hilly regions, especially, north-eastern hill areas are grossly neglected, as many of the facilities are not adequately provided. The state of Sikkim must ensure the establishment of pollution-resistant small scale industries to preserve its ecological balance.

The analysis of various indicators of infrastructural facilities in the state viz., communication, transport, banking, education etc. indicates inequitable distribution. Deficiencies in these areas are to be eradicated by proper redistribution of existing facilities or raising equitable distribution.

It is observed that on an average 50.0 per cent of the plan outlay is earmarked for power and communication sector. This affected other social and economic needs of the people.

Considering the analysis of sectoral growth pattern in Sikkim, it can be concluded that the growth since 1975 is phenomenal. The Net State Domestic Product (NSDP) at current prices was estimated at Rs.250.2 crore in 1993-94 registering a growth of 5 times since 1980-81.

It is observed that more than 80.0 per cent of the units are concentrated only in the east district, which is only 13.4 per cent of the total geographical area of Sikkim. The Corporation has depended primarily on 'Walk-in' business for the growth in its operations. Thus, the growth in its operations has been mainly concentrated in the developed areas i.e. the east district of the state where infrastructure has been reasonably developed. The performance of the Corporation in other districts has not been of the desired level.

Though there are many financial and service institutes in Sikkim, barring SIDICO, IDBI and Directorate of Industries all others' performance is below expectation. Geographic limitation, entrepreneurial indifference and other societal constraints appeared to be the main impediments to their optimal performance.

It is found that the flow of funds was fettered causing yawning situation in the operation of loan sanction and disbursement.

The managerial personnel of the Corporation is to be selected and trained keeping in mind the gravity of a financial institution. The organisation structure must be well equipped with recovery wing. The Entrepreneurial Development Programme (EDP) conducted by various institutions like Directorate of Industries, SISI etc. did not yield the desired result because of primordial factors, unwillingness of banks to entertain first generation entrepreneurs, lack of post-training, and inefficiency in conducting EDPs by the institutions themselves. The Corporation has no Entrepreneurial Guidance Cell and as such they have no ready Project Profiles, prepared after due study of industrial potential of the State for the prospective entrepreneurs.

Analysis of lending policies divulged procedural delays in enabling one to obtain loan. The appraisal method is to be strenghtened to lessen default.

Considering the categorywise disbursement, it is found that small-scale industries were given the highest priority.

It is perceived from the industrywise assistance of the Corporation that, service industries of a small nature shared the highest amount. This indicates a tilt towards non-manufacturing industry.

The mainstay of Sikkim is agriculture. Village and Small Scale industries grew up with and for the development of agriculture. The growth of the Seventh five year plan outlay on village and SSIs (1985-90) was 1.7 times while the growth of SIDICO assisted village and SSIs for the same period was 4.2 times.

It is observed that the Corporation laid a solid foundation for village and small-scale industries, in this infant state. However, many small scale units are in morbid condition. Nevertheless, the Corporation has created a large section of first-generation entrepreneurs.

Based on the results of ratios, it can be substantiated that the overall performance of the SIDICO is not satisfactory. The management of funds is not upto the desired level.

The social cost benefit of the Corporation is phenomenal. It has been successful in extending a network of industries, sizeable amount of employment, exploring new avenues for the socio-economic development of the state.

The banks in Sikkim are concentrated in urban areas. The Banking system is confined to providing working capital loans. The term loan is not provided to set up industrial establishments. All-India banking institutions are only confined to deposit-mobilisation. A meagre 27.3 per cent of the total deposits was provided for advance. The concept of Rural Banking is conspicuously absent in Sikkim. This has adversely affected development of those areas.

The upsurge of an unrecognised Stock Exchange in Sikkim in the recent past resulted in small-scale deposit mobilisation through securities. However, the exchange dealt in the securities of the industries situated outside the state. The exchange could not sustain the pace of inceptional activities as it was not linked with the industrial development of Sikkim.

The upsurge of a neo-middle class in the state was evident since its integration with the main-stream of India. Government developmental agencies enlisted a group of entrepreneurs. In this process, political and bureaucratic pressure is a considerable factor. Most of the industries, hotels and tourist-vehicles are owned directly or indirectly by top officials and politicians. Thus, loan assistance for one account was sometimes diverted for other purpose.

Tourism in Sikkim is having a significant impact on the State's economy especially in the trade, hotel and transport. This is supported by the fact that the inflow of tourists has gone up substantially over the years. The number of foreign tourists has since increased remarkably following the easing out of restrictions so far imposed upon them. As the tourists continue to dominate the economic aspirations of a large cross section of the people of the state, the Government of Sikkim is preparing a 'Master Plan' for the all round development of this sector. The SIDICO, since its inception, has played a vital role in the growth of tourism by providing loans to all the related sectors.

RECOMMENDATIONS

I. For SIDICO

1. The IDBI and SIDBI should reduce lending rates or allow rebates on interest rates.
2. The Banking Sector needs to be extended to rural areas with immediate opening of Rural Banks. Proper co-ordination is to be established between commercial banks and the Corporation.
3. The Corporation must launch an efficient recovery drive exerting all possible social and legal pressures.
4. Central Investment Subsidy is to be re-instituted. It can be raised to 33.0 per cent on Capital Investment.
5. The Corporation must develop a potential workforce to generate resources for its survival and growth.

II. General

1. To support industrial marketing in the state, some of the government purchases may be made of the state's products.
2. Diseconomies existing in the state should not overwhelmingly surpass the fiscal incentives provided to the entrepreneurs.
3. The primordial factors responsible for uncongenial industrial atmosphere must be removed on a priority basis.
4. Joint ventures need to be encouraged to promote harmony and non-local entrepreneurs.

The Corporation must give preference in loan sanction to the industries dependent on each other. The output of one industry would be the input to another industry. This polar effect in industries is very helpful in catering to the needs of people in backward areas.

The National Committee on the Development of Backward Areas headed by B. Sivaraman, 1981, recommended strategies to develop hill areas, through "basic approach" and "watershed approach".

The basic approach emphasises increase in the productive capacity of the hill economy by encouraging income-generating activities like horticulture, animal husbandry, social forestry and tourism. This may mean a change from a subsistence food crop to possible cash crops for more returns. To slow down the out-migration, generation of gainful employment locally has to receive high priority.

The change-over in cropping priority can be effective by providing suitable marketing facilities to buy the products at fair prices and arranging the supply of foodgrains commonly consumed in the area in fair price shop.

On the other hand, the watershed approach stressed the necessity of the watershed area as the basis for making developmental plans. In hilly areas communication follows the streams. Social groups and village boundaries are generally coterminus with watersheds as communication across watersheds is difficult because of the terrain. The committee recommended that the watershed should be the primary planning unit rather than a block or a district. The approach provides a sound basis for programming of soil-conservation, water harvesting and harnessing of land-use and planning social institutions. It is also possible to delineate watersheds into micro and mini watersheds. A mini watershed may be equated with the concept of a focal-point i.e., area cum beneficiary approach, and may cover an area of a cluster of villages with a population coverage of a fifth or sixth of a block population and the micro watershed may cover an area of 1000 to 1500 hectares.

Forest covers in the hill slopes are ideal and should get priority. Cultivation of hill slopes should be discouraged as far as possible as this causes erosion. There should be a long term policy for covering such areas under perennial crops. The committee has recommended that degrees of slopes beyond which cultivation should not be allowed may be specified for different regions.

As far as possible, horticulture should be encouraged in combination with soil cover. Soil cover should preferably comprise grass-cover mixture suitable to the locality. This would provide a very good combination for horticulture and animal husbandry, both of which can be complementary. The watershed approach also involves the development of irrigation. High-yielding variety foodgrains should be produced. Thus, the strategy must be to increase irrigated areas in the zone taken up for a change-over to horticulture, pasture development, vegetable growing etc.

Industrial development in the hill areas has to be based essentially on the promotion of such activities in which hills offer a distinct advantage like forest based vegetables and food processing industries. Another area in which hill areas offer an advantage in terms of climate and dust and pollution free environment is electronic and precision goods, as they do not involve heavy transportation cost. These are skill-based industries where the value added is substantial. Necessary steps have to be taken for training and skill development so as to prepare the environment for location of such industries.

is substantial. Necessary steps have to be taken for training and skill development so as to prepare the environment for location of such industries.

The industrial development in any region is dependent on the primoridal factors including culture, language, religion, orientation of people etc. Unfortunately, the said factors are conspicuously deficient with the tradition-bound society of Sikkim. Writing on the socio-cultural differences in the north-east, B.P. Singh (North-East India: Demography, Culture and Identity Crisis, Indian Journal of Public Administration, 1987, 33(4), pp. 991-1010) identifies two key factors with regard to this region— "limited socialisation" and "rapid modernisation". These two factors are responsible for the situation in Sikkim also. But "limited socialisation" is actually an effect rather than a cause. Socialisation may have been limited not only because of various primordial differences but also due to factors like attitude and orientation. Therefore, the second factor is the most important determinant of the ill-adaptation in societies. When a region is rapidly exposed to the forces of modernisation and development, the local people and the migrants do not get the opportunity to understand each other properly and develop networks of social and cultural relations.

One is compelled to extol the Elwin-Nehruvian Policy of 'Protected Development' or 'Hastening Slowly'. Both Elwin and Nehru were aware of the consequences of exposing a backward region rapidly to the forces of development and modernisation.

The limited feudalistic development in Sikkim has intrinsic impact in the process of industrial development. The social-transformation has not taken place with a fear of losing limited resources in hand of original inhabitants. The age-long laws and the agreement of merger allowed some privileges under Article 371F of the Constitution of India which causes a separation and doubtful credibility between the local and non-local. Such feelings have restricted mainstream industrialists from investing in Sikkim with a sense of security. This sort of fear psychosis has jeopardised the influx of technology and expertise in Sikkim. The Central Government is also in favour of protected development without any serious effort to social-reform. On the contrary, the Central Government can not afford to have its border state with strategic importance fretting with ethnic tension.

In the existing state of affairs, the Corporation must be emphatic on the promotion of mini-industrial estates based predominantly on livestock and agricultural resources. The large variety biological plants need to be explored for commercial purposes. The state must accommodate itself to the process of liberalisation which is necessary in the era of globalisation.

It is necessary for the SIDICO to adopt a shift in its approach and strategy to cope with the industrial development in such a way that the pace of industrialisation gets accelerated with the removal of regional disparities and maintenance of the required ecological balance.

APPENDIX- I

STATEMENT SHOWING SOURCES OF FUNDS

(Rs. in Lakh)

	1977-1978	1978-1979	1979-1980	1980-1981	1981-1982	1982-1983	1983-1984	1984-1985	1985-1986	1986-1987	1987-1988	1988-1989	1989-1990	1990-1991	1991-1992	1992-1993	1993-1994	1994-1995
1a. Increase in paid-up Capital																		
i. State Govt.	8.3	7.0	16.0	10.0	10.0	18.0	22.0	20.0	18.0	27.0	63.0	51.7	85.5	60.0	80.0	50.0	60.0	50.0
ii. IDBI	—	—	—	—	—	—	60.0	20.0	49.3	27.0	63.0	50.0	57.5	60.0	—	—	—	—
b. Increase in Reserves	0.3	0.9	2.0	2.4	2.9	14.0	3.4	3.5	3.9	4.7	5.7	7.9	—	16.7	43.8	—	—	—
2. Borrowings (gross)																		
i. State Govt.	4.6	—	—	—	—	—	—	—	—	0.4	—	—	—	—	—	200.0	—	—
ii. IDBI	—	—	12.6	20.1	8.0	44.2	23.8	70.5	132.3	157.9	330.8	145.3	242.3	213.5	272.4	73.7	—	—

cont...

	1977-1978	1978-1979	1979-1980	1980-1981	1981-1982	1982-1983	1983-1984	1984-1985	1985-1986	1986-1987	1987-1988	1988-1989	1989-1990	1990-1991	1991-1992	1992-1993	1993-1994	1994-1995
3. Repayment of Loans	—	—	0.1	0.1	2.3	8.2	13.3	18.2	19.1	55.4	63.2	58.6	117.0	59.3	56.6	46.8	53.2	46.1
4. Other Cash in-flow	—	—	—	—	—	—	—	12.9	1.0	4.0	4.6	18.7	0.2	—	5.2	6.2	6.3	3.9
5. Others	1.0	19.8	—	—	—	—	—	14.3	13.9	—	59.0	—	—	14.7	—	30.9	—	2.8
6. Opening cash & bank balance	—	13.5	37.2	38.3	32.1	16.3	37.9	24.7	18.7	33.7	15.0	142.4	26.9	52.8	49.1	11.1	17.0	44.3
Total	14.2	41.2	67.9	70.9	55.3	100.7	160.4	180.1	256.2	310.1	604.3	416.0	529.4	477.0	507.1	418.7	136.5	147.1

APPENDIX-I

STATEMENT SHOWING USES OF FUNDS

(Rs. in Lakh)

	1977-1978	1978-1979	1979-1980	1980-1981	1981-1982	1982-1983	1983-1984	1984-1985	1985-1986	1986-1987	1987-1988	1988-1989	1989-1990	1990-1991	1991-1992	1992-1993	1993-1994	1994-1995
1. Disbursement of assistance by way of (gross)																		
i. Loans	0.7	3.7	17.4	31.6	23.8	43.0	51.3	130.3	138.7	210.2	369.2	246.9	269.8	281.5	257.9	321.6	48.1	94.6
ii. Subscription to shares	—	—	0.5	1.7	3.2	1.8	36.3	—	45.0	11.9	33.5	4.0	57.0	16.7	43.5	—	—	—
2. Repayment of loans to																		
i. IDBI /SIDBI	—	—	0.1	0.9	3.8	5.4	11.5	18.9	32.9	43.6	51.1	87.9	104.4	128.7	166.1	73.4	2.1	23.2
ii. Others (State Govt.)	—	0.3	0.3	0.3	0.3	—	—	—	—	0.4	—	—	—	—	—	—	—	—
3. Other Cash outflow	—	—	—	—	—	—	13.7	12.2	5.9	6.4	8.1	7.7	24.0	1.0	6.7	6.7	8.3	8.8

	1977-1978	1978-1979	1979-1980	1980-1981	1981-1982	1982-1983	1983-1984	1984-1985	1985-1986	1986-1987	1987-1988	1988-1989	1989-1990	1990-1991	1991-1992	1992-1993	1993-1994	1994-1995
4. Others	—	—	11.3	4.3	7.9	12.6	22.9	—	—	22.6	—	42.6	21.4	—	21.8	—	33.7	—
5. Closing cash & bank balance	13.5	37.2	38.3	32.1	16.3	37.9	24.7	18.7	33.7	15.0	142.4	26.9	52.8	49.1	11.1	17.0	44.3	20.5
Total	14.2	41.2	67.9	70.9	55.3	100.7	160.4	180.1	256.2	310.1	604.3	416.0	529.4	477.0	507.1	418.7	136.5	147.1

Note: Differences between the sides of sources and uses of funds have been accounted for under the item "others" in Sl. No. 5 and Sl. No. 4 respectively.

APPENDIX-II

PERFORMANCE OF SOME ASSISTED INDUSTRIES

(Rs. in Lakh)

Name	*Product*	*Total Inv.*	*Loan from SID-ICO*	*Turn-over (1992 -93)*	*Produc-tion (1992 -93)*	*Net Pro-fit (1992) - 93)*	*No. of Emplo-yees*
1. M/s. Denzong Rubber Indus. (P) Ltd.	Hawai Chappals & Straps	79.0	33.6	38.6	58.1	—	60
2. Oriental Manufacturing Co.(P) Ltd.	G.I. Wire, G.I. Barbed Wire & Other Wire Products	65.0	35.4	389.7	NA	NA	65
3. i. Sikkim Packaging & Marketing (P) Ltd. ii. Sikkirn Snacks Food (P) Ltd.	Snacks and Packaging	150.0	62.7	NA	NA	NA	16
4. Atlas Mfg. Co. (P) Ltd.	Luggage Bags	2.8	1.5	NA	3.6	0.6	5
5. Photo-media (P) Ltd.	Photographs	35.0	29.5	NA	13.0	2.7	7
6. Trend Apparel (P) Ltd.	Ready-made Garments	20.0	5.0	3.5	3.6	NA	42
7. Usha Industries	Room Purifier, Cleaning Powder etc.	3.1	1.2	NA	NA	NA	13

Name	*Product*	*Total Inv.*	*Loan from SIDICO*	*Turnover (1992-93)*	*Production (1992-93)*	*Net Profit (1992)-93)*	*No. of Employees*
8. Kanchanjunga Steel Furniture	Steel Furnture, Fabrication	14.5	9.3	9.0	6.7	NA	5

N.A. = Not available.
Source: Based on Questionnaire.

APPENDIX-III

QUESTIONNAIRE TO SSIs

A. Name of the Entrepreneur
B. Name of the Unit/Firm
C. Place
D. Product

Questions

1. What is the total investment?
2. What are the sources of raising finance?
3. How much loan obtained from the SIDICO and in which year?
4. How much time was taken in sanctioning the loan?
5. Do you think the procedures/requirements to be complied with for loan taking is satisfactory?
6. What is your annual production? (Unitwise/Amountwise)
7. How do you procure raw material for production?
8. What type of subsidies availed of from the SIDICO?
9. What is the No. of employee in your unit?
10. Where do you market your products?
11. What is the annual profit?
12. Did you receive any guidance other than loan assistance from the SIDICO?
13. Do you repay loan instalments in time? If not, Why?
14. Is the unit sick? If so, reasons therefore.
15. Do you have any complaint/suggestion on the workings of the SIDICO?
16. Do you have any suggestion to the SIDICO/Govt. for the development of your unit?

APPENDIX-IV

PERFORMANCE OF SOME MAJOR HOTELS FINANCED BY SIDICO AS ON 31.3.94

(Rs. in lakh)

Name of the Hotel	*Year of Establishment*	*Total Inv.*	*Loan from SIDICO*	*Capacity*	*Av. Room Rent (Rs)*	*Annual Income*	*No. of Employee*
1. NORBU GANG	1993	25.0	9.0	32 Bed (16 Rooms)	400.0	3.0	20
2. CENTRAL POINT	1991	12.5	7.5	40 Bed (20 Rooms)	200.0	2.0	7
3. HOTEL ORIENT	1986	12.0	4.0	—	—	0.2	5
4. MOUNT VIEW	1991	10.0	5.0	60 Bed	350.0	—	7
5. PUSHPANJALI HOTEL, Jorethang	1984	7.0	4.0	15 Bed (9 Rooms)	80.0	0.4	6
6. CHUMILA	1986	6.6	2.6	17 Bed (8 Rooms)	300.0	0.8	6
7. WINDSOR	1993	6.0	1.6	20 Bed (9 Rooms)	250.0	2.0	4
8. MADAVI	1993	4.5	4.0	24 Bed (12 Rooms)	400.0	1.6	6

Source: Based on Questionnaire.

APPENDIX-V

QUESTIONNAIRE TO HOTELIERS

A. Name of the Owner

B. Name of the Hotel & year of establishment

Questions

1. Do you own the building of the hotel?
2. What is the capacity of the hotel?
3. What is the average room rent?
4. How many months the hotel remain full?
5. What is your total investment on it?
6. What are the sources of capital?
7. How much loan obtained from the SIDICO?
8. How much time taken to obtain such loan?
9. What is the no. of employees?
10. What is your annual income?
11. Do you repay instalment regularly? If not, why?
12. Do you have any suggestion/complaint to the SIDICO?

Select Bibliography

Books

1. Avadhani, V.A., *Studies in Indian Financial System,* Jaico Publishing House, Bombay, 1978.
2. Basnet, L.B., *Sikkim — A Short Political History,* Sultan Chand and Company Private Limited, New Delhi, 1974.
3. Basu, S.K., *Theory and Practice of Development Banking — A Study in Asian Context,* Asia Publishing House, Bombay, 1965.
4. Bhasin, V., *Ecology, Culture and Change: Tribals of Sikkim Himalayas,* Inter-India Publication, New Delhi, 1989.
5. Bhole, L.M., *Financial Markets and Institutions,* Tata McGraw Hill Publishing Company Ltd., New Delhi, 1982.
6. Das, B.S., *The Sikkim Saga,* Vikas Publishing House, New Delhi, 1990.
7. Dasgupta, M., *Sikkim: Problems and Prospects of Development*, Indus, New Delhi, 1992.
8. Datta, Amal, *Sikkim Since Independence,* Mittal Publications, New Delhi, 1991.
9. Doig, Desmond and Jean Perrin, *Sikkim,* Oxford and IBH Publishing Company, Calcutta, 1971.
10. Goyal, O.P., *Financial Institutions and Economic Growth of India,* Light and Life Publishers, New Delhi, 1979.
11. Gupta, L.C., *The Working Structure of Industrial Finance in India,* Oxford University Press, 1969.
12. Harry, C. Sanvani, *Investment Management,* Prentice Hall Inc., New York, 1963.

13. Karan, P.P. and Jenkins, W.N., *The Himalayan Kingdom Sikkim, Bhutan and Nepal,* D. Von Nostrand Company, New Jersey, 1963.

14. Malhotra, Keshavi, *Development Banks and Industrially Backward Areas,* Deep and Deep Publications, New Delhi, 1991.

15. Naidu, L., *Bank Finance for Rural Development,* Ashish Publishing House, New Delhi, 1988.

16. Pal, A. (ed.), *The Himalaya — Environment, Economy and Society,* Vikas Publishing House, New Delhi, 1995.

17. Ramkrishna Sharma, K., *Financial Institutions and Regional Development in India,* Chug Publication, Allahabad, 1986.

18. Rao K.V., and Venkatramaih, *Bank Finance to Industries,* Printwell, Jaipur, 1991.

19. Rao, P. Kallu, *Development Banking — SIDCs in India,* Anmol Publications, New Delhi, 1993.

20. Risley, H.H., *Gazetteer of Sikkim,* Bengal Secretariat Press, Calcutta, 1894.

21. Salisbury, Charlotte, Y., *Mountain Kingdom, Sikkim,* Horton and Company, New York, 1972.

22. Sarkar, R.L. and M.P. Lama, *Eastern Himalayas, Environment and Economy,* Atma Ram and Sons, New Delhi, 1986.

23. Shirley, Boskey, *Problems and Projects of Development Banks,* John Hopkins Press, Baltimore, 1959.

24. Sikider, Sujit, *Development Banking,* S. Chand and Company, New Delhi, 1985.

25. Singh, N. Prabhu, *Role of Development Banks in a Planned Economy,* Vikas Publishing House Pvt. Ltd., New Delhi, 1974.

26. Singh, Vimal Shankar, *Development Banking in India,* Deep and Deep Publications, New Delhi, 1985.

27. Srivastava, R.M., *Management of Indian Financial Institutions,* Himalaya Publishing House, Bombay, 1984.

28. Tripathi, A.R., *Bank Financing of Industries in India,* Tiwari Publications, New Delhi, 1991.

29. Viswanathan, R., *Industrial Finance,* S. Chand and Company, New Delhi, 1985.

30. William, Diamond, *Development Banks,* Johns Hopkins Press, Baltimore, 1957.

Reports and Journals

1. SIDICO, *Annual Report,* 1977-95.
2. SIDICO, *Scope of Financing and Guidelines for Entrepreneurs* 1991.
3. IDBI, *Performance Evaluation Study Reports of SIDICO,* 1978-94.
4. IDBI, *Organisation Study of the SIDICO,* 1993, WEBCON.
5. IDBI, *Report on Development Banking in India,* relevant issues.

Government of Sikkim Publications

6. *Annual Plan Documents,* relevant issues.
7. *Sikkim Companies Registration Act, 1961.*
8. *Industrial Development in Sikkim,* 1979.
9. *Report on the Availability of various Amenities in Rural Areas of Sikkim,* 1979.
10. *Agriculture Census,* 1980-81.
11. *District Industries Centre (Action Plan), 1983-84.* 1987-88.
12. *Draft Annual Plans,* Department of Industries, 1984-85, 1988-89.
13. *Sikkim Compendium of Achievement,* 1987.
14. *Sikkim Public Demand Recovery Act,* 1988.
15. *A Profile of Planned Development in Sikkim* (1975-76 to 1988-89), 1989.
16. *Report on Economic Census,* B.E. and S., 1990.
17. *Industrial Economy of Sikkim,* B.E. and S., 1991.

18. *Assistance to Industrial Entrepreneurs in Sikkim,* 1991.
19. *Sikkim — An Economic Survey,* B.E. and S., 1991-92.
20. *Report on Tourists in Sikkim,* B.E. and S., 1992.
21. *Twelve Years of Bhandari Government, An Appraisal of Achievement* (1979-92), 1993.
22. *Sikkim — A Statistical Profile* (1979-80 and 1991-92), B.E. and S., 1993.
23. *Economic Survey,* B.E. and S., 1993-94.

Government of India

24. Report of the Technical Team, Planning Commission, 1971.
25. Report of the Study Team on Institutional Arrangements for Agricultural Credit in Sikkim, Datey Committee, 1976.
26. Report of the Study Team — Economic Development of Sikkim State, 1978.
27. Report on General Issues relating to Backward Areas Development, National Committee on the Development of Backward Areas, B. Sivaraman Committee, Planning Commission, 1981.
28. State Bank of India, *Lead Bank Survey,* Gangtok, 1985.

Articles

29. Boot, D.P., "A Note on Urbanisation in Sikkim," *Indian Journal of Regional Sciences,* Vol. 1, 1988.
30. Dasgupta, M., "Structure of Sikkim's Economy," *Indian Journal of Regional Sciences,* Vol. XII, No. 2, 1980.
31. Dasgupta, M., "Some Demographic Characteristics of Sikkim — A Study of Census of 1971," *Himalaya: Man and Nature,* 4 (9), 1981.
32. Joshi, M.S., Financial Institutions and Financial Policies for Economic Development, *Pragnan,* National Institute of Bank Management (NIBM), April-June, 1972.

33. Karan, P.P., *Economic Development in Sikkim, Pacific Community*, Vol. 8, 1970.

34. Menon, N.C., "Contemporary Development in Sikkim: An Appraisal," *Indian and Foreign Review*, 12(3), 1974.

35. Misra, B.N., "Development Banks and Financing of New Entrepreneurship in India," *Pragnan*, NIBM, Oct-Dec., 1982.

36. Rao, S.B., SFCs and Management of Assisted Units, *Commerce*, Vol. 141, July-Sept., 1980.

37. Sarma, K.R., "Role of Andhra Pradesh SFC in the Industrial Development of the State," *Pragnan*, NIBM, April-June, 1980.

38. Singh, B.P., "North-East India: Demography, Culture and Identity Crisis," *Indian Journal of Public Administration*, No. 33 (4), 1987.

Index

U

W

Y